AF779249

# Governing Artficial Intelligence

# Issues in Online Dispute Resolution

VOLUME 3

The titles published in this series are listed at *brill.com/iodr*

# Governing Artificial Intelligence

*By*

Leah Wing, Chris Draper, Scott Cooper,
and Daniel Rainey

BRILL | NIJHOFF

LEIDEN | BOSTON

Library of Congress Cataloging-in-Publication Data

Names: Wing, Leah author
Title: Governing artificial intelligence / by Leah Wing, Chris Draper, Scott Cooper, and Daniel Rainey.
Description: Leiden ; Boston : Brill Academic Publishers, Inc, 2025. | Series: Issues in online dispute resolution, 3050-9378 ; volume 3 | Includes bibliographical references and index.
Identifiers: LCCN 2025020946 (print) | LCCN 2025020947 (ebook) | ISBN 9789004736290 hardback | ISBN 9789004737389 pdf
Subjects: LCSH: Artificial intelligence--Law and legislation | Artificial intelligence--Safety measures | Artificial intelligence--Government policy | Online dispute resolution
Classification: LCC K564.C6 W56 2025 (print) | LCC K564.C6 (ebook) | DDC 340.0285/63--DC23/ENG/20250721
LC record available at https://lccn.loc.gov/2025020946
LC ebook record available at https://lccn.loc.gov/2025020947

Typeface for the Latin, Greek, and Cyrillic scripts: "Brill". See and download: brill.com/brill-typeface.

ISSN 3050-9378
ISBN 978-90-04-73629-0 (hardback)
ISBN 978-90-04-73738-9 (e-book)
DOI 10.1163/9789004737389

Copyright 2025 by Koninklijke Brill BV, Plantijnstraat 2, 2321 JC Leiden, The Netherlands.
Koninklijke Brill BV incorporates the imprints Brill, Brill Nijhoff, Brill Schöningh, Brill Fink, Brill mentis, Brill Wageningen Academic, Vandenhoeck & Ruprecht, Böhlau and V&R unipress.
All rights reserved. No part of this publication may be reproduced, translated, stored in a retrieval system, or transmitted in any form or by any means, electronic, mechanical, photocopying, recording or otherwise, without prior written permission from the publisher. Requests for re-use and/or translations must be addressed to Koninklijke Brill BV via brill.com or copyright.com.
For more information: info@brill.com.

This book is printed on acid-free paper and produced in a sustainable manner.

*For* DGM
Leah Wing

*"Even if we do not know where we will arrive,*
*we do know how we will get there."*
Chris Draper

*For Sheila, Preston, and Colleen.*
*As always.*
Scott Cooper

*For Julia*
*My North Star*
Daniel Rainey

# Contents

# Notes on Authors

*Leah Wing*

Ed.D., is Director of the National Center for Technology and Dispute Resolution (NCTDR) and Senior Lecturer II and Honors Director, Department of Legal Studies, University of Massachusetts Amherst, USA. Co-founder, board member and 2023 President of the International Council for Online Dispute Resolution (ICODR), Leah co-led the development of the NCTDR-ICODR Online Dispute Resolution Standards. She served as a researcher on early interdisciplinary experiments in online dispute resolution and her present research projects focus on ODR ethics and AI and on technology and disaster response. Leah serves on the editorial boards of the *International Journal of Online Dispute Resolution* and *Conflict Resolution Quarterly*. As a trainer and consultant, Leah has worked with hundreds of agencies and organizations both in the U.S. and internationally.

*Chris Draper*

Ph.D., P.E., is a technologist whose career has focused on reducing human errors using novel technologies in safety critical environments. He has held roles from computational modeler in the aerospace industry to C-suite positions in the renewable fuels industry, and supported entrepreneurial and intrapreneurial efforts at companies ranging from startups to Fortune 100 companies in industries including real estate to automotive to education. In the LegalTech space, he has been a longtime contributor and leader to problems of data security, confidentiality, and equitable information use for applications ranging from dispute resolution to access to justice. He is a Visiting Scholar at the Indiana University Ostrom Workshop focusing on blockchain governance and intangible valuation and a Fellow of the National Center for Technology in Dispute Resolution.

*Scott Cooper*

has been involved in global governance issues most of his career; on consumer protection issues in the US House of Representatives; working on global electronic commerce issues reporting to the CEO of Hewlett-Packard; and as Vice President for Policy at the American National Standards Institution. He was federal government affairs manager in the Washington D.C., office of Hewlett-Packard and was responsible for global electronic commerce, Internet and advanced network services issues for HP. Scott has worked closely on U.S. legislation dealing with nanotechnology, electronic signatures and authentication, telephone competition, Internet taxes and consumer protection issues, such as privacy. Before joining HP, Scott was director of Electronic Commerce at the American Electronics Association (AEA), and manager of Telecommunications Policy at Intel. He also worked for many years for the U.S. Congress. As professional staff for the Commerce Committee of the House of Representatives he had responsibility for the Federal Trade Commission (FTC), the Federal Communications Commission (FCC), and the Interstate Commerce Commission (ICC).

*Daniel Rainey*
is a founder and principal in Holistic Solutions, Inc. (HSI), which he and his wife/partner Julia Morelli founded in 1996 as a home for their practice in dispute resolution, organizational development, and communication. He is a Fellow of the National Center for Technology and Dispute Resolution, housed at the University of Massachusetts Amherst. He is a founding member of The International Council for Online Dispute Resolution (ICODR), an international consortium that drives the development, convergence, and adoption of open standards for the global effort to resolve disputes and conflicts using information and communications technology. He has developed graduate level ODR courses for several universities, in addition to skills-based ODR training for dispute resolution centers and professional associations. As a consultant, he has worked with clients in the development of ODR resources, ADR programs, intercultural negotiation skills, Ombudsman programs, and organizational conflict engagement programs in the public, private, and non-profit sectors. In September, 2017, he retired as the Chief of Staff for the National Mediation Board, and in October, 2017, at the Association for Conflict Resolution annual conference, he received the Mary Parker Follett Award for innovation in dispute resolution.

# Introduction and Rationale

The key questions that any authors beginning work on a book should ask themselves are rather simple: why are we writing this book, at this time? In our case, for this book, the answers are both straightforward and complex. We are, as a society, embarking on a radical change in the way we relate to information and communication technology, a change that we think is as profound as the development of the printing press or the onset of the Industrial Revolution. Geoffrey Hinton, a recipient of a 2024 Nobel Prize for the development of neural network capabilities in AI, suggests that the inevitable direction of the evolution of AI should be a matter of concern.

> [Development of AI that thinks like humans] will be comparable to the Industrial Revolution. Instead of exceeding people in physical strength, it's going to exceed people in intellectual ability. We have no experience of what it's like to have things smarter than us.[1]

In the recent past, artificial intelligence (AI) has advanced to a degree that is surprising even to the experts and developers who are responsible for the advancement. And it is advancing in largely uncontrolled and unregulated environments in a context in which the future is unknown and the present already has revealed some significant risks to the use of AI. Put simply, the foundation idea of this book is that making some effort to put guardrails around AI development and use is a game worth the candle.

If Hinton is correct, who will be affected? In a word, everyone. As Hinton and his co-Nobelist John Hopfield suggest, most of us will feel the impact of AI in relatively positive ways, with improved health care and improvements in productivity. But they add:

> ... we also have to worry about a number of bad consequences, particularly the threat of these things getting out of control.[2]

1 Geoffrey Hinton, in Dereck Bryson, Taylor Cade Metz, and Katrina Miller, "Nobel Physics Prize Awarded for Pioneering AI Research by 2 Scientists," The New York Times, October 8, 2024, available at https://www.nytimes.com/2024/10/08/science/nobel-prize-physics.html

2 Ibid.

© KONINKLIJKE BRILL BV, LEIDEN, 2025 | DOI:10.1163/9789004737389_002

Basically, arguments about governance of AI center on how to 'control' AI: how to prevent or blunt the 'bad' uses of AI, and how to encourage and guide the 'good uses' of AI. Put simply, the question that often surfaces is simply, can we control Artificial Intelligence? The answer is No, and Yes. Depending on the way one defines "control."

If by "control" one means the ability to put a protective fence around AI platform development, adoption, and use in such a way that disruptive and harmful uses are impossible, the answer is a very hard No. The very nature of AI development to date has meant that at least some basic AI tools are generally available to users who can adapt AI platforms or use existing platforms to engage in socially and politically negative ways. AI will certainly amplify existing on-line concerns, and will no doubt add new ones to the mix, such as:

- Fiction posing as fact – getting single documents tentatively accepted as *bona fide* will be easier with AI tools.
- Security, privacy, protected personal information (PPI), sensitive information – the techniques of data protection and the definition of what data must be protected are issues that have been in the public domain for decades, but the emergence of AI will add to the concerns around these issues. AI's ability to provide higher fidelity context to data whose protection could previously have been thought safe to ignore will bring both unexpected complexities and practical solutions.
- Trustworthiness – the ability of malign AI programs to deliberately misconstrue public requirements for accuracy, safety, reliability and security, is of great concern.

Some of the negative uses of AI may be simply extensions of bad behaviors that already exist in social media. For example:

> The fake [pornographic] images of Taylor Swift that spread like wildfire on social media in late January [2024] likely began as a chatroom challenge to bypass filters meant to stop people from creating pornography with artificial intelligence ….[3]

The uses of AI to create fake political content are already almost too numerous to count, even at the local political level.

3 Kate Gibson, CBS MoneyWatch, "Fake and Graphic Images of Taylor Swift Started with AI Challenge," available at https://www.cbsnews.com/news/taylor-swift-artificial-intelligence-ai-4chan/, last accessed in April 2024.

> In Chicago [in 2024], the runner-up in the mayoral vote in April complained that a Twitter account masquerading as a news outlet had used AI to clone his voice in a way that suggested he condoned police brutality.[4]

The lesson that can be taken from the current nefarious uses of AI is that AI technology is already available to a degree that ensures that even non-governmental bad actors have access to potentially harmful tools and are willing to use them. Further, the open nature of AI development so far has '... triggered concerns that the tech could be used by America's geopolitical rivals or by criminals or fraudsters.'[5] Unfortunately, those concerns no longer belong in the future – they are relevant now, and throughout the world. And, as history has proved time and time again, bad actors will act badly no matter how diligently mainstream society tries to thwart their bad behavior. Total control, we argue, is not possible.

However, if by 'control' one means: 1) that there are sufficiently clear and transparent guidelines, regulations, and standards in place to guide AI developers as they create products that can be used by governments and private entities, and 2) information about AI platforms is accessible to consumers as they seek to make an informed choices, and is sufficiently understandable to guide potential users as they choose to adopt or reject AI products, the answer to 'can we control AI?' is a qualified Yes. At least in these basic senses, AI may be governed if not totally controlled. Govern*ance* of AI, we argue, is not the sole realm of govern*ment*, but is rather a responsibility that merges government action with self-regulation through the adoption of accepted international and professional standards.

In this book we argue first that governance, in the sense of guidelines for those developers and users of AI who want to operate ethically, has to cross a boundary between laws and regulation (which are mandatory and bound by venue) and voluntary standards (which can be universal but not legally binding). We further argue that the most effective controls on AI will be those that coordinate between and among law, regulation, and

4 Tiffany Hsu and Stephen Lee Meyers, "A.I.'s Use in Elections Set Off a Scramble for Guardrails," The New York Times, https://www.nytimes.com/2023/06/25/technology/ai-elections-disinformation-guardrails.html, last accessed in April, 2024.

5 Gerrit De Vynch and Naomi Nix, "META Releases Open-Source AI Model It Says Rivals OpenAI, Google Text," The Washington Post, July 23, 2024. Available at https://www.washingtonpost.com/technology/2024/07/23/meta-new-ai-llama-open/, last accessed in July 2024.

standards. We further argue that there are existing standards of practice addressing AI within fields of practice, and which cross professional and jurisdictional borders to guide ethical behavior generally. The standards of practice developed in the field of online dispute resolution will serve as our north star for standards that cross borders, both professional and national, and which can be coordinated with law and regulation to create effective guidance for developers and users of AI for dispute handling. Ultimately, avoiding the 'bad consequences' of which Hinton and Hopfield warn us will depend on regulations and standards to guide the developers of AI, the providers of AI services and applications, and the consumers who will choose to use or not use the plethora of AI options that inevitably will be available as AI advances.

## 1 A Review of Disruption and Responses to New Technology

At the risk of diverting from our main argument that governance of AI must be a cooperative effort between and among governments and standards creators, it is interesting to note that the excitement about the possibility of AI adding positively to society echoes the optimistic tone set by early researchers, *and* that the anxiety about the disruptive and negative aspects of AI development have seeds in earlier anxiety about technological change, and the need for some standardization.

The transit from mainframe to minicomputers to PCs was helped by a consensus ultimately reached, with IBM as an outlier, on the use of the American Standard Code for Information Interchange (ASCII), developed by ANSI (American National Standards Institute) in 1963.[6]

Based on the ASCII consensus code, the internet started as a mostly self-regulated academic and research body that grew exponentially. In the early days with the sky's the limit thinking and few guard rails, Vint Cerf (and many others) felt that *ad hoc* consensus governance could (and would) take on the wicked problems that the nation-states had ignored.

> [I]t is expected that we will also uncover important social, economic and political issues. Over the long run, our objective is to seek resolution of these issues ..."[7]

6 "Because of its beachhead in minicomputers, ASCII would prevail in the personal computer and workstation environment...". A History of Modern Computing. Paul Ceruzzi. MIT Press 2000. p. 152.

7 ISO TC 6.1 on global internet standards . Vent Cerf. Jan 15, 1974. Quoted,. Open Standards. Andrew Russell. Cambridge 2014. p. 175.

At the birth of the World Wide Web, in the 1990s, Tim Berners-Lee realized that the human remit was not just about creating revolutionary technologies such as the Web. Behind such exciting technical breakthroughs was the realization that:

> ... computers could also follow and analyze the tentative connective relation, unveiling entirely new ways to see our world. A system able to do that would be a fantastic thing.[8]

We have, as a society, benefited by the scope and depth of the technical breakthroughs laboriously gained over the past sixty years: electrical switching circuits, the transistor, the transit from analog to digital, the silicon computer chip, the internet, the Web. All are tools that help supply ubiquity and universality to modern communications and information sharing, opening up new ideas, opportunities and challenges.[9] But behind each of these invaluable tools was an even richer concept – that of using the advantage these tools gave us to extend the power of the human mind. Truly stealing fire from the gods.

This concept with AI and with other technologies in the past has been at once exciting, disruptive, and frightening.

Galileo's discovery of the moons of Jupiter through the use of an adjustable machine (the telescope) in one motion made old theories of time and distance in the universe obsolete, disconcerting many in authority who saw their worldview, and often their authority, slip away.

Behind the visible stars were infinite others, which could not be seen, except through a machine. As Milton described in Paradise Lost, 'The secrets of the hoary Deep – a dark Illimitable Ocean, without bound, Without Dimension.'[10] Human intelligence before Galileo was, in fact, upended, and we still have not caught up with the universe as first revealed by Galileo and most recently captured by Hubble and Webb.[11]

---

8 Weaving the Web. Berners-Lee. NY. 1999. p. 5.

9 The euphoria of new technological systems however often leads to 'Utopia fatigue'. In October 1945, President Truman told Congress that atomic power "may someday prove to be more revolutionary in the development of human society than the invention of the wheel, the use of metals, or steam, or internal combustion engines" Seventy years later, still a work in progress. (Message to Congress 10/3/45) Endless Frontier p. 296.

10 The Sleepwalkers Arthur Koestler London 1959 (PB 1982) p. 373 Quoting Paradise Lost Book ii p. 890.

11 Only forty years after Galileo's invention, a Danish astronomer Roemer tracked Jupiter's moons and found that sunlight reflected from the one closest to Jupiter lagged by 1320 seconds when the moon's position was farthest from earth than that when closest. This fact induced from the Rev. 1 telescopes of the day gave Roemer a very

Another adjustable machine, the printing press, made the written word available to a growing literate public, not just the Great and the Good. To Erasmus, print would build 'a library which has no other limits than the world itself.'[12] While the technical concept of movable type was well received, it also released malign and aggressive usages. Books were burned as well as martyrs.

The invention of movable type did not just create a better, more efficient system of literary distribution; it also empowered a growing middle class to participate in the *de facto* Republic of Letters. To have opinions about governance (political and personal) was to be part of an enlightenment that has made the world modern. 'Books were just the vehicles by which ideas escaped from the private libraries of the elite, and circulated among the population.'[13] Where the telescope forced human thought to confront a three-dimensional (maybe four?) universe, the printing press pointed to a new world where access to ideas was now cheap, accessible and fungible.

As with AI, books (and the ideas they hold), were suspect and subject to close scrutiny in most nation-states.[14] When print was finally released from legal fetters in Queen Anne's England at the beginning of the 18th century,[15] among the first to emerge as producers of print information were the 'hacks of Grub Street,' who mixed fact with fabrications (and hallucinations, a term currently applied to questionable output from AI).

> Sheer poverty compelled them to work – were it political pamphlets, scandal sheets, pornography ... or any of the other chores associated with starvation scribbling.[16]

And yet closely following were the works of Swift, Dafoe, Pope, Steele, and Addison who charted a golden age of English literature, poetry, and commentary.[17]

---

close approximation of the speed of light... Again, in 1676... Michelson and the Speed of Light Bernard Jaffe Wesleyan U. 1960 pp. 24–27.

12 The Printing Press as an Agent of Change Elizabeth Eisenstein Cambridge 1979 p. 219.

13 Tools for Thought Howard Rheingold NY 1985 p. 14.

14 Printers in Venice, Amsterdam, and some American colonies kept the Republic of Letters dialogues alive.

15 Queen Ann Copyright Act 1710; gave copyright to authors.

16 Authors by Profession. Victor Bonham-Carter Society of Authors. London. 1978. p. 28.

17 Before Queen Anne, authors would have to seek out noble patrons who would receive effusive dedications (and free books), for their patronage.

The art historian Kenneth Clark defended photography from those who accused it of being an artificial technology that demeaned the Art of painting. He pointed out that Leonardo da Vinci encouraged Renaissance artists to:

> ... catch and set down correctly every gesture and expression ... They would, we may be sure, have taken the invention of photography very seriously.[18] [If Photography can come] ... so close to achieving what many good judges have believed to be the aim of painting, why do we hesitate to consider it as a branch of art? What essential quality does it lack?[19]

Clark pointed out that it was English landscape painters (not French impressionists) who were so outraged by the technical temerity of photography to intrude on their idylls with nature. Their favorite subject, as described by Clark in "The Machine in the Garden," was a vision of a static, unchanging 'Golden Age of grazing flocks, unruffled waters and a calm luminous sky, images of a perfect harmony between man and nature.'[20]

The telegraph, as the first electronic medium, had a difficult birth. In 1838 over sixty patent applications claimed founding rights to the technology.[21] The telegraph did find wide acceptance in the marketplace. What was sent over it however, could be controversial.[22] In its early years the telegraph faced little regulatory oversight.[23] But scams were a problem, as uniform (and official-looking) telegrams could pass on fiction disguised as fact. There were concerns at inception that people would have access to this new technology, without adequate safeguards for fraud, deception, privacy and security.[24] The telegraph could be tapped, signals intercepted and telegraph operators bribed. By 1851 in the US over 70% of all telegraph traffic was commercial messages, as a contemporary telegraph operator described

18 Kenneth Clark Lecture given before the Royal Photographic Society on 13 October 1953.

19 Ibid "Further, I think that Goethe's favorite doctrine – that the nature of a thing can be understood only in its growth is particularly true of photography" Ibid.

20 The Machine in the Garden" Leo Marx Oxford UK 1964 [PB 1967] p. 89.

21 Ruling the Waves Deborah Spar NY 2001 p. 63.

22 The ubiquity of the telegraph and railroad schedules are considered the forcing mechanism that ultimately sent armies to the borders in August 1914.

23 Ruling the Waves p. 66.

24 Open Standards and the Digital Age. Andrew Russell U of Cambridge 2014.

it, 'conveying secrets of the rise and fall of markets.'[25] The fears and reservations are strikingly like those surrounding AI.

The lack of government oversight of the telegraph was initially countered by voluntary private standards (including Morse Code), that created a rough consensus among unruly groups from business, governments (federal, state and local), farmers and consumers.

In every case, new technology has appeared to offer new possibilities, and simultaneously has generated worries about significant problems and various attempts at preventing and resolving them. AI is no different.

In the world of eCommerce that emerged after the National Science Foundation lifted the ban on commerce on the Internet in 1992, an early form of AI, basically a process driven by algorithms, was created using decision trees to handle the millions upon millions of disputes generated by the act of buying and selling online. eBay's online dispute resolution program was and is the poster child for that type of algorithmic decision tree-based AI.[26]

The algorithms and AI that are in use in the bounded universe of online commerce, where there are a finite number of things that can go wrong (it did not arrive, it was not what was advertised, etc.) and a finite number of things that can be done to 'make peace' (give a refund, replace the item, etc.) the disruptive technology can work very well and concerns can be addressed when it doesn't. In a less bounded universe there are complicating issues that are relevant both to developers and users of the AI platforms. In Spain, an algorithm that rates the relative risk to spouses who have been victims of abuse uses 35 yes/no questions about the abuse and the abuser to give a score that indicates whether further protection for the abused is necessary. A case that made headlines involved an abused woman whom the algorithm judged was not in immediate danger. Her husband was released from jail and less than a week later she was dead.[27]

This is an example of what one of the authors of this book, Daniel Rainey, has called the "Colgate/Crest Caveat": if the universe is three hundred million people, it is possible to predict which toothpaste they will

25 What Hath God Wrought. Daniel Howe. Oxford 2007. p. 695.

26 For an overview of eBay's dispute resolution development, see Colin Rule, "Resolving Consumer Disputes: Making Peace on eBay," AC Resolution, Fall 2008, pp. 8–11.

27 Adam Satariano and Roser Toll Pifarre, "An Algorithm Told Police She Was Safe. Then Her Husband Killed Her," New York Times, July 18, 2024. Available at https://www.nytimes.com/interactive/2024/07/18/technology/spain-domestic-violence-viogen-algorithm.html?smid=em-share, last accessed in July 2024.

buy, within a point or two, over the next year. If one takes a single individual from that three hundred million, prediction becomes risky at best. Risk is acceptable when predicting the purchase of toothpaste. Not so acceptable when individual lives are at risk or access to justice hangs in the balance. The issue of governance this raises is related to the data set from which the AI learns, how the AI is taught to interact with that data set, and the risks of its use or misuse. These basic issues – what data set the AI uses, how it learns from that data set, and the implications of its usage – are key to the notion of governing AI in a way that is ethical and understandable.

The history of reaction to disruptive technology mirrors patterns today of excitement about new possibilities and increased access to them as well as concerns about the dangers AI is already manifesting and risks of others unknown. Crafting governance mechanisms for harnessing the positive potential of AI and restricting its threats are challenges for today and likely many tomorrows.

## 2 Issues of Governance for AI

Transparency is a common feature of discussions surrounding the control or governance of AI as it continues to develop. The assumption being that if the development of AI platforms is open to review by regulators and potential users, the likelihood of "dangerous" AI will be reduced and potential users of AI platforms will be better able to select products that fit their ethical and procedural needs. In an open letter to the SEC, OpenAI staff argued that, '[it isn't possible] that AI companies can build technology that is safe and in the public interest if they shield themselves from scrutiny and dissent.'[28]

But absolute transparency has its negative side and the doubtful possibility of achieving it at present is illustrated by the results of a review of transparency in available AI platforms. In 2023, Stanford University published a study using several indices of transparency, measuring on a scale of 100 the relative transparency of ten of the AI platforms available at the time.[29] The

28 The open letter can be found at https://www.washingtonpost.com/documents/83df0e55-546c-498a-9efc-06fac591904e.pdf?itid=lk_inline_manual_4, last accessed in July 2024.

29 Current as of 2023.

best score was 54, barely half of the arguably desirable one hundred percent transparency that was set as the ideal for the study.[30]

There are three common arguments suggesting that total transparency regarding data sets and internal programming is not a good idea.

First, it is argued that complete transparency regarding programming and the data set on which the AI is learning would undercut a platform's competitive advantage in the marketplace. This seems a reasonable argument given the past performance of the tech sector in protecting, or failing to protect, intellectual property.

Second, it is thought that complete transparency would benefit bad actors who wish to take the best ideas and approaches from commercial AI and adapt them for nefarious purposes. This also seems a reasonable argument, but, as we have said, any attempt to keep bad actors from behaving badly, no matter how opaque development may be, is probably a losing battle. Ethical guidelines and regulations may be effective for those who wish to operate in a responsible manner, but bad actors will find a way to act badly. Not all will have ethical and societally beneficial uses in mind.

Third, complete transparency would accelerate the advancement of AI. This is seen by some as a potential problem because there is a growing fear that in an open, transparent environment, AI will more rapidly become an independent actor in many spheres, and will pose an increased threat to humans. Sam Altman, CEO of OpenAI, has suggested that some restrictive controls on AI, including the guarding of developmental information, is critical for at least slowing the spread of AI expertise to countries and actors who do not have the best interests of the United States at heart.[31]

> So AI nationalism – the idea that a country must develop its own tech to serve its own interests – is spreading. Countries have enacted new laws and regulations. They've formed new alliances. The United States, perhaps the best positioned in the global AI race, is using trade policy to cut off China from key microchips. In France, the president has heaped praise upon a startup focused on chatbots and other tools that excel in French and other non-English languages. And in Saudi Arabia,

30 Katherine Miller, "Introducing the Foundation Model Transparency Index, October 18, 2023, Stanford University. Available at https://hai.stanford.edu/news/introducing-foundation-model-transparency-index, last accessed in December 2023.

31 Sam Altman, "Who Will Control the Future of AI?", The Washington Post, July 25, 2024. Available at https://www.washingtonpost.com/opinions/2024/07/25/sam-altman-ai-democracy-authoritarianism-future/, last accessed in July 2024.

> Crown Prince Mohammed bin Salman is pouring billions into AI development and striking deals with companies like Amazon, IBM and Microsoft to make his country a major new hub.[32]

A basic challenge for those wishing to govern AI exists surrounding governments' use of it in their own national interests, and engaging private corporations to develop applications. As one of its closing acts, on January 13, 2025, the Biden administration issued new export controls on computer chips and technology critical to the development of AI and AI systems.[33] Peter Harrell, a nonresident Fellow at the Carnegie Endowment for International Peace argued:

> This is definitely a departure from how we've thought about technology since the early '90s and the growth of the Internet .... It is in many ways conceptually more consistent with the way we thought about the role of technologies ... during the Cold War.[34]

It would be easy to dismiss the threat of radical harm from unchecked AI development, or the compounding or creating of bias and other harms, as a paranoid sci-fi delusion, but, as we have seen from Dr. Hinton's comments and the Biden administration's actions, it is serious and taken seriously by many in government and the AI community. For a current example of radical change generated by AI, even before the advancement of AI to human-like thought, consider AI controlled targeting applications, even with humans in the loop, making decisions about whom to bomb. Steven Feldstein, a Senior Fellow at the Carnegie Endowment who studies the use of AI in war, notes that

---

32 Adam Satariano and Paul Mozur, "The Global Race to Control AI," The New York Times, August 14, 2024, available at https://www.nytimes.com/2024/08/14/briefing/ai-china-us-technology.html?smid=em-share

33 Ensuring U.S. Security and Economic Strength in the Age of Artificial Intelligence: https://www.whitehouse.gov/briefing-room/statements-releases/2025/01/13/fact-sheet-ensuring-u-s-security-and-economic-strength-in-the-age-of-artificial-intelligence/ The fate of the Biden administration's actions were reversed by the incoming Trump administration but they signal a growing concern about the link between national security and AI security, and they demonstrate the political and volatile nature of governance by governments.

34 Gerrit De Vynch and Eva Dou, "Biden's New AI Export Controls Cover Most of the World," The Washington Post, January 13, 2025: https://www.washingtonpost.com/technology/2025/01/13/ai-export-controls-chips-china/

> [If] you combine … [targeting decisions] with the acceleration these systems offer – as well as the questions of accuracy – … the end result is a higher death count than was previously imagined in war.[35]

The notion of AI making judgements that affect humans, based on an advanced ability to seek and use data and then reason from that data, is not far-fetched, and is, in fact, a reality now.

What faces developers, legislators, regulators, and ethicists regarding the openness of AI development, is a continuum for AI governance that runs from total transparency to total opacity. If we have total transparency, we know what we are getting with AI platforms, but the issues noted above are real and will affect development. If we have total opacity, AI platforms will be developed in the classic black box, and we as consumers or users of the platforms, will be, as the saying goes, buying a pig in a poke. But in this case, the developers will be creating the poke and the pig that is in it. And there are no guarantees that either the pig or the poke will be free of bias or unethical behavior. In fact, even with what are to date very basic uses of AI, bias has been a feature, not a bug, in AI systems. As Forbes has reported:

> [A US Dept. of Commerce Study] found that facial recognition AI often misidentifies people of color. If law enforcement uses facial recognition tools, this bias could lead to wrongful arrests of people of color. [And] Several mortgage algorithms in financial services companies have also consistently charged Latino and Black borrowers higher interest rates, according to a [study by UC Berkeley].[36]

The problems with the COMPAS system in use by Federal courts in the United States is well known,[37] and the study of a sentencing algorithm in Virginia revealed an amplification of the bias inherent in the data set from

35 Steven Feldstein, The Washington Post, December 30, 2024, available at https://www.washingtonpost.com/technology/2024/12/29/ai-israel-war-gaza-idf/

36 Bernard Marr, "The Problem with Biased AIs (and How to Make AI Better)," Forbes, https://www.forbes.com/sites/bernardmarr/2022/09/30/the-problem-with-biased-ais-and-how-to-make-ai-better/?sh=31993ada4770, last accessed in April, 2024.

37 See Jeff Larson, Surya Mattu, Lauren Kirchner and Julia Angwin, "How we Analyzed the COMPAS Recidivism Algorithm," available at https://www.propublica.org/article/how-we-analyzed-the-compas-recidivism-algorithm, and Ed Yong, "A Popular Algorithm Is No Better at Predicting Crimes Than Random People," The Atlantic, January 17, 2018, available at https://www.theatlantic.com/technology/archive/2018/01/equivant-compas-algorithm/550646/, last accessed in July 2024.

which it drew its sentencing recommendations.[38] These and other concerns about AI bias are explored more in depth in the chapters that follow.

Beyond transparency, governance must consider the roles that governments, businesses, consumers, and professional organizations should play in determining what are the risks faced in the use of AI, and what are the protections that should be in place.

As AI systems become more and more advanced and complex, their benefits and dangers will increase. So, in this book, our modest aim is to suggest ways to use the mechanisms of technology standards within disciplines, regulation, and international standards to impact those who wish to develop AI platforms ethically, protect the public, and, importantly, to guide those who wish to choose from the menu of available AI programs.

## 3 Approaches to Governance

What we suggest is that the approach to building governance for AI cannot effectively come from one direction. Any one approach from law or regulation or standards to setting limits, controls, or guardrails brings advantages and disadvantages, so that a comprehensive approach to AI has to involve approaches from those multiple directions. And, importantly, must be done in a way that both gives developers an understanding of what ethical users want in their AI systems, and gives potential users a framework for understanding and evaluating the AI systems among which they may choose. We think an approach that merges governance development strategies for ethics and standards of practice in existing technology-based fields (such as online dispute resolution), international standards, and traditional regulation, offer the best and most effective way to govern AI.

Altman has argued that, "If we want to ensure that the future of AI is a future built to benefit the most people possible, we need [an] innovative new strategy to make it happen."[39] This book does not pretend to be

---

38 Andrew Van Dam, "Algorithms Were Supposed to Make Virginia Judges Fairer. What Happened Was More Complicated," The Washington Post, November 19, 2019, available at https://www.washingtonpost.com/business/2019/11/19/algorithms-were-supposed-make-virginia-judges-more-fair-what-actually-happened-was-far-more-complicated/, last accessed in July 2024.

39 Altman, "Who Will Control the Future of AI?," https://www.washingtonpost.com/opinions/2024/07/25/sam-altman-ai-democracy-authoritarianism-future/

exhaustive, but rather seeks to contribute to further development of ethical AI governance, and in this spirit, offers one such innovative strategy.

The "regulatory" chapter of this book will address the various regulatory and legal approaches to controlling AI that are underway around the world. It will discuss the various approaches to regulation and legislation, and suggest why regulation works in some situations and does not work in others. The basic argument will be that regulation can be effective, but due to the nature of regulations as proscriptive guardrails based within national or local boundaries, regulations are problematic by being insufficient in the control of technology like AI and quickly becoming obsolete as technology rapidly advances. AI can and will cross borders as a matter of course, rendering an effective regulation in one venue impotent in another venue unless the regulations are associated with broadly accepted standards.

On 21 April 2021, the EU issued a 108-page draft law to address AI – 'Proposal for a Regulation Laying Down Harmonized Rules on Artificial Intelligence.'[40] At the time, it was hailed as visionary. Magrethe Votager, head of digital policy for the EU, called it 'landmark' and 'future proof.'[41] Unfortunately, nineteen months later, in November of 2022, the future caught up with the EU in the form of the release of ChatGPT, the underlying programming of which was not considered in the draft EU regulation. Svenja Hahn, a member of the EU Parliament, noted that, regarding legislation, '... we will always be lagging behind the speed of technology.'[42]

More recently, the European Parliament passed the Artificial Intelligence Act in March, 2024, and the Council approved the Act in May, 2024. The Act addresses risk, transparency, and innovation support for those countries affected by the Act. Time will tell whether the Act is effective at supporting good uses of AI and thwarting bad uses, but it is limited to the EU.[43]

---

40 The published draft can be found at: https://digital-strategy.ec.europa.eu/en/library/proposal-regulation-laying-down-harmonised-rules-artificial-intelligence

41 A review of the EU regulation and comments from drafters can be found at: Adam Satariano and Cecilia Kang, "How Nations are Losing a Global Race to Tackle AI's Harms," The New York Times, December 12, 2023. Online at: https://www.nytimes.com/2023/12/06/technology/ai-regulation-policies.html

42 Ibid.

43 For information on the Act: https://www.europarl.europa.eu/topics/en/article/20230601STO93804/eu-ai-act-first-regulation-on-artificial-intelligence#ai-act-different-rules-for-different-risk-levels-0

The first of two "standards" chapters will address the international standards development process and discuss examples of standards that easily cross borders and jurisdictions. Our basic argument will be that standards, if they are developed with a range of interested parties and are accepted internationally, have the ability to provide robust guardrails for all types of technology development and use, including AI.

Some efforts are already underway in the international community. In June 2022 (again some months before the release of ChatGPT) the International Standards Organization (ISO) published ISO/IFC 23053:2022, "Framework for Artificial Intelligence (AI) Systems Using Machine Learning [ML]."[44] The introduction to the document set forth the goal of the developers:

> This document aims to provide a framework for the description of AI systems that use ML. ML is a branch of AI that employs computational techniques to enable systems to learn from data or experiences.[45]

Yet, a weakness of formal standards is that they take a long time to develop, and perhaps a longer time to gain international consensus. If they are not regularly updated, they can be just as out of date as regulations. And, so far, they tend to be aimed at development more than at use.

The second "standards" chapter is devoted to standards of practice that have been created for the field of online dispute resolution (ODR) that set baseline requirements for dispute resolution system designers, practitioners, and platform providers who handle disputes in any sector within or across multiple societies. This chapter takes the existing standards of practice for online dispute resolution[46], which include specific references to AI, and suggests how those standards can be adapted in practice. The utility of the ODR Standards is that anyone who wishes to use technology, including AI, has a consensus-based set of guardrails for the adoption and use of technology platforms. And developers have a blueprint of what issues are of importance to practitioners and users. Although not all users of AI will be involved in dispute resolution, the standards have relevance to a broad range of

44 The published document can be obtained through: https://www.iso.org/standard/74438.html

45 Ibid.

46 The National Center for Technology and Dispute Resolution and the International Council for Online Dispute Resolution Online Dispute Resolution Standards can be found at https://icodr.org/standards/ and https://odr.info/standards/

professions, not solely lawyers, judges, mediators, and arbitrators, but also vendors, other service providers, and government agencies who use technology in their engagement with clients, customers, and the public at large. Essentially, dispute resolution involves managing communication, handling and understanding data, and managing group dynamics, all of which are core to human interaction and affect every sector of society. Basic technology already has been impacting each of those functions and AI will do so further, thus, the ODR Standards hold promise in having relevancy across both national and professional boundaries.

In the conclusion we will highlight how we have sought to reconcile the strengths and weaknesses of these three approaches to creating a governance environment for AI, and we will offer some recommendations about how to approach governing AI, based on the arguments that:

- International standards of practice for individual professions and other interested groups, like practitioners in the field of online dispute resolution, can be helpful across borders and professional fields even though they do not carry the force of law or regulation;
- International standards are particularly effective when developed in ways that mirror the reality of how technology disrupts silos, and when they are created by international entities attending to the importance of making the standards thin enough to be locally interpretable and jurisdictional relevant.
- Standards from international organizations may address the issue of cross border impacts, and may be more regularly updated, but may be slow in development and adoptions. While they lack the force of law or regulation, international consensus can be a powerful marketplace force.
- Regulations alone, based in a nation or locale, may initially be effective, but are usually behind the curve, are difficult to update, and may not work across borders or jurisdictions.

Again, our basic argument is that taking one approach to governing AI will not be sufficient. Essentially, it is clear to us that the most effective way to create guardrails that guide development and adoption of AI is to coordinate disciplinary standards that look beyond discipline and national borders with international standards that address general development and use, and with regulations and laws that mirror the disciplinary and international standards.

It is undoubtedly not possible to keep bad actors from using AI for nefarious purposes. It *is* possible to provide governance for those who wish to develop and use AI in a responsible and ethical manner.

Since ChatGPT landed like a technology bomb in 2022 it has been the case that discussions, praise, and hand wringing about AI has focused on generative AI. But that's not the whole story of AI. Prior to delving into the three chapters on regulation and standards, we set the context in Chapter One that will offer a look back (and forward) to set some boundaries about what we mean by AI, and indeed what needs governing. In Chapter Two we will examine how the AI industry views AI with the goal of highlighting key issues that governance mechanisms need to address.

CHAPTER 1

# Governing What? What Is AI?

So, what is it we suggest needs governance? AI is generally considered the simulation of human intelligence in machines that are programmed to think and learn. AI as a concept is certainly not new. One could begin the story of AI's evolution with the publication of Claude Shannon and Warren Weaver's *The Mathematical Theory of Communication* in 1949, wherein they discussed the problems of meaning and noise in communication channels.[1] Their book was part of a body of work that led to the development of digital communication as we know it, and which began to flourish in the 1950's. Among other significant work was the publication of Alan Turing's *Computing Machinery and Intelligence*. Turing's conclusion was:

> We may hope that machines will eventually compete with men in all purely intellectual fields .... We can only see a short distance ahead, but we can see plenty there that needs to be done.[2]

In 1942 Turing collaborated with Claude Shannon from Bell Laboratories and started a friendship that lasted until Turing's suicide a dozen years later. Both were influential in cryptography, with Shannon counseling Roosevelt and Turing advising Churchill during World War II. Wartime secrecy rules dictated that they could not confer about code making (or breaking) in their personal discussions, but what they shared were their ideas on artificial intelligence. As Shannon recounted later: 'We had dreams. Turing and I used to talk about the possibility of simulating entirely the human brain. Could we really get a computer [to be] the equivalent of the human brain?[3] Turing did seminal work in developing computer feedback loops[4], and

---

1 Claude Shannon and Warren Weaver, The Mathematical Theory of Communication, The University of Illinois Press, 1949.

2 A. M. Turing, *Computing Machinery and Intelligence*, Mind 49, p. 460, 1950.

3 A Mind at Play – How Claude Shannon invented the Information Age. Rob Goodman & Jimmy Soni. NY. 2017. p. 107.

4 Norbert Weiner had early on identified developing "feedback" mechanisms as a basic software requirement – (certainly for AI). "This control of a machine on the basis of *actual* performance rather than its *expected* performance ...". The Human Use of Human Beings. Norbert Wiener. ....... NY 1950. p. 24. Further, with the *lack* of feedback mechanisms, "Disastrous results are to be expected. ... whenever two agencies essentially foreign to each

© KONINKLIJKE BRILL BV, LEIDEN, 2025 | DOI:10.1163/9789004737389_003

Shannon on communications theory, but AI eluded them. 'We both thought that it should be possible in not very long, in ten or fifteen years. Such was not the case.'[5]

The decades of work that have followed Shannon and Weaver and Turing's work have illuminated the 'plenty that needs to be done,' and in fact researchers and developers have done many of the things that early theorists looking forward to the future of AI could only dimly envision.

The term Artificial Intelligence, or AI, was coined at a conference held at Dartmouth College during the Summer of 1956. The conference, *Dartmouth Summer Research Project on Artificial Intelligence*, hosted by Marvin Minsky, John McCarthy, and Claude Shannon, was an opportunity for a range of researchers to come together to discuss the possibility of creating intelligent machines.[6] The conference itself did not result in the creation of an AI platform, but following closely on the heels of the conference was the development of the first acknowledged AI program: Logic Theorist.[7]

In the decades that followed, 'intelligent' systems were slowly developed on an increasingly large scale. The 1960s were a time of attempted development, with little success in creating the machines that would 'compete with men' as Turning phrased it. The 1970s and 1980s were something of a down time in the development of AI, but in 1997 Deep Blue defeated chess champion Garry Kasparov, proving that in a bounded universe like chess, machines could more than merely compete with humans. By 2016, Google DeepMind's AlphaGo victory over then world champion Lee Sedol proved AI could win in, arguably, the world's most complex simple game.[8] In these victories we see the power of brute-force, computational advancement directed towards tasks where human computational capability was previously considered synonymous with intelligence.

---

other are coupled in the attempt to achieve a common purpose". "Blind Date" Norbert Weiner. 1960. in "Visions of Technology". Richard Rhodes. ed. NY 1999. p. 218 [Having a third-party mediator – such as AI – could be very useful in such situations ...].

5 Interview with Shannon, February 1977. Quoted in "A Mind at Play". p. 107.

6 For a retrospective view of the Dartmouth conference a half century later, see James Moor, *The Dartmouth College Artificial Intelligence Conference: The Next Fifty Years*, AI Magazine, Vol. 27, No. 4 (2006), pp. 87–91.

7 For a discussion of the development of *Logic Theorist, see Logic Theorist - Everything You Need to Know*, on History-Computer, found at https://history-computer.com/logic-theorist/, last accessed in December 2023.

8 AI's Victories in Go Inspire Better Human Game Playing: https://www.scientificamerican.com/article/ais-victories-in-go-inspire-better-human-game-playing/

Machines, or in the broad view, technology, creating disruption is not a new occurrence and certainly did not begin with AI. As early as 1961, a computer *savant* from MIT, Marvin Minsky, outlined 'Steps Toward Artificial Intelligence'[9] Minsky cautioned that those following the challenging path to AI attainment will 'be warned that these machines must be restrained, lest they overwhelm us by might, persuasion or even the revelation of truths too terrible to be borne.'[10] More than 60 years later, AI has proven to be an invaluable tool for a wide range of positive applications. But indefinite fears about the use of AI persist.

Beyond a focus on AI competing or outdoing humans at computationally intensive tasks, its history also reveals an interest in the relationship between the two, including seeing the former as an extension of the latter. Even before the Dartmouth Project, Vannevar Bush, in July 1945, proposed that we:

> ... consider a future device for individual use, which is sort of a mechanized private file ... so that it can be consulted with exceeding speed and flexibility ... [as] an enlarged intimate supplement to ... memory.[11]

Bush's comment gives wings to the issue of AI now before us with an interesting choice of words – not 'artificial,' but 'intimate,' a view of AI interacting with the intimate contemplations and observations that populate our memory.

Intuitively, Bush realized that creating knowledge from information was not to be dependent on artificial categories (alphabetization, Dewey Decimal, etc.), but on recognizing that ideas are formed by association with other ideas, creating concepts that had not existed before. He explains:

> I conceived the idea of a machine that could be an extension of the personal memory and the body of knowledge belonging to an individual, and would work in a fashion analogous to the working of the human brain – by association rather than by categorical classification.[12]

9 Steps Toward Artificial Intelligence Marvin Minsky in "Computers and Thought" Edward Feignenbaum (ed.) NY 1963 pp. 406–450.

10 Ibid p. 406 (copyright 1961).

11 "Atlantic Monthly". Vannevar Bush July 1945. Boston. Quoted in What the Dormouse Said. John Markoff. NY 2005. p. 7.

12 Pieces of the Action Vannevar Bush NY 1970 p. 190.

Using dynamic associations as the driver of knowledge creation, Bush forecast the goal of AI that is still being pursued: intelligent machines using relationships as the driver of evolutionary change.[13] It will be, he argued, 'a new form of inheritance, not merely of genes, but of intimate thought processes.'[14]

Joseph Licklider, an early computer pioneer, wrote in 1960:

> The hope is that in not too many years, human brains and computing machines will be coupled together very tightly and that the resulting partnership will think as no human brain has ever thought and process data in a way not approached by the information-handling machines we know today.[15]

Vint Cerf looked to see where new communications technologies would become a forcing mechanism for developing collaborative human/machine intelligence. Looking back, the pioneers who designed ARPANET (the Advanced Research Projects Agency Network) in 1969, which morphed into the Internet, built 'the first [successful] attempt to bridge that gap among theory, simulation and engineering.'[16]

The concept that allowed so many to dream of the possibilities related to AI started to take shape near the end of the twentieth century. Gains in computing power and coding efficiency gave way to the tools and techniques that have become what we know of as AI today. Advances in machine learning (ML) using artificial neural nets (ANN) and other deep learning techniques in the early 2000s, like the ImageNet classification breakthrough widely attributed to the work of Geoffrey Hinton while at Google,[17] empowered a whole host of other AI use case advances from computer vision to natural language processing (NLP). A non-exhaustive map

13 Endless Frontier: Vannevar Bush, Engineer of the American Century Pascal Zachary MIT 1999 "By mechanization the process of association, [Bush's computer] would extend the powers of the human mind." p. 262.

14 Ibid p. 401 [Quoting Bush from "Science Pauses" Fortune May 1965].

15 Man-Computer Symbiosis J.C. Licklider "IRE Transactions on Human Factors in Electronics HFE-1 March 1960.

16 Inventing the Internet Jane Abbate. MIT 2000 p. 229 Further, "Our approaches and philosophies have often differed radically, [but], we have found our collaboration to be extremely rewarding.) p. 72.

17 https://papers.nips.cc/paper/2012/hash/c399862d3b9d6b76c8436e924a68c45b-Abstract.html

showing examples from the wide tapestry of what make up modern AI technologies, methods, and strategies can be seen in Figure 1.1, with Narrow AI[18] systems integrated into products impacting nearly every aspect of our lives completing a wide range of specific use cases by combining various mixtures of these elements.

The official release of OpenAI's ChatGPT LLM on November 20, 2022, made AI tangible in a way that both simplified and mystified the public's views of the technology in near equal measure. Once the general public began interacting with the ChatGPT application and saw its ability to respond in a nearly instantaneous, human-like manner, debates on whether the tool was "sentient" clouded the reality and challenges the tools actually posed.[19] In many ways, ChatGPT allowed many to project the hopes and expectations discussed above, developed over decades of visioning and research, to see intelligence and creativity in the algorithms. This hype slowed the opportunity for thoughtful regulation, and in some cases has put discussions on, at best, tangential paths through a misunderstanding of what AI truly is.

Currently, AI is a mimic. Period.

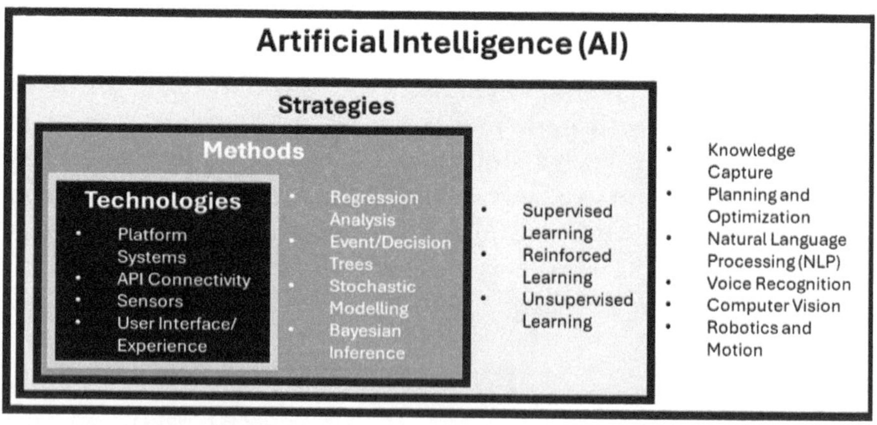


FIGURE 1.1 Layers making up AI
REVISED FROM ODR THEORY AND PRACTICE, SECOND EDITION

18 Narrow AI, which is also considered Weak AI, is designed to perform a specific task or a set of tasks, including virtual personal assistants like Siri or Alexa, recommendation systems on Netflix, and system functions like hazard recognition for autonomous vehicles. While thought leaders routinely speak about General AI, also considered Strong or Superintelligent AI systems that can mimic human action more broadly, it is important to realize that no General or Superintelligent AI systems exist as of 2024.

19 https://www.cbc.ca/radio/spark/bots-like-chatgpt-aren-t-sentient-why-do-we-insist-on-making-them-seem-like-they-are-1.6761709

This argument that AI is a mimic will often conflict with the perception that AI is augmenting intelligence in a manner that produces new innovation or new insight. Yet examining how AI produces outputs to which many have affixed perceptions of innovation or insight can be instructive for understanding the fundamental limits of the technology. For example, astronomers have been using AI for decades to help identify and refine views of distant galaxies that could not be seen with telescopes alone.[20] In this use case, where the physical limitations of pixel-based digital tools are fundamentally incapable of producing more clarity of such distant objects, AI is often interpreted by the public as a tool that is capable of boosting the telescope's ability to "zoom in" on these blurry items. But that is not what is happening. In this case, the pixels that can be captured to represent the distant object are too large relative to what is needed to provide additional clarity, leaving visual gaps that cannot be filled because the data needed to see better just doesn't exist. The AI is not providing higher resolution of the observed item. It is filling in these gaps in its vision of the obscured item by observing everything it has greater resolution of, expecting that what is missing should look like what it can see, and projecting a representation of what it has seen into the gaps. The output is interpreted as a view of something that has not been seen before, yet the reality is that it still remains unseen. The improved vision is not the item but a projection of the image created by mimicking what is expected to be seen.

As an alternative example, the Royal Swedish Academy of Sciences's inclusion of Demis Hassabis and John M. Jumper from Google DeepMind as equal recipients of the 2024 Nobel Prize in chemistry with biochemistry professor David Baker for their work on the AlphaFold provides support to arguments that AI exhibits creativity.[21] In this case, it is clear that AlphaFold was able to produce an innovative breakthrough in an area where a human mind could not operate fast enough to find what was previously unknown or unimagined. However, it did not arrive at this innovation through imagination, but like astronomers filling in the gaps with projections of their observations, it arrived at a novel representation of prior associations found through brute force evaluations unconstrained by human bias. Where creative processes led by humans are hampered with bias for what each feels is known, AI can offer new combinations of old realities in

20 https://www.pbs.org/newshour/science/analysis-how-ai-is-helping-astronomers-study-the-universe

21 https://www.technologyreview.com/2024/10/09/1105335/google-deepmind-wins-joint-nobel-prize-in-chemistry-for-protein-prediction-ai/#:~:text=Google%20DeepMind%20leaders%20share%20Nobel,to%20help%20design%20new%20proteins.

ways that spark human identification of advances beyond the limits of their prior knowledge. Yet these advances are not actually creative, rather they are merely produced in ways not borne of traditional, iterative innovation by humans. Therefore, they are artifacts of the AI tool mimicking truth in a manner that would be considered a "hallucination" if it could be proven incorrect.

The exact design of each AI tool will vary, with major architectural components or concepts remaining relatively similar. For example, ChatGPT is a Narrow AI LLM that is built on the Transformer architecture, introduced by Vaswani, *et al.*, in 2017.[22] Transformers use a mechanism called self-attention to weigh the importance of different words in a sentence, allowing them to capture long-range dependencies and contextual relationships. The probabilities within the ChatGPT Transformer are iteratively replaced with upgrades using increasingly larger datasets and are continually optimized for dialogue through Reinforcement Learning with Human Feedback (RLHF) that determines quality based on user ratings or regeneration requests of system outputs.

In a general sense, this technology is a massive probability model through which sentences are assembled word by word based on how likely each word would be related to each other based on the data that has been ingested. This random walk through these probabilities is how AI models like ChatGPT both appear human and also "hallucinate" falsehoods. The "brain" of the system is continually attempting to find an appropriately likely string of words, yet cannot truly know the perfect answer since it does not actually know what any of the words really mean. In cases where there is an underlying model that can be uncovered through ML or deep learning, this continually retraining of the Transformer or its equivalent component on larger and larger datasets produces a system that is able to "think" more precisely by randomly walking more tightly down more likely paths, even if it will never prevent the generation of factually inaccurate statements since randomness can never be removed from the system. Attempts to address this continue (but have yet to accomplish it) and include when factual or algorithmic accuracy are vital, hybrid strategies like retrieval-augmented generation (RAG) that essentially offer an LLM a library from which it can

22 Ashish Vaswani, Noam Shazeer, Niki Parmar, Jakob Uszkoreit, Llion Jones, Aidan N. Gomez, Lukasz Kaiser, Illia Polosukhin "Attention Is All You Need," 31st Conference on Neural Information Processing Systems (NIPS 2017), Long Beach, CA, USA https://arxiv.org/abs/1706.03762

retrieve precise data once it recognizes that part of its highest probability answer is referring to something precise.

Beyond the challenges of misperceptions of AI as sentient, its hallucinations presented as facts, and its (re)production of biased data (which will be discussed in more depth in later chapters), it is important to remember that the costs of training these models with larger and larger datasets is exorbitant in the face of the reality of climate change and high energy costs. Beyond the hardware cost where the calculations that build the AI models are performed, the energy required to build and run these models is multiples of nearly any other computational architecture that produces a similar benefit for the humans deploying it. By the third quarter of 2024, investors were already starting to question the economic viability of these ever-growing training exercises, fearing few viable pathways for returning their investments.[23]

With every modification or AI breakthrough up through 2024 came greater acceptance that we may be falling into the "Turing Trap" described by Erik Brynjolfsson, a senior fellow at the Stanford Institute for Human-Centered AI: 'that measuring the "machine's ability to exhibit intelligent behavior equivalent to a human … was the wrong goal all along.'[24] The limitations that this Turing Trap placed upon the general public's view of AI's value enabled a focus on the opportunities and fears of AI technology separate from its applications, preventing many from focusing on AI's true power and danger when used within its appropriately or inappropriately limited application contexts.

These limits of the technology are not broadly understood by the general public from which most legislators emerge, and regulators too often depend upon industry expert guidance which can be merely self-serving. In the case of AI, a seemingly magic technology masks the fact that it is merely amplifying and accelerating human directions. This obfuscation of the boundary between human direction and the sentient-like actions of AI allows many to direct blame on a technology that is working as directed, instead of strengthening the protections against those humans who are initiating societally damaging actions through the technology.

23 https://www.ft.com/content/42bad56f-02cc-4b32-b9ac-1af5dbc7bc83
24 https://www.ft.com/content/42bad56f-02cc-4b32-b9ac-1af5dbc7bc83

CHAPTER 2

# How the AI Industry Views AI Safety

The explosive growth of generative AI tools between 2022 and 2024 woke much of the public up to both the dangers and limitations of seemingly transformative tools that depend on LLMs. Response to this awakening, especially from those like Anthropic's Claude platform, focused on safety in an attempt to find new angles for capturing market share from OpenAI's dominating position as it went for-profit in late 2024. In the response to this need for safety can be seen the designer perspective on what makes these systems unsafe. Understanding what the industry considers "safety" offers a window into what the designers see as solvable problems. This window into these perceptions of safety by the AI industry, especially when balanced against the unaddressed risks left at the feet of our communities, can contribute to arriving at the root challenges with which any meaningful regulation, or governance in general, must grapple.

Most industry conversations around "AI safety" revolve around system reliability. For example, in the Center for Security and Emerging Technology 2021 series authored by Tim G. J. Rudner and Helen Toner, the authors propose 'three categories of AI safety issues: problems of robustness, assurance, and specification.'[1] These issues are presented in a series of papers which identify that:

> one of the most significant current challenges in AI safety is creating machine learning systems that are robust to adversarial examples,[2] rendering modern machine learning systems like deep neural networks interpretable will help us ensure that any such system deployed in safety-critical settings works as intended,[3] [or] being able to interpret a model's uncertainty estimates, determining the level of uncertainty in machine learning systems that human operators are comfortable with, and understanding when and why a system's

1 https://cset.georgetown.edu/publication/key-concepts-in-ai-safety-an-overview/

2 https://cset.georgetown.edu/publication/key-concepts-in-ai-safety-robustness-and-adversarial-examples/

3 https://cset.georgetown.edu/publication/key-concepts-in-ai-safety-interpretability-in-machine-learning/

© KONINKLIJKE BRILL BV, LEIDEN, 2025 | DOI:10.1163/9789004737389_004

> uncertainty estimates may be unreliable is extremely important for safety-critical application settings.[4]

The positions of these leaders in the field provides support for the argument that the industry generally considers AI safety to be framed as system performance, with the broader societal risks that could be posed by the systems themselves being contained within misspecification errors. These types of errors are revealed through observation of system performance, with the authors observing that the

> revealed specification typically differs from both the design and ideal specifications, and it is often difficult to find a design specification that leads to the intended outcomes – that is, for the revealed specification to match the ideal specification – which can lead to unintended and harmful consequences.[5]

This framing of "safety" as system reliability and appropriateness is echoed by OpenAI's statement that:

> our approach to AI safety ... includes "[age gating] use of our AI tools ... [prohibiting our technology from being] used to generate hateful, harassing, violent or adult content, among other categories ... respecting privacy ... improving factual accuracy ... [and] collaboration and open dialogue among stakeholders to create a safe AI ecosystem."[6]

This statement appears to reflect the safety guidance co-authored by Toner, above. Yet the turmoil around safety at OpenAI which subsequently led to Toner's departure from the OpenAI board raised questions regarding how effectively OpenAI was complying with its stated safety intent.[7]

This turmoil at OpenAI, despite the indications that the intentions of the AI industry regarding its definition of AI safety as being akin to platform reliability and output appropriateness are relatively homogeneous, turned

4 https://cset.georgetown.edu/publication/key-concepts-in-ai-safety-reliable-uncertainty-quantification-in-machine-learning/

5 https://cset.georgetown.edu/publication/key-concepts-in-ai-safety-specification-in-machine-learning/

6 https://openai.com/index/our-approach-to-ai-safety/

7 https://fortune.com/2024/10/24/openai-miles-brundage-suchir-balaji-ai-safety-copyright-sam-altman-chatgpt/

the focus on safety towards reliable implementation of these objectives. This is what allowed the market leader in "safety" as of late 2024 to be generally considered Anthropic's Claude AI model. Like its competitors, Claude uses a transformer architecture that processes large volumes of text using self-attention mechanisms that capture dependencies across words, sentences, and larger chunks of language. Like its competitors, Anthropic has taken the public stance that it implements a pseudo-opt-in approach to user data, stating the following in its terms of service:

> We will not use your Inputs or Outputs to train our models, unless: (1) your conversations are flagged for Trust & Safety review (in which case we may use or analyze them to improve our ability to detect and enforce our Usage Policy, including training models for use by our Trust and Safety team, consistent with Anthropic's safety mission), or (2) you've explicitly reported the materials to us (for example via our feedback mechanisms), or (3) by otherwise explicitly opting in to training.[8]

These claims made by Anthropic acknowledge that it does store performance data that could be used for evaluating system performance, it is able to identify the sources of data both used by its training model and supplied by its users, and data sources can be uniquely flagged or segregated by the system. Making these claims in their contract with their users indicates systems making these claims could take three actions that would likely be broadly supported by the communities they serve. First, these claims demonstrate that AI providers could publicly release data on system reliability, when reliability is considered historic system output as a function of input. Second, these claims demonstrate that dataset transparency is attainable, when transparency is considered a summary of the data sources used and their relative importance within any dataset being used by the model. And third, these claims demonstrate that these platforms can conform to restrictions on data ownership, when ownership is considered the ability to identify and appropriately respect the ownership rights of data sources. The relative ubiquity of these claims within most system user agreements indicates these capabilities are broadly shared across industry platforms and could be included as a mandatory aspect of the industry's expected base level of safety, with a majority of the public believing these

---

8 https://support.anthropic.com/en/articles/7996868-i-want-to-opt-out-of-my-prompts-and-results-being-used-for-training-models (retrieved October 7, 2024).

minimum levels of transparency should be required.[9] That Anthropic is placing a marketing wager on these basic capabilities remaining the standards defining safety demonstrates a significant challenge to shifting industry focus towards meaningful safety efforts.

For example, industry consensus tends to diverge when it comes to how AI system reliability should be evaluated or managed. Design strategy for AI systems nearly universally starts with choosing the desired level of human involvement. The three main types of human involvement strategies are illustrated in Figure 2.1 below and can be considered 'human-in-the-loop,' where a system cannot complete a process without human intervention; 'human-on-the-loop,' where a system operates autonomously until a human observing the system steps in to correct the automation; or 'human-out-of-the-loop,' where the human has no ability to influence the system while it is operating.[10]

From a design strategy level, examples of each system do exist as of 2024, even though implementation of each may not be complete. For example, Waymo is an operating, self-driving car technology that employs a human-out-of-the-loop design strategy for the vehicle while operating. This technology does still feature human-on-the-loop characteristics as Waymo can step in and correct system failures, but the design strategy of Waymo is to perfect its product until its operation is fully human independent. This differs from examples in manufacturing or logistics, where it is expected that a human will be checking the AI system outputs. For example, while AI will

FIGURE 2.1 AI safety strategies defined by the level of human involvement
PREVIOUSLY PRESENTED IN ODR THEORY AND PRACTICE, SECOND EDITION

9 https://www.pewresearch.org/short-reads/2024/03/26/many-americans-think-generative-ai-programs-should-credit-the-sources-they-rely-on/

10 Raymond, A.H., Draper, C.H. & Schubauer, J., "Artificial Intelligence Governance and Policy: A Practical Guide to Identifying, Understanding, and Mitigating Legal Risks Associated With AI Integration," Leading Legal Disruption: Artificial Intelligence and a Toolkit for Lawyers and the Law, Thomson Reuters, 2021, pp. 357–375.

now determine what packages must go into the back of which delivery vehicles for eCommerce giants like Amazon, it is expected that the humans ranging from order pickers to delivery drivers will provide sufficient oversight that any mistake made by the AI system will be caught before a package is considered delivered. LLM strategy regarding RLHF is often less clear, since making the regenerate function so easily accessible in most systems provides support to the argument that RLHF is essentially a human-in-the-loop technology, placing responsibility for the appropriateness of any output squarely on the user who accepted the output as appropriate.

Claude attempts to differentiate itself from other models that could be considered human-in-the-loop designs by focusing on automating ethical output generation review, a human out-of-the-loop strategy guided by a concept Anthropic calls *Constitutional AI*. Constitutional AI attempts to ensure responses adhere to ethical guidelines by integrating a set of predefined ethical principles, referred to as "constitutional principles," into the model during its training process. These principles provide a framework for the AI's decision-making, allowing it to autonomously evaluate the ethical implications of its responses as it generates them by evaluating how well a generated response aligns with this framework. Anthropic argues that implementation of this approach ensures the outputs adhere to socially acceptable standards, prioritizing fairness, inclusivity, and the avoidance of harmful or biased content. Embedded in this solution is recognition that system reliability can be viewed as model output variability, with unreliability often recognized by the general public as "hallucinations" when they produce something that is considered "wrong." The fundamentals of how Anthropic does this is not uncommon, and understanding how this is done will help regulators understand what core risks exist and how they should be managed.

Anthropic's ethical decision-making process begins like most others approaching this problem with the initial output generation phase. When Claude receives a user prompt, it utilizes its transformer architecture to produce a response, drawing on patterns it has learned from vast datasets during training. At this stage, Claude functions similarly to other language models, generating a coherent response based on its deep learning capabilities, which predict the most likely continuation of the input text. Unlike models that rely solely on traditional, human-in-the-loop approaches, like reinforcement learning from human feedback (RLHF), Claude immediately follows this by evaluating its output for ethical alignment.

After generating the initial response, the model enters a self-supervision phase where Claude compares its output against the ethical guidelines encoded within its constitution. These principles were integrated during training and represent a comprehensive framework that fundamentally operates much like a RAG, yet instead of focusing on factual accuracy, this constitution is the system truth against which the AI checks if a response aligns with values such as safety, non-discrimination, and factual accuracy. Claude evaluates the output across several dimensions, including the potential for harmful language, misinformation, or bias. For instance, if the response contains violent language or perpetuates harmful stereotypes, the model flags the output for review based on how far it deviates from its constitutional principles. This step assesses the degree to which the response is ethically appropriate, using a defined tolerance threshold. If the response crosses this threshold, it is marked as problematic.

Once a response is flagged, Claude proceeds to the self-critique and adjustment phase. In this stage, the model reassesses the flagged output in light of the identified ethical violation and makes necessary modifications. If the violation is minor, the model might adjust the response by refining the tone or rephrasing certain elements. For more significant deviations – such as content that could cause harm or is overtly offensive – the model may reformulate the entire response. This adjustment often involves reweighting the importance of certain words or ideas that contributed to the problem. Through this self-critique process, Claude seeks to ensure that it can autonomously refine its outputs to better align with its ethical guidelines, without the need for human intervention.

This is not to say that Claude does not depend upon human review. It instead demonstrates a strategy that more closely aligns with human-on-the-loop systems. Beyond these individual instances of flagging and correction, Claude incorporates feedback over time to continuously improve its ethical decision-making. This is where reinforcement learning comes into play. Human trainers evaluate the model's outputs and provide feedback on whether its ethical judgments are too lenient or overly restrictive. Claude uses this feedback to adjust its tolerance levels and refine how it handles future responses. For example, if certain phrasing is consistently flagged as problematic, the system learns to apply stricter standards to similar outputs in the future. This continuous learning process enables Claude to adapt to evolving ethical standards and improve its ability to manage complex ethical dilemmas.

Claude's real-time self-supervision that automatically compares each output against its constitutional framework is considered the feature that enhances the model's ability to prevent harmful outputs before they reach the user. Yet these ethical principles are not static. Claude's ethical principles are developed from a range of sources, including human rights protocols, fairness doctrines, and safety standards that are curated and considered widely accepted by the system designers. If it is assumed that these generalized principles are capable of addressing a wide spectrum of ethical issues from avoiding discriminatory language, steering clear of misinformation, or ensuring its responses promote inclusivity, it must be accepted that its ability to respond appropriately to complex moral or ethical questions without requiring detailed task-specific rules for each scenario is predicated on the appropriateness of the system constitution.

This mechanism that allows Claude's AI to evaluate its responses in real time and actively assess their ethical implications as they are generated, moving away from reliance on post-output human correction, requires us to accept that human influence on constitution design and appropriateness thresholds are in many ways more important when the use of RLHF on an output-by-output basis is minimized. As system standards become the kernel from which the system starts growing and exploring what is appropriate by autonomously completing its own evaluation of what is inappropriate, we start to arrive at two vital conclusions. First, the rate at which our society pivots its attention away from solely focusing on AI as the source of harm and accepts the role of the designer and operator as the root cause of many challenges made evident through the unique qualities of AI will define the pace and success of any regulatory effort. Second, the jurisdictional framework for prior technology regulation is not sufficient for protecting the public once a system is allowed to grow in an unsupervised manner bounded by nothing but its perceptions of its operational jurisdiction.

The true danger of AI, which in many ways accelerates if we accept that Anthropic's "human-on-the-loop" approach to output validation is "safe," is that AI tools can generate actions at rates exceeding a human's ability to validate their suitability. Exactly like Tesla's driver assist technology being sold as "autopilot," Anthropic's Constitutional AI increases the risk that users will be lulled into complacent acceptance of any system output because the effort to maintain the human's responsibility as a component of the safety system protecting against erroneous output exceeds our capabilities. It is this reality that humans are outmatched when attempting to protect against dangerous AI products that is leading to recent examples of the application-associated dangers from which any AI regulation must be prepared to protect society.

## 1 How Society Must Begin to View AI Danger

On December 4, 2024, at 6:40 a.m. on a busy Midtown Manhattan, New York City street in front of the New York Hilton hotel, it was reported that Luigi Mangione pulled out a 3D printed ghost gun and shot

UnitedHealthcare (UHC) CEO Brian Thompson to death.[11] Before his capture, the clearest indication of Mangione's motive was interpreted from the phrase etched onto the shell casings left at the scene and popularized by Jay Feinman's 2010 book: "Delay, Deny, Defend."[12] It was not AI that pulled the trigger in this case of Thompson's death. Yet it is reasonable to read the manifesto found with Mangione as a call to take down a healthcare system using AI as UHC did in a manner that could be interpreted as akin to stochastic terrorism.[13]

In the case of UHC, indications from a Minnesota lawsuit filed on behalf of two deceased UHC patients purport that UHC deployed AI:

> in place of real medical professionals to wrongfully deny elderly patients care owed to them under Medicare Advantage Plans by overriding their treating physicians' determinations as to medically necessary care based on an AI model that [UHC knew to have] a 90% error rate ... because they know that only a tiny minority of policyholders (roughly 0.2%)[14] will appeal denied claims, and the vast majority will either pay out-of-pocket costs or forgo the remainder of their prescribed post-acute care.[15]

The damages being pursued in that case were merely financial. Yet the harms inflicted on the public by these types of tools in pursuit of a 'clear financial windfall in the form of policy premiums without having to pay for promised care' range from 'the elderly [being] prematurely kicked out of care facilities nationwide or forced to deplete family savings to continue receiving necessary medical care.'[16] Given the likelihood of death in the absence of care or the fact that medical bills account for 40% of bankruptcies' at the time of the shooting,[17] these outcomes have provided most Americans with an earned fear of the healthcare system, including feelings of being

11 https://abcnews.go.com/US/unitedhealthcare-ceo-shooting-suspect/story?id=116460289

12 https://apnews.com/article/unitedhealthcare-ceo-shooting-delay-deny-defend-depose-ee73ceb19f361835c654f04a3b88c50c

13 Amman, M., & Meloy, R. (2024). Incitement to violence and stochastic terrorism: Legal, academic, and practical parameters for researchers and investigators. *Terrorism and Political Violence, 36*(2), 234–245. https://doi.org/10.1080/09546553.2022.2143352

14 Karen Pollitz, et al., Claims Denials and Appeals in ACA Marketplace Plans in 2021, KFF (Feb. 9, 2023) https://www.kff.org/private-insurance/issue-brief/claims-denials-and-appeals-in-aca-marketplace-plans/ (last visited Nov. 13, 2023).

15 https://cdn.arstechnica.net/wp-content/uploads/2023/11/class-action-v-unitedhealth-and-navihealth-1.pdf

16 https://cdn.arstechnica.net/wp-content/uploads/2023/11/class-action-v-unitedhealth-and-navihealth-1.pdf

17 https://pmc.ncbi.nlm.nih.gov/articles/PMC1127305/

"trapped" once they experience medical debt.[18] The intentional use of AI tools that are capable of putting individuals in these harmful mental, physical, and financial states through no fault of their own with no effective recourse accessible through the human experts managing traditional safety channels is where terror-inducing sentiments like those reflected through Mangione's alleged actions and writings provide an opening to take root in our society. Despite there rarely being a direct link between a specific system action and a proved individualized consequence that can be tied to direct economic and health damages, the system's ability to overpower its community can generate the kind of hopeless terror from which individuals lash out.

Like a politician engaged in stochastic terrorism, a recently defined term akin to incitement, where intentional harm can be expected due to the creation of an environment that inspires harm instead of calling for harm, the AI is not directly responsible for the harm that befalls the victims. The AI often is, though, responsible for the environment that creates the danger. For example, multiple cases involving Character.ai include its AI urging one young user to kill his parents over screen time limits,[19] and successfully convincing another to take his own life.[20] Even more challenging, however, are applications where AI algorithms are allowed to operate on behalf of their operators in a manner that incites unrelated AI tools to commit crimes. For example, research on AI trading bots demonstrated the ability for the bots to:

> autonomously learn to sustain collusive supra-competitive profits without any form of agreement, communication, intention, or any interactions that might violate traditional antitrust regulations.[21]

In the same way the damages can be expected from the environment facilitated by the AI systems, the crime being committed was not perpetrated

18 https://www.lls.org/news/nearly-1-2-patients-medical-debt-feel-trapped-new-poll-leading-healthcare-orgs-finds

19 https://www.npr.org/2024/12/10/nx-s1-5222574/kids-character-ai-lawsuit

20 https://www.nytimes.com/2024/10/23/technology/characterai-lawsuit-teen-suicide.html

21 Dou, Winston Wei and Goldstein, Itay and Ji, Yan, AI-Powered Trading, Algorithmic Collusion, and Price Efficiency (May 30, 2024). Jacobs Levy Equity Management Center for Quantitative Financial Research Paper, The Wharton School Research Paper, Available at SSRN: https://ssrn.com/abstract=4452704 or http://dx.doi.org/10.2139/ssrn.4452704

in a manner that could be prevented with the community's traditional protections.

In all of these cases, the underlying danger that is unique to AI is its ability to perform its human-like functions at a rate greater than any human charged with system safety is capable of verifying their appropriateness. This risk, potentially ironically, is greatest when using "human-on-the-loop" systems where users are often lulled into complacency by systems operating within the bounds of traditional safety measures or evaluation standards. As AI's speed and complexity increase, so does the need for innovative oversight mechanisms suitable for inclusion into regulatory frameworks that must define when and how human oversight remains essential to ensure safe, ethical AI deployment.

## 2 Inclusively Reframing Safety

The current acceptance of Anthropic as an industry leader representative of how its peers define "safety," when recent examples prove human-on-the-loop protections like its Constitutional AI in themselves can often increase access to harmful outcomes, demonstrates a need to be more inclusive in our definition of safety. This current representation of safety is more akin to platform reliability and property protection, yet provides no outcome derived targets for contemplating the impacts of system use. Pulling back from these restrictions that view an AI platform in isolation to viewing the safety of these components within the context of the societal systems where they are deployed requires a reframing of safety more generally.

For example, defining "safety" as "the iterative reduction in the probability or consequence of any negative outcome" requires a wider view of the accessible hazards and the rate at which AI will force us to encounter such hazards. In many ways, safety is confined by the industry to misuse of data and the creation of responses that the human operator may find inappropriate. Issues like the reduced capacity for a human operator to meaningfully validate or even evaluate the output of these systems due to the sheer volume of their output is currently ignored. For example, the limited adaptations made by the legal industry to how terms and conditions in end user license agreements are presented and accepted by end users who are typically laymen can be reasonably argued as rendering meaningful elocution nearly inaccessible in our modern society. By keeping the terms and conditions of use so long, presented in traditional legal prose, and acceptable with a mere button click virtually guarantee that the vast majority of users will neither read nor understand what is being agreed to when clicking 'Accept.'

In addition to expanding the definition of safety, it is also important to examine the nature of its iterative implementation. For example, the types of decisions regarding human oversight structure and human observation rate examined above are often made in isolation at the internal design stage where a holistic view of the system's wider hazards is difficult to view in the context of the AI tool's likely end application. As the focus on safety must shift from traditional measures of information technology safety like Service Organization Control Type 2 (SOC2) or Information Security Management Systems and Cybersecurity ISO 27001 compliance, its implementation must also begin to include best practices like AI Safety Overview Boards that effectively implement the types of independent reviews proposed by efforts like the OpenAI Safety and Security Committee.[22] Many of the best practices on how to operationalize these independent oversight boards in an AI context when starting from accepted frameworks like those provided by the National Institute of Standards and Technology (NIST) are explored by the Responsible Artificial Intelligence Institute in its 2024 guide *Operationalizing Independent Review in AI Governance: A Guide for AI Practitioners*. These types of measures when meaningfully implemented allow for the continual hazard identification and reevaluation necessary for iteratively producing safety advances and mitigating hazards within rapidly changing societal contexts.

Continual iteration ungrounded by targets or standards, however, will often allow for complacency. This makes it vital that the AI industry and standards and regulation developers examine risk acceptability measures these safety efforts can work within like those provided in other high technology industries. For example, Draper and Raymond proposed the *Draper Catastrophic Value Curve* in 2019 as a measure for identifying failure probability and consequence value combinations that would result in adoption of a particular technology for a specific legally sensitive purpose being considered an unethical use case.[23] The thresholds proposed in the Draper Catastrophic Value Curve would allow independent oversight boards, guided by accepted frameworks, to definitively value and prioritize specific safety iterations in their systems against combinations of objective risk acceptability thresholds and traditional business metrics such as return on

22 https://openai.com/index/openai-board-forms-safety-and-security-committee/

23 Draper, C.H. and Raymond, A.H., "Ethical Technology Risk: How to identify what is reasonable data protection for ODR," 12 Int'l J. Dispute Res., 2019.

investment (ROI). The presented relationships were based on catastrophe models that are widely accepted in the aerospace, nuclear, and petrochemical industries, and calibrated against court judgements, insurance claims, and US government awards for events ranging from wrongful death to reduced capacity life events. The Draper Catastrophic Value Curve presented in Figure 2.2 concludes that any technology application evaluated as being in the upper right region would be considered unethical, and any evaluation resulting in a use case in the far bottom left would be clearly ethical. Between these regions is where ethical behavior is defined as continual, iterative improvement of the technology use case in the downward or leftward direction within the region, corresponding to a reduction in the probability or value of a negative outcome.

The reason it is vital that the AI industry and those governing it immediately adopt an iterative, independent, and risk-based strategy towards safety is because the societal risks are likely already exceeding our awareness. AI is already producing outcomes driven by unfettered demand for productivity where the sheer volume of what AI can generate effectively lulls any human-on-the-loop into a sense of accepting comfort. When a system is designed with the assumption that the human-in-the-loop or human-on-the-loop is a safety critical system with a known estimate of its reliability, changes in the reliability of that safety component (i.e. the human) due to design choices embedded in the wider system must be evaluated and protected against. For example, the arguably fraudulent marketing behind Tesla's driver assist features being sold as "autopilot" produced systemic performance reductions in its human-on-the-loop safety

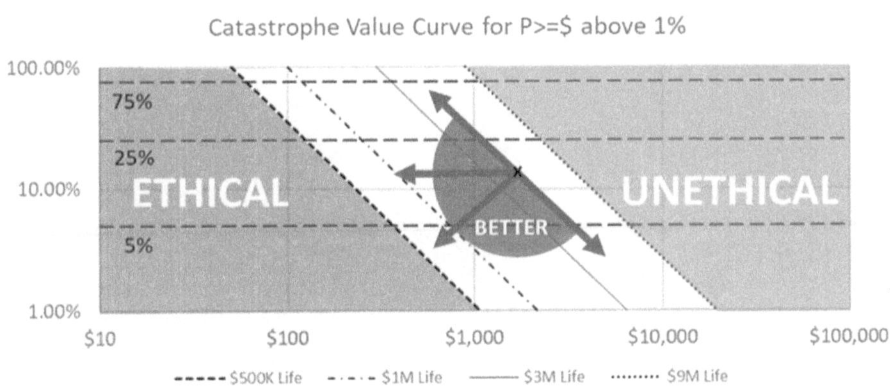


FIGURE 2.2 The Draper Catastrophe Value Curve for evaluating the ethical use of novel, legally sensitive technologies
REPRODUCED FROM DRAPER AND RAYMOND, 2019.

system (i.e. the driver) resulting from driver inattentiveness. This issue of human adaptation resulting in diminished safety system performance was evident through the rise of products designed to allow the humans to more easily thwart their safety responsibilities, like weighted pouches that could be attached to the steering wheel for simulating driver interaction. By retaining focus solely on the failure of its safety features and not on the broader safety strategy of the system, the probability and consequence of negative outcomes consistently increased over time.

This same issue of safety reductions due to human adaptation will likely be even more prevalent in AI systems that are economically sustained through engagement-dependent business models. Identical to the reduced oversight afforded terms and conditions, expanding human exposure to content at volumes that become unmanageable for human oversight will erode attentiveness thereby diminishing the value of human engagement from a safety perspective. This reality of the competing forces that will be present in most AI systems will require an outcome focused view on safety that must be pulled far enough back to account for the entire societal context of system use.

Background on the origins and development of artificial intelligence, and the perspective on safety that is held by AI developers is the first step toward understanding the challenges and complexities of governing what has rapidly become an integral part of our society. The next two chapters will examine the role of regulations and the role of standards as they have been applied to past developments, and as they may be applied to the governance of AI.

CHAPTER 3

# The Role of Regulation

Most major problems are solved best by working backwards from your ideal outcome to where you are now. AI is no different in this regard. This chapter starts from the perspective that the ideal end state is a safe, equitable, uniform implementation of a level playing field for AI use and innovation across all national borders. Therefore, it is reasonable to assume that effective government strategies will include legislatively authorized, internationally harmonized, and locally implemented regulations across all the world's jurisdictions, in coordination with widely accepted international and professional standards. Such a task is so immense that its completion currently borders on imperceivable. This chapter explores why society would be benefited by pursuing this end state of internationally harmonized regulations, discusses the most likely paths for arriving at this end state, and offers strategic guidance on where regulatory progress could be made most rapidly and meaningfully. This exploration is divided into sections that:

- Explore core aspects of the shared culture across technologists designing AI-powered solutions,
- Highlight the sovereignty reframing that is necessary to appropriately define the jurisdictional strategy behind any regulatory initiative,
- Review a roadmap for how society will likely move towards AI regulation,
- Highlight key "shocks" that are likely to arise where leaps in progress could be made,
- Propose regulatory strategies that could provide cures to these shocks while moving towards appropriate regulations, and
- Conclude that any path towards this desired end state must start with inclusive standardization efforts informed by specific use cases.

## 1 Regulating the Transparently Opaque

One of the loudest arguments made against regulating AI is that even its practitioners do not fully understand what is happening within many of its core systems. Where public safety is typically bettered through transparency, the AI industry is incredibly transparent about the fact that it believes the products themselves are fundamentally opaque.

© KONINKLIJKE BRILL BV, LEIDEN, 2025 | DOI:10.1163/9789004737389_005

OpenAI CEO Sam Altman's comments at the 2024 International Telecommunication Union AI for Good Global Summit in Geneva, Switzerland, that 'we certainly have not solved interpretability' perfectly represent the most significant challenge facing AI regulation at the time he was quoted.[1] Most legislators or regulators will hear such an assertion and be lost in the idea that it represents a process of discovery that is ongoing yet not out of hand. *The Observer*'s summarizing headline of this comment offers insight that is far more accurate: 'Sam Altman Says OpenAI Doesn't Fully Understand How GPT Works.'[2] Like the rest of the industry, Altman is effectively saying: we can't tell you what's happening because we don't know, yet if we keep doing more of it, we'll figure it out. Hopefully.

This is not an unusual approach for innovative technologies to take. Most innovations from Coca-Cola to financial derivatives started with hidden ingredients that were essentially allowed to be publicly trialed at their onset. When the dangers of opiates were better understood, regulations could prevent Coca-Cola from including cocaine in its soda. When the exponential damage of financial derivatives was accepted, regulations could restrict who was able to readily use them on whose behalf. The challenge that makes regulating AI unique is also what makes its risks identical to those which have come to market before it: its deployment is occurring when it exhibits more "unknown unknowns" than "known knowns."

Regulations are fundamentally restrictions our communities place on how community members interact with each other for the benefit of our wider community. Food safety regulations define the materials that can be used and processes that must be followed in order to offer food for sale to the public, but their purpose is to prevent food manufacturers from poisoning the public for profit. Financial regulations define the types of contracts and levels of risk allowed in publicly available financial instruments, but their purpose is to prevent financiers from defrauding the public for profit. Regulations may be placed on products or services, but the intent is to reasonably protect each other from the actions taken by creators, operators, or providers of those products or services. Regulations protect society from the actions of individuals or organizations within society, (including government agencies) requiring regulation of a product or service to account for the culture of the community associated with that product or service.

1 https://observer.com/2024/05/sam-altman-openai-gpt-ai-for-good-conference/

2 https://observer.com/2024/05/sam-altman-openai-gpt-ai-for-good-conference/

Despite efforts in the European Union to blunt the progression of AI into risk sensitive industries and applications, the use of AI tools is accelerating around the world often with little of the stress testing one would expect from technologies that demonstrate a more evident danger. Although all of the issues related to AI are international in nature, the societal willingness to allow acceleration of AI innovation in the face of so many unknown risks is heavily rooted in American technology culture. Many of the blind spots observed in the front-line engineers and business leaders driving the rollout of AI are likely rooted in three major "truths" that have driven decades of innovation.

First, software development now typically starts from an Agile worldview. Agile software development was first proposed in 2001 through release of the *Manifesto for Agile Software Development*[3] by *The Agile Alliance*.[4] The core innovation of Agile development is its collaborative approach to discovering customer needs through testing tangible iterations. Agile design philosophy favors engaging interdisciplinary teams that explore user needs by offering small changes that are tested for suitability, with the best performing option being adopted as an accepted iteration. This philosophy is possibly easiest for many to see in the A/B testing that has become a staple of online advertising. For example, once a digital advertiser has identified a demographic it is hoping to target, it must optimize the appearance and language of its ads to ensure its messaging is most effective. This is done by creating two or more options per element that could be changed, like making red, blue, or yellow backgrounds; running each version of the ad to statistically identical subsets of the target demographic, so that metrics like open or click-through rates can be used to determine relative effectiveness; and then redirecting ad spending to the version of the ads that perform best. Agile is so effective at delivering cost efficient innovation that it has become the default world view of modern developers.

The risk of this worldview is that hard design boundaries are rarely as thoughtfully considered in advance as they would have been using previous waterfall style project management strategies. Where prior design strategies typically involved fully defining all aspects of the software before any programming commenced, exactly like one would build houses, roads, or cars,

3 Kent Beck; James Grenning; Robert C. Martin; Mike Beedle; Jim Highsmith; Steve Mellor; Arie van Bennekum; Andrew Hunt; Ken Schwaber; Alistair Cockburn; Ron Jeffries; Jeff Sutherland; Ward Cunningham; Jon Kern; Dave Thomas; Martin Fowler; Brian Marick (2001). "Manifesto for Agile Software Development". Agile Alliance.

4 "What is Agile?". Agile Alliance. Retrieved 16 July 2024.

Agile keeps pushing system capabilities in little, iterative steps. For low-risk systems, this approach can let the design team find new opportunities for previously unidentified customer needs and help the customer discover new needs it had not previously considered. For high-risk systems, this continual, iterative, envelope expansion makes it very easy to accidentally cross ethical boundaries that become less visible when the design team is focusing on specific deliverable sprints. This ingrained culture of rapid, continual testing within the technology community reduces perceptions of risk in AI systems that are continually pushing operational boundaries but often allows hallucinations to be seen as manageable features more often than they are interpreted as symptoms of inherently dangerous root issues.

Second, the vast majority of tech workers have spent their entire professional career under the protections of 'Section 230 of the Communications Act of 1934, enacted as part of the Communications Decency Act of 1996, [that] provides limited federal immunity to providers and users of interactive computer services.'[5] Section 230 is often best known for protecting social media platforms from liability associated with user or other third-party content, limiting the cost of content moderation that would need to be provided if the platforms were considered traditional publishers. This immunity from liability has allowed these platforms to rapidly scale using user generated content, empowering engagement-based business models that offer users content supported by targeted advertising.

The risk of this protected worldview is twofold. Platforms see themselves as neutral facilitators who provide an environment defined by and whose safety is the responsibility of its users. In the United States, this worldview is very much reinforced by the limited government regulations impacting the American technology sector. At the same time, these platforms see their facilitation role as taking actions and making modifications which will maximize user engagement with the platform. Removing liability allows the platforms to focus on building 'digital twins'[6] of its users that are then tested in an Agile manner using digital nudges. These nudges and the manner in which users respond to them become datasets owned by the platform, with the platforms financially incentivized to continually refine these models while protected from any actions that push the users to take unethical

5 https://crsreports.congress.gov/product/pdf/R/R46751

6 This word is used as it has been colloquially modified over the past decade. Historically, a digital twin was restricted to a physics-based fast running model, while recent usage in the tech community has expanded it to include nearly any digital representation of a physical object or its actions or intentions.

actions. This ingrained culture of indemnity allows technologists to see their users as datasets independent of the humans that created or are impacted by the actions that created them.

Third, there is a widely accepted general assumption that more data will always lead to better information.[7] Like a hidden picture that is revealed one pixel at a time, many of the relationships underlying complex interactions in our world can be discovered with more observations of their outputs for any given inputs. This is only true if there is an underlying pattern. Many natural environments, despite decades worth of attempts to find discernible models, are fundamentally chaotic.[8] The greatest surprise for many was the relative simplicity of human language, allowing increases in computing power to directly relate to improvements of large language models (LLMs). But most of the problems we dream to solve with AI are not as simple as language. The natural, physical world rarely conforms to patterns. Organizations of people working with communities have no decipherable pattern to their interaction, with many of the simplifications for concepts like economic rationality routinely proved inaccurate.[9] Many of these systems at a macro level are fundamentally chaotic, absent the type of overarching simplification we see in language. When a system is fundamentally chaotic, as seen in many natural systems, no amount of additional data or AI processing will arrive at an underlying model where it does not exist.

The risk of this "more is better" worldview is again twofold. The assumption that an underlying model must always be discoverable will lead those who have not discovered the model to needlessly expand their datasets, centralizing informational risks for no attainable gain. Compounded with a belief in indemnity and a mission to deliver continual improvement for a customer whose needs are not yet met, this pressure to find an underlying reality through data accumulation will lead many to justify incorporating datasets they would not otherwise have a right to use. When there is pressure to use unapproved datasets, while there is currently strong copyright law that can be looked back to for resolutions, the pace at which such law can be ignored by modern AI tools requires further exploration of whether

7 It is important to note that this assertion employs the data science framing of data being the fragments of data that, when interpreted within meaningful context, offer interpretable insights about the object or actions that produced the data.

8 Meadows, Donella H. The Limits to Growth: the 30-Year Update. White River Junction, Vt: Chelsea Green Pub. Co., 2004.

9 https://pmc.ncbi.nlm.nih.gov/articles/PMC9351500/

current enforcement strategies and tools are still sufficient means for protecting creator rights.

The more dangerous presentation of this risk is the access to confirmation bias when a chaotic system is hoped to have order. The expectation of finding rules based patterns from which human actions can be interpreted has driven researchers for generations, with an AI culture of pattern expectation leading to a dangerous pursuit of securing or generating data through any means necessary to prove that pattern exists. Once accessible data has been exhausted and no pattern has been found, there is a significant risk that the problem could be viewed like the blurry galaxies discussed earlier, with representations given despite the gaps in a reality that astronomers but not the general public know are there. Not challenging such beliefs is likely to give rise to synthetic data reflecting that expectation being fed into a system so that the results conform to the modeler's expectations, accelerating the representation of the chaotic system to a highly refined model that deviates drastically from its reality. For example, while many communities are informed by economic rules, it seems difficult to argue that the actions of individuals managing their economic choices within society are not irrational or chaotic. Arguing the simplicity of economic rationality is sufficient for understanding the economic perspective and choices of society, an assumption many in the AI community essentially require when justifying the riches spent seeking an "AI for everything," flies in the face of societal reality. Volumes of work have been produced on the economic irrationality of humans as both individuals and groups, producing direct challenges to the desired assumptions that underpin the desired model many would like to find.[10] These volumes of work demonstrate that modelling humans as economically rational will lead to incorrect results, but one seeking to find economic rationality will consider these "incorrect" results to be "hallucinations." The danger here lies in the modeler's choice of the reality it wishes to accept. If modelers were to "correct" what they could consider irrational "hallucinations" of the model by providing synthetic representations of the data they felt must be missing, their models would then be considered "correct" while they are in fact accelerating further from reality. This acceleration away from reality due to synthetic data that increases bias towards a model that the modelers expect, yet have not observed, would be expected to cause rapid acceleration towards economic injustice.

10 Thaler, Richard, H. 2000. "From Homo Economicus to Homo Sapiens." *Journal of Economic Perspectives*, 14 (1): 133–141.

Combining Agile thinking, indemnity entitlement, justification for aggressive data accumulation, and access to confirmation bias in situations where an underlying model may not exist into the culture of those responsible for building AI applications provides an environment where regulation must be an end goal.[11] Especially when the profit motive is as overpowering as it was following the launch of ChatGPT-3.5 in November of 2022, with AI-driven companies representing 32% of the US Stock market in the second quarter of 2024.[12] It is vital that the cultural drivers behind the risks posed by AI application design are acknowledged when exploring effective regulatory solutions in the context of the systems being built.

It is vital to remember that regulations placed on AI technology are intended to address permissible actions of the community that is building, deploying, and using AI technologies. This means that any regulations placed on any AI serving a community must account for the context of the community when evaluating the requirements that can be applied to the technology.

## 2 Reframing AI Functionality

There is an entrepreneurial adage that the customer in a hardware store who is looking for a drill bit actually wants a hole. There are many ways to create a hole, with many types of holes best made using a drill bit. The ability to clearly define the kind of hole the drill bit will produce in the material where the hole will be located under the specific conditions when the hole will be made allows the drill bit designer to specify everything from the material that the drill bit will be made of to the design it must follow to create a drill bit appropriate for the user's needs. We then approach regulation around the drill bit from two directions simultaneously. First, we make sure the product is fit for its purpose of creating an intended hole. Second, we ensure the product is capable of producing an intended hole that is societally appropriate. The delicate balance that must be maintained along these two simultaneous paths is seen in everything from bug spray to handguns, with those products capable of producing catastrophic

11 This exploration of the design culture exhibited by the technologists working on these systems represent root problems argued here to be even more fundamental than the well documented lack of diversity in dataset inputs and curation.

12 https://www.reuters.com/markets/echoes-dotcom-bubble-haunt-ai-driven-us-stock-market-2024-07-02/

outcomes being the most challenging to regulate when there is lack of clarity on what the user actually wants and when there is societal controversy of the levels of safety that should be required.

The lack of clear intention around AI is seen in the range and severity of public fears around its adoption.[13] Unlike general public consensus on how, when, and what types of holes hardware store drill bits should make, most do not know how AI will make their lives either better or worse. Regulatory progress is not possible until the core utility of AI is understood in a standardized manner which can be correctly applied to solve problems for which it is the most appropriate technological solution. This same challenge led to the boom, bust, and reframing around the use of blockchain[14] and its rediscovery as a powerful tool when used within an extremely narrow use case for fighting many deepfake challenges brought on by generative AI.[15]

Customers looking for AI want to augment human intellect through the amplification and accelerating of those processes that produce our current interpretation of intelligence. Where a human can put one hundred handwritten cards into the correct envelopes in an hour, AI customers want the ability to put one million cards into the correct envelopes in that same hour. Where a truck driver can only drive for twelve hours per day, AI customers want the truck driving twenty-four hours per day. If a social media consultant needs half a day to come up with one social media calendar for one client, AI customers want to create one thousand social media calendars for five hundred customers every day. The AI customer is looking for a product that will replicate actions previously requiring human intellect that are now limited by nothing but compute capacity. Unlike a hole, successfully discerning when an AI product has achieved customer expectations is often challenging. And unlike a drill bit, an AI product is constantly self-optimizing in an agile manner. This means that both the customer expectation and the product being sought out to deliver those expectations are moving targets.

---

13 Pew Research Center. "Growing Public Concern About the Role of Artificial Intelligence in Daily Life." Pew Research Center, August 28, 2023. https://www.pewresearch.org/short-reads/2023/08/28/growing-public-concern-about-the-role-of-artificial-intelligence-in-daily-life/

14 The Economist. "Bitcoin and Other Cryptocurrencies Are Useless." The Economist, August 30, 2018. https://www.economist.com/leaders/2018/08/30/bitcoin-and-other-cryptocurrencies-are-useless

15 World Economic Forum. "How Blockchain Can Help Combat Threat of Deepfakes." World Economic Forum, October 2021. https://www.weforum.org/agenda/2021/10/how-blockchain-can-help-combat-threat-of-deepfakes/

Agreeing that the product of AI is an amplifying accelerant for human intellect, though, means it is possible to find regulatory parallels along which safety can be achieved without stifling societally accepted innovation. If AI was to be viewed not as a constantly changing product, but instead an exoskeleton for the mind, regulatory strategies could find consensus more quickly. For example, if a normal human arm can deliver one hundred pounds of force, a customer may want an exoskeleton that would allow that arm to direct the delivery of two-thousand pounds of force. Specifications could be developed that state how the pounds of force delivered would be calculated, verification standards could be developed so that the customer can be comfortable knowing when the product has been delivered upon the request, or product safety regulations could be developed to ensure such a force can be delivered safely. For the customer operating the exoskeleton, training could be required to ensure the user is capable of safe operation, age gating could be required for any operating license just like for any car or boat, or use restrictions could be imposed by local ordinances so that such an exoskeleton is not operated the same way in all settings the same way bike riders must walk their bikes through a crowded pedestrian plaza.

In this hypothetical case of the exoskeleton, regardless of how significant any laws, regulators, or ordinances are around its design, construction, and operation, damage caused by an appropriately operating exoskeleton would not be attributed to the technology. If the user walked into a crowded room and started causing the exoskeleton to strike people, the actions of the user would not rally the public to deny the technology's use by nurses who need such a device to safely move patients. The exoskeleton, like the drill bit, is a tool through which the actions of its user must ultimately be responsible, with the user protected from any dangerous or deceptive actions taken by the product designer or supplier. As a tool for amplifying and extending human intellect, AI regulation must avoid the trap of focusing restrictions or blame on the technology, and instead address the interactions and actions between the provider and the user that pass through the AI technology.

Historically, when faced with new technology that presented incalculable risks to a small portion of a willing community, from passengers on Virgin Galactic to thrill seekers on the Titan Submersible, the operators and providers of the unproven technologies were allowed to operate at their own risk. The technology in these cases was allowed to evolve so long as the risks and responsibilities flowed through to the willing and informed providers and users. The actions of the operators and users were clearly the focus. Now that it is becoming clear that AI is merely an amorphous technology layer through which harms, whether by misuse or negligence, can pass from a small number of individuals more rapidly and broadly throughout society as a whole than nearly any technology before, the focus on protection or control must remain trained on the actions being amplified and accelerated by the humans who initiated any actions causing harm.

## 3 Reframing AI Sovereignty

Current regulatory frameworks for AI often focus on digital sovereignty, emphasizing control over digital technologies, data, and infrastructure. While this has been effective in addressing some concerns, it is increasingly clear that digital sovereignty alone is inadequate in tackling the unique challenges AI presents, such as systemic bias, transparency, and intellectual property concerns. A more nuanced framework – informational sovereignty – offers a potential solution. Informational sovereignty prioritizes the jurisdictional appropriateness of the information used by AI systems, ensuring that these systems produce outcomes that are not only legally compliant but also culturally relevant to the communities they serve.

Adopting informational sovereignty brings its own set of challenges, particularly in cross-border applications. Many AI systems rely on datasets that span multiple jurisdictions, raising questions about how to ensure compliance with local legal norms when the data itself may be sourced globally. For example, a system trained in one jurisdiction may be applied in another, where legal and cultural expectations differ significantly. As a result, the shift to informational sovereignty could complicate AI projects, particularly in sectors where international collaboration or global datasets are the norm.

Despite these challenges, the necessity of jurisdictionally appropriate data is evident. A compelling example comes from the European Union's Artificial Intelligence Act (EU AI Act), which stresses the importance of using datasets that reflect the specific geographical, behavioral, or functional setting of the communities where AI is deployed. This provision represents a departure from the traditional focus on the physical location of data, instead emphasizing the need for AI systems to be trained on information that aligns with the local legal and cultural context. By focusing on the jurisdictional relevance of data, the EU AI Act illustrates how informational sovereignty could mitigate many of the shortcomings of digital sovereignty, particularly in preventing the use of inappropriate or biased data.

The implications of this shift are particularly striking in the legal field, where jurisdiction-specific precedents and legal norms are paramount. For instance, in the case of Mata v. Avianca Inc., a lawyer unwittingly submitted a court brief containing fabricated citations produced by ChatGPT, which had blended fragments of real training data but failed to produce accurate legal references.[16] While it is argued from the OpenAI perspective that this is a case of the user misusing ChatGPT outputs, the AI system produced an unreliable answer because it had not been constrained by jurisdictionally appropriate data, leading to unreliable and potentially damaging legal outcomes. This case underscores the critical need for AI systems to be grounded in data that is not only accurate but also jurisdictionally relevant. Informational sovereignty, by ensuring that AI systems are trained on data that adheres to the legal norms of the jurisdiction in which they are used, would reduce the likelihood of such errors occurring. If an AI system used in legal decision-making is trained on data from foreign jurisdictions, it risks applying legal precedents that are incompatible with local laws, leading to unpredictable or even unlawful outcomes. Informational sovereignty ensures that AI systems respect the legal boundaries and cultural norms of the communities they serve, preserving the integrity of local legal systems.

Another example of the risks associated with unrepresentative data comes from the Dutch childcare benefits scandal (Kinderopvangtoeslagaffaire).[17] In this case, an AI system used by the Dutch government disproportionately flagged minority families as fraudulent, largely due to the unrepresentative training data it was fed. The system's bias led to widespread harm, affecting thousands of families. Had the AI system been trained on data that appropriately reflected the diverse population it was tasked with evaluating, such outcomes might have been avoided. Informational sovereignty would address these concerns by ensuring that AI systems are trained on data that is not only legally relevant but also demographically representative of the communities they serve, thereby reducing the risk of systemic bias.

Informational sovereignty also has broader implications beyond specific cases. By grounding AI systems in jurisdictionally appropriate data, it ensures that the outcomes produced by these systems align with the legal and cultural frameworks of the jurisdictions in which they operate.

At the same time, the move toward informational sovereignty presents new challenges for AI regulation, particularly in cross-border applications.

---

16 https://www.nytimes.com/2023/05/27/nyregion/avianca-airline-lawsuit-chatgpt.html

17 https://www.politico.eu/article/dutch-scandal-serves-as-a-warning-for-europe-over-risks-of-using-algorithms/

Many AI systems, especially those developed by multinational companies, rely on global datasets to train their models. Ensuring that these datasets comply with the jurisdictional requirements of each country in which the AI will be used introduces significant complexity. For example, a healthcare AI system developed using medical data from one country may be deployed in another, where patient privacy laws and medical protocols differ. Informational sovereignty requires that AI systems be trained on data that is not only compliant with local regulations but also reflective of local practices and norms, a requirement that could significantly impact the development and deployment of AI across borders.

Despite these challenges, the benefits of informational sovereignty are clear. By ensuring that AI systems are trained on jurisdictionally appropriate data, this framework addresses many of the key challenges posed by AI, such as bias, transparency, and accountability. The examples of the EU AI Act, the Mata v. Avianca Inc. case, and the Dutch childcare benefits scandal illustrate the necessity of grounding AI systems in data that is both legally and culturally relevant to the communities they serve. Informational sovereignty offers a more robust and context-specific framework for AI regulation than digital sovereignty, one that better reflects the nuanced and jurisdiction-specific nature of AI's impact on society.

As AI continues to permeate various sectors, the need for regulatory frameworks that ensure the quality and relevance of information will become increasingly important. By prioritizing jurisdictionally appropriate and representative data, informational sovereignty provides a foundation for future iterations of AI regulation that can more effectively balance innovation with the protection of fundamental rights and the rule of law. While the shift to informational sovereignty introduces new complexities, particularly in cross-border applications, it offers a necessary evolution in the regulatory approach to AI, ensuring that these systems serve the communities they impact in a fair, transparent, and accountable manner.

## 4 The Roadmap to Regulation

Regulations are crafted under the authorities delegated to any relevant administrative agency by that society's legislative bodies. Legislative bodies grant these authorities to administrative agencies that have the ability to be staffed with apolitical, subject matter experts who can craft regulations that routinely encompass a diverse array of rules, standards, and directives promulgated by governmental bodies, industry associations, or international organizations to become relevant and enforceable rules that carry the weight of law. Effective regulations that are appropriately representative of thoughtful legislation have the ability to serve many purposes at once, from safeguarding public interests to mitigating risks, or from promoting societal welfare to fostering innovation.

The authority to delegate regulatory responsibility to administrative agencies often stems from constitutional provisions, statutes, or executive mandates. This authority fundamentally derives from the sovereign power vested in governmental entities to enact and enforce laws for the welfare of society, with disagreements over the intent of legislation or how that legislative intent is incorporated into any associated regulation being handled by a judiciary that will typically be the body responsible for facilitating the resolution of any such disputes. When regulations produce clear rules and standards, they provide certainty to individuals, businesses, and other stakeholders, empowering informed decision-making and risk management on a level playing field that prevents unfair advantages, monopolistic practices, or exploitation of vulnerable populations.

Technology-dependent industries often see significant benefit from the level playing field that can be created through clarifying acceptable uses, intellectual property rights, research boundaries, or even system operation or design limitations that strike a balance between private profit, societal progress, and public safety. Successfully achieving this delicate balance is heavily dependent upon understanding the fundamentals of a new technology, including any of its fundamental dangers, and employing a regulatory strategy that is appropriate both for the technology's development and society's risk acceptability given its biases towards the specific nature or context of that developing technology.

AI poses an extremely unique challenge for regulators. By sitting at the intersection of societal visions that excite and scare in near equal measure a population that has largely to date misidentified the acceleratingly developing technology's greatest threats, strategic consensus is difficult to find, and will likely remain bogged down by superficial understandings of AI's role in the expanding number of less visible, highly consequential failures. The depth of this problem is seen in the shortcomings of current efforts to meaningfully define AI in currently proposed regulations, it is seen in the misalignment of the regulatory and design strategies for protecting the public from these systems, and it is resulting in regulatory efforts that are focusing on ancillary applications of specific AI augmented processes when they should instead be acknowledging the fundamentally ultrahazardous nature of the technology. Taking all of these challenges into consideration is why most communities will struggle to start governing AI through regulation, and will likely only arrive at thoughtful, collaboratively developed regulations after pursuing a more conventionally organic approach to demonstrating regulatory need. This is why most paths towards regulation in many jurisdictions are already starting to proceed along this organic approach as follows:

- Legislate by Lawsuit,
- Free Market Regulation,
- Regulate by Waiver,
- Regulation through Incorporation, and then
- Performance to Prescriptive Regulation

### 4.1 *Legislate by Lawsuit*

In industries where technological advancements often outpace the development of formal regulations, an increase in lawsuits serves as a critical indicator of the need for legislative action. This phenomenon, commonly referred to as "legislate by lawsuit," occurs when governments allow industries to operate with minimal oversight, leaving the courts to resolve disputes and, eventually, guide policy. Lawsuits in these situations not only provide a path for those seeking justice but also shape future regulatory frameworks. The uptick in legal disputes can act as a feedback loop, reflecting societal concerns and corporate behavior, which in turn pushes legislators to act. The legal outcomes of these disputes help establish standards and practices that may eventually be codified into law, especially in rapidly evolving sectors like AI.

By 2024, the AI industry began experiencing a surge in lawsuits, with many targeting harms allegedly caused by AI systems. These cases, addressing fundamental questions of accountability, intellectual property, privacy, and safety, are set to shape the future of AI regulation. One of the most prominent legal battles involves author Sara Silverman, among other writers, suing OpenAI and Meta for copyright violations. The plaintiffs claim that these companies used their copyrighted works to train AI models without obtaining proper permissions. These lawsuits highlight the growing tension between the vast datasets AI systems require for training and the intellectual property rights of content creators. If the courts rule in favor of Silverman and others, it could prompt stricter copyright laws, requiring companies to secure licenses before using copyrighted material for AI training.

In another significant legal front, AI-related data privacy issues are also emerging. Several lawsuits have been filed against companies for using personal data without consent to train AI models. These cases typically involve accusations of scraping personal data from social media platforms and other online sources without individuals' explicit permission. If courts find in favor of the plaintiffs, the legal precedent may lead to tighter regulations on the collection and use of personal data for AI development. Companies may also be required to establish transparent data usage policies to avoid legal repercussions.

Additionally, class action lawsuits are being pursued in California, where law firms have been recruiting plaintiffs who claim to have suffered harm from AI-amplified content, such as misinformation or deep fake images. These cases represent a shift in legal theory, attempting to hold companies accountable for the unintended consequences of their AI technologies. Should these lawsuits succeed, it could spur new regulations that obligate AI companies to mitigate the risks associated with harmful or misleading content generated by their systems.

This strategy of relying on litigation to regulate industries is not unprecedented and has proven effective in several sectors where risks once outpaced formal regulation. A notable example is the tobacco industry, which faced a wave of lawsuits in the 1990s. These legal actions led to massive financial settlements, stricter advertising regulations, and more comprehensive labeling requirements. The lawsuits also contributed to a broader public health initiative aimed at reducing smoking. Through the legal system, tobacco companies were held accountable for deceptive practices, and the outcomes helped catalyze future legislative efforts that further regulated the industry.

Similarly, litigation involving asbestos provided another powerful example of how lawsuits can drive industry reform. Asbestos-related health risks led to numerous lawsuits against companies that used the material, particularly in construction and manufacturing. These legal battles forced companies to compensate victims and adopt safer practices. Over time, the litigation played a crucial role in prompting federal regulatory agencies to implement protective measures for workers and consumers, ensuring better safety standards in industries where asbestos exposure had been common.

Environmental litigation also demonstrates how legal actions can enforce existing regulations and drive stricter enforcement. Lawsuits against corporations responsible for pollution have often resulted in substantial cleanup efforts and have set legal precedents for protecting natural resources. For example, legal challenges based on violations of the Clean Water Act forced companies to take remedial action for dumping hazardous waste into waterways. These cases strengthened environmental protection efforts by ensuring that companies adhere to stricter regulatory oversight, showing how legal pressure can serve as an effective tool for enforcing regulations that might otherwise be neglected.

While litigation has proven to be an effective tool for driving industry change, there are significant drawbacks to over-relying on this approach, especially in rapidly evolving fields like AI. One of the main issues is the delay in action. Legal proceedings are notoriously slow, often taking years or even decades to reach a resolution. In the case of AI technologies, where advancements occur at a rapid pace, relying on the courts to address issues retroactively means that harmful practices may persist long before meaningful legal outcomes are achieved. This lag time can expose the public to unnecessary risks, underscoring the need for more proactive regulatory approaches.

Moreover, litigation outcomes are inherently unpredictable. The results of legal cases can vary significantly depending on the specifics of the case, the jurisdiction in which it is tried, and the judges presiding over the cases. This unpredictability leads to inconsistency in how legal standards are applied across different regions and industries, making it difficult for companies to navigate and adhere to uniform guidelines. Furthermore, litigation is costly. Bringing a lawsuit, especially against well-funded corporate defendants, can be prohibitively expensive, creating barriers for individuals or smaller organizations seeking justice. The high costs associated with legal action may prevent important cases from being heard, allowing harmful practices to continue unchecked.

Another major criticism of regulating through litigation is that it often focuses on compensating victims after harm has already occurred, rather than preventing the harm in the first place. This reactive approach can leave the public vulnerable to the emerging risks posed by AI technologies, as it emphasizes remediation rather than prevention. The burden of regulating dangerous technologies should not fall solely on the judicial system, as it is neither equipped to proactively oversee complex industries nor designed to bear the brunt of technological regulation. Over-reliance on the courts places unnecessary strain on the judicial system and diverts resources from other important legal areas.

As the AI industry continues to grow, litigation will undoubtedly play a crucial role in shaping its future. However, the limitations and risks associated with this strategy highlight the urgent need for comprehensive legislative frameworks that can address the unique challenges posed by AI technologies proactively, rather than relying on the slow and often unpredictable nature of litigation.

### 4.2 *Free Market Regulation* (*i.e. Insurance*)

The rise in lawsuits within an industry often leads to a significant shift in how the insurance sector interacts with that industry. As legal disputes become more frequent, insurance companies, which are typically responsible for covering the costs of these lawsuits, begin to adjust their strategies to mitigate financial risk. This shift results in what can be described as a form of "free market regulation," where the insurance industry plays a crucial role in influencing behavior through the power of its coverage decisions. Essentially, insurers act as *de facto* regulators, using their market influence to shape industry practices based on what they are willing to insure.

The insurance industry's expertise in risk management positions it as a key player in regulating behavior. Insurance companies specialize in assessing and managing risks, allowing them to identify potential hazards and set conditions for coverage that incentivize companies to adopt safer and more compliant practices. This expertise allows insurers to step in where regulatory oversight may be lacking, indirectly enforcing standards across various sectors. For businesses, the potential to reduce insurance premiums by managing risks more effectively creates a financial incentive to comply with best practices and safety measures. As a result, the insurance industry's influence helps align economic interests with regulatory goals, encouraging companies to make improvements without the need for direct government intervention.

One example of insurance-driven regulation can be seen in the environmental protection space. Many insurers require companies to adopt stricter environmental safeguards as a condition for receiving coverage. These conditions effectively enforce environmental standards, as companies that fail to comply may face higher premiums or even become ineligible for coverage. In this way, insurers can compel businesses to implement practices that reduce their environmental impact. Similarly, in the realm of workers' compensation, premiums are often tied to a company's safety record. Businesses with a lower incidence of workplace accidents and injuries typically enjoy lower insurance premiums, incentivizing them to invest in safety measures that protect workers and reduce claims. This dynamic encourages businesses to prioritize safer working environments in order to reduce costs.

Cybersecurity is another area where the insurance industry plays a regulatory role. Cyber insurance policies often mandate that companies implement specific security practices and protocols before they can obtain coverage. For instance, businesses may be required to adopt multi-factor authentication, encryption, or regular system audits to reduce the risk of cyberattacks. These conditions not only mitigate the financial risk for insurers but also promote better cybersecurity practices across industries, ensuring that businesses are better protected against cyber threats.

One of the major benefits of using the insurance industry as a regulatory mechanism is its flexibility and adaptability. Unlike traditional government mandates, which can be slow to respond to emerging risks, insurers can quickly adjust their coverage requirements to account for new technologies or evolving threats. This flexibility allows the insurance sector to provide a more responsive approach to regulation, keeping pace with fast-changing industries like AI and cybersecurity. Additionally, the economic incentives inherent in the insurance model encourage voluntary compliance. Businesses are motivated to adopt safer and more compliant practices in order to reduce their insurance costs, leading to more cost-effective risk management overall.

Furthermore, insurance can offer comprehensive coverage for a wide array of risks, including those not explicitly addressed by existing regulations. This broad scope enables businesses to mitigate potential liabilities in areas where formal regulatory frameworks may be lacking. In this sense, insurance fills a regulatory gap by providing a safety net for risks that may otherwise go unregulated.

However, there are also challenges and risks associated with relying on insurance as a regulatory tool. One concern is the potential for inequity in coverage. Businesses that can afford comprehensive insurance coverage may be able to comply with best practices and manage risks more effectively, while those that cannot afford such coverage may struggle to meet the same standards. This could create inequalities within industries, where smaller or less well-funded companies are at a disadvantage.

Another risk is the possibility of market failures within the insurance industry itself. For example, insurers may underprice risks or lack sufficient capacity to cover certain high-risk industries, which could undermine the effectiveness of insurance as a regulatory mechanism. If insurance companies fail to accurately assess and price risks, the entire system could become unstable, leading to gaps in coverage that leave businesses and the public exposed to unforeseen dangers.

Moreover, there is a risk that businesses may come to view insurance simply as a cost of doing business, rather than actively engaging in risk management. In this scenario, companies might opt to pay higher premiums rather than investing in preventative measures, relying on insurance payouts to cover any potential losses or liabilities. This over-reliance on financial compensation rather than risk mitigation could erode the intended regulatory effect of the insurance industry, allowing unsafe or non-compliant practices to persist.

Using the insurance industry as a "regulator of last resort" represents a novel approach to achieving regulatory objectives through market-based mechanisms. It offers several advantages, including greater flexibility, economic efficiency, and the ability to leverage the insurance industry's specialized expertise in risk management. However, it also presents challenges, such as potential inequities in coverage, market failures, and the risk of businesses becoming complacent about managing risks. To ensure that this approach effectively protects public interests without exacerbating inequalities or introducing market distortions, regulatory agencies must strike a careful balance. As markets and risks continue to evolve, the interplay between traditional regulation and insurance-driven regulation will shape the future of risk management and compliance.

### 4.3 *Regulate by Waiver*

Regulation by waiver refers to the practice in which federal agencies grant exemptions from existing regulatory requirements under specific circumstances. This approach allows agencies to navigate situations that may not have been anticipated when the original regulations were established, and it often provides the necessary flexibility to accommodate emerging technologies or unique industry practices. Over time, as waivers become more common in response to particular regulatory challenges, they can serve as a testing ground for new approaches, which may eventually be formalized into regulations. The cumulative effect of these waivers helps to shape and refine regulatory frameworks to better align with industry standards and technological advancements.

One of the key reasons agencies grant waivers is that they are able to address gaps or limitations in regulations without the need for immediate legislative changes. In industries where innovation moves rapidly, such as artificial intelligence (AI), insurance, or communications, regulations often lag behind. Waivers provide a mechanism for regulators to maintain oversight while giving companies room to innovate and adopt new technologies. Over time, the logic behind these waivers – often influenced by accepted industry practices – can pave the way for broader regulatory reform. For instance, if certain industry standards are consistently accepted through waivers, regulatory bodies may use these standards to inform the development of new rules.

An example of this can be found in the aviation industry. For many years, the Federal Aviation Administration (FAA) routinely granted waivers to airlines and aircraft manufacturers concerning noise regulations. As newer, quieter aircraft technologies emerged, existing noise regulations became outdated. Instead of immediately rewriting the regulations, the FAA issued waivers for companies adopting the new technologies, allowing them to bypass outdated noise standards. As these waivers became common practice, the FAA used the data and experiences from the waivers to inform new noise regulations. Eventually, the regulations were amended to reflect the advancements in aircraft design, and the need for waivers in this area diminished.

Similarly, the financial services sector has seen the use of waivers influence long-term regulatory change. In the wake of the 2008 financial crisis, the Dodd-Frank Act introduced sweeping reforms to the banking industry, including stringent capital requirements for financial institutions. However, many small and regional banks found these regulations overly burdensome. As a result, federal agencies, such as the Federal Reserve, began granting waivers to these smaller banks, exempting them from some of the strictest capital requirements imposed on larger institutions. Over time, as these waivers were issued repeatedly, it became clear that a more tailored approach was needed. The logic behind these waivers led to a legislative amendment in 2018, easing some of the capital requirements for smaller banks while still maintaining the core regulatory protections for the broader financial system.

The insurance industry plays a key role in how these industry standards emerge and gain acceptance. For instance, in the cybersecurity sector, insurance companies have been instrumental in establishing best practices by mandating that companies adopt the kinds of security protocols mentioned in the preceding section: requirements for multi-factor authentication, encryption, and incident response plans. Initially, many of these practices were not formalized in regulations, and companies seeking insurance were granted waivers from existing, outdated rules. However, as the insurance industry consistently enforced these standards through its coverage policies, regulators began to take notice. Over time, the cybersecurity standards set by insurers became the basis for new regulations, eliminating the need for continued waivers.

Waivers also played a significant role in the early stages of environmental regulation. In the automotive industry, manufacturers were routinely granted waivers from fuel efficiency and emissions standards as new technologies like hybrid and electric vehicles emerged. These technologies did not fit neatly into existing regulatory frameworks, which were primarily designed around traditional internal combustion engines. Rather than stifling innovation, agencies such as the Environmental Protection Agency (EPA) granted waivers to companies developing these new technologies, allowing them to operate outside the constraints of outdated regulations. As the technologies became more widespread and proven effective, the EPA revised the regulations to accommodate these advancements, incorporating the lessons learned from the waiver process. For example, the Clean Air Act standards were eventually updated to reflect the capabilities of electric and hybrid vehicles, reducing the need for waivers and establishing new emissions benchmarks.

The strategic use of waivers allows agencies to address challenges that were not anticipated when the original regulations were written. Waivers provide a controlled environment in which regulators can test new technologies and approaches while maintaining overall regulatory objectives. By granting waivers and monitoring their outcomes, agencies gain valuable data that helps inform future policymaking. The process of refining regulations based on waiver experiences has been seen across numerous industries, including healthcare. The Department of Health and Human Services (HHS) routinely granted waivers to states experimenting with new healthcare delivery models, such as Medicaid expansion waivers under the Affordable Care Act. These waivers allowed states to pilot new approaches to healthcare that did not strictly comply with federal standards. Over time, the experiences of these states provided valuable insights, which influenced future healthcare policies and even led to amendments in federal healthcare regulations.

The iterative nature of regulation by waiver also helps build a body of precedents that influence future regulatory changes. As more waivers are issued, agencies begin to see patterns in how industry practices evolve. Over time, these patterns contribute to a body of informal precedents that reflect the agency's evolving approach to certain issues. This body of precedent can ultimately lead to the development of new regulations or amendments to existing ones, codifying practices that had previously been exempted through waivers.

While regulation by waiver offers many advantages, including flexibility and fostering innovation, it also presents challenges. One key concern is the consistency and fairness of waiver application. Waivers may be applied differently across various entities, leading to concerns about fairness and equal treatment under the law. This inconsistency can undermine public trust and raise questions about whether certain companies are receiving preferential treatment. Additionally, the waiver process is often opaque, with decisions made through internal agency deliberations that may not be fully transparent to the public or the entities being regulated. The lack of transparency can hinder public participation and accountability in the regulatory process, further contributing to perceptions of unfairness.

Another potential risk of over-relying on waivers is the possibility of circumventing formal regulatory processes. While waivers provide a mechanism for flexibility, they can be seen as a way to bypass the formal rulemaking process, which involves public input and thorough review. This reliance on waivers could weaken the integrity of the regulatory framework if it leads to significant changes in how industries operate without sufficient public scrutiny or input.

The examples of the FAA's noise regulations, financial capital requirements, cybersecurity standards, automotive emissions regulations, and healthcare waivers demonstrate how the consistent application of waivers can shape long-term regulatory policy. As these examples show, waivers are not merely temporary fixes but rather tools that help agencies and industries adapt to changing realities. By gradually building a body of precedents, waivers provide a foundation for new regulations that reflect current industry practices and technological advancements. Ultimately, this process ensures that regulatory frameworks remain flexible and responsive, while maintaining their core objectives of protecting public interests and fostering innovation.

## 4.4 *Regulation through Incorporation*

Once regulatory agencies determine that there is enough consistency across the waivers they have granted, it becomes evident that full regulation is necessary to establish uniform standards across the industry. However, agencies often lack the depth of experience and technical expertise required to develop highly specialized regulations on their own, particularly in fast-evolving fields like artificial intelligence. To overcome this challenge and to ensure that regulations remain flexible and up to date, agencies frequently turn to a strategy known as regulation through Incorporation by Reference (IBR). This method allows agencies to adopt industry standards, guidelines, or technical documents created by external organizations directly into the regulatory framework. By doing so, the agency can rely on the expertise of these organizations while providing the regulated entities with the flexibility to adapt to the latest technological advancements more quickly than the agency could if it developed the regulations independently.

Regulation through incorporation by reference operates by selecting a set of established standards and incorporating them into the regulatory framework by reference rather than reproducing their text within the regulation itself. This method allows regulators to effectively say, "These standards have been agreed upon by experts – let's go with them." However, this approach can raise challenges, particularly when there are borderline cases where the appropriateness of specific standards is in question. In these instances, determining which standards are the most applicable requires careful judgment. Nevertheless, the key advantage of IBR is that it allows regulations to remain dynamic and agile, as updates to the referenced standards can be incorporated into regulations more efficiently than would be possible through traditional regulatory revisions.

Historically, the practice of incorporation by reference dates back to the early 20th century, emerging as a practical solution to the problem of maintaining relevant and timely regulations in the face of rapid technological progress. At first, IBR was used sparingly, but as the pace of innovation accelerated in the latter half of the 20th century, its use expanded. Regulatory bodies realized that the increasing complexity of industrial and technological standards made it impractical for them to develop the requisite technical expertise internally. Thus, they began relying more heavily on external standards-developing organizations, such as professional associations and industry-led technical committees, to establish the necessary technical frameworks. This allowed regulators to ensure that their rules reflected the latest industry best practices without the need to create new regulatory texts from scratch.

In the United States, the legal framework for incorporation by reference has evolved over time, with the Administrative Procedure Act (APA) and guidelines from the Office of the Federal Register (OFR) establishing procedures for federal agencies to follow when using IBR. These rules ensure that when agencies adopt external standards, they do so in a manner that remains accessible and transparent to the public. For instance, the APA requires that materials incorporated by reference must be made available to the public so that regulated entities and other stakeholders can review and understand the requirements they are subject to. This accessibility is a cornerstone of maintaining accountability in the regulatory process.

The advantages of incorporation by reference are numerous. First and foremost, IBR provides significant efficiency. Instead of undergoing a lengthy regulatory revision process every time an industry standard is updated, agencies can simply reference the most current version of a technical document, which is often updated by the external organization responsible for it. This ensures that regulations remain up to date with the latest developments in technology and industry practices without requiring constant regulatory overhaul.

Moreover, IBR allows agencies to leverage the expertise of specialized standards-developing organizations. These organizations often consist of experts with deep knowledge of their respective fields, making them better suited to create highly technical standards than a general regulatory agency might be. By adopting these standards, regulatory agencies can ensure that their rules are informed by the latest innovations and expert consensus, rather than relying solely on the agency's internal capabilities.

Additionally, incorporation by reference promotes harmonization across regulatory environments. By adopting internationally recognized standards, for example, IBR can help align regulations across different jurisdictions. This is particularly beneficial in industries with global reach, such as telecommunications, AI, and financial services, where consistent standards across borders facilitate international trade and cooperation. This harmonization reduces the regulatory burden on companies that operate in multiple countries by allowing them to adhere to a common set of standards, rather than navigating conflicting regulations in each jurisdiction.

In practice, incorporation by reference is widely used across a variety of regulatory fields. In environmental protection, for example, regulators frequently incorporate standards for pollution control, emissions, and environmental testing procedures that are developed by national or international organizations such as the International Organization for Standardization (ISO). By referencing these standards, agencies can ensure that their regulations reflect the latest environmental technologies and best practices.

In the realm of health and safety, workplace safety regulations often incorporate standards for equipment, materials, and practices that are developed by organizations like the Occupational Safety and Health Administration (OSHA) or the American National Standards Institute (ANSI). This incorporation ensures that safety measures are informed by the most current research and industry expertise, providing better protection for workers and the public.

In the financial services sector, regulatory agencies may incorporate accounting standards, risk management practices, and audit procedures developed by organizations like the Financial Accounting Standards Board (FASB). This ensures that financial regulations remain aligned with the latest accounting principles and risk management techniques, helping to maintain the stability and transparency of financial markets.

Similarly, in technology and telecommunications, regulations often reference standards for data security, interoperability, and technical specifications developed by international organizations such as the Institute of Electrical and Electronics Engineers (IEEE) or the International Telecommunication Union (ITU). These references ensure that regulations keep pace with the rapid advancements in technology and cybersecurity, areas where staying current is critical to maintaining public trust and system integrity.

Despite its many advantages, incorporation by reference is not without its challenges. One of the primary concerns is accessibility. Because many of the documents referenced in regulations are created by external organizations, they may not always be freely available to the public. Critics argue that when these referenced standards are not easily accessible, it can create barriers for businesses, stakeholders, and the public who need to understand the regulatory requirements. This issue of accessibility must be carefully managed to ensure that regulations remain transparent and inclusive.

Another concern relates to oversight and accountability. When agencies rely heavily on externally developed standards, there is a risk that they may cede too much regulatory authority to industry-led organizations, potentially reducing the rigor of public oversight. If these standards are primarily developed by industry groups, they may prioritize the interests of their members over broader public concerns, raising questions about whose interests the standards ultimately serve.

Finally, the legal and practical complexities of incorporation by reference can create challenges. When external documents are updated, determining which version is officially incorporated into the regulation can be difficult, especially if changes are made frequently. Agencies must be vigilant in ensuring that the most current and relevant standards are being referenced, while also maintaining clarity about which version of a document is in effect at any given time.

In conclusion, regulation through incorporation by reference is an essential tool for modern regulatory agencies. By adopting external standards into their regulations, agencies can keep pace with rapid technological and industry changes, ensure that regulations reflect the latest expertise, and promote efficiency and harmonization across sectors. While IBR offers significant benefits, it also requires careful management to address concerns around accessibility, accountability, and complexity. As industries like AI continue to evolve, the use of IBR will remain a critical mechanism for ensuring that regulatory frameworks remain both flexible and robust.

## 5 Performance to Prescriptive Regulation

Recent regulatory practices increasingly recognize that regulation is necessary even before a technology is fully mature, acknowledging that not all specific issues can be identified at the outset. In such cases, regulators often begin with performance-based regulations, setting broad goals rather than prescribing specific methods of compliance. As the technology evolves and more is understood about potential failures, regulators shift toward prescriptive regulations when it becomes clear that certain methods or technologies are the most effective in addressing specific issues. This progression reflects the growing confidence of regulatory bodies to define exact processes that must be followed to protect public health, safety, and welfare, moving from reliance on industry standards to more concrete regulatory mandates.

Performance-based regulation focuses on the outcomes or goals that need to be achieved, allowing industries the flexibility to innovate and explore how best to meet these objectives. This is particularly important in fast-moving sectors like AI, where rapid technological change can make prescriptive regulations outdated almost as soon as they are issued. However, while this approach encourages innovation, it presents several challenges. A key challenge is the difficulty in defining and measuring certain outcomes, especially when it comes to complex, emerging technologies like AI.

A clear example of the challenge posed by rapid technological advancements in AI is seen in the development of large language models, such as OpenAI's GPT-4 and subsequent iterations. When these models were first introduced, there were no clear performance targets for transparency or bias mitigation, as the technology was relatively new. As these models became more powerful, their capabilities outpaced the regulatory frameworks designed to manage them. The initial performance-based regulations that focused on general outcomes like reducing bias or ensuring transparency quickly became outdated as newer, more complex versions of the models were released. This rapid evolution made it difficult for regulators to keep performance standards relevant and effective without stifling innovation. In response, regulatory frameworks must now be more dynamic and forward-looking, capable of adapting to such unforeseen advancements.

Another major challenge comes from the complexity and opacity of AI systems, particularly those based on machine learning and deep learning. These systems often function as "black boxes," making it difficult to understand how they arrive at specific decisions. For example, recent controversies around AI systems used for predictive policing and criminal justice have highlighted the difficulty in assessing whether these systems produce fair and unbiased outcomes. The opacity of these systems complicates compliance monitoring and enforcement because regulators cannot easily verify whether the AI's decision-making process adheres to ethical standards. This issue was underscored by the public outcry over the use of AI in determining parole or sentencing recommendations, where the lack of transparency made it nearly impossible to assess the fairness of the system's recommendations. These situations demonstrate the need for sophisticated methodologies and greater regulatory expertise to evaluate AI technologies properly, pushing regulatory bodies to seek advanced tools and knowledge to understand the intricacies of such systems.

The ethical and social implications of AI technologies further complicate performance-based regulation. AI's impact on privacy, bias, and surveillance raises significant concerns, as seen in the widespread use of facial recognition systems. In recent years, cities like San Francisco have enacted bans on the use of facial recognition technology in policing and public spaces due to concerns about privacy violations and racial bias. These ethical issues show that regulation cannot merely focus on technical outcomes but must also address the broader societal impacts of AI systems. Establishing performance standards that adequately reflect these concerns requires a multidisciplinary approach, incorporating insights from technology, law, ethics, and social sciences. This kind of holistic view ensures that the broader societal consequences of AI systems are considered alongside their technical performance.

One of the biggest regulatory challenges in AI is international coordination. AI technologies often operate across national borders, and regulatory approaches differ significantly from country to country. This has been highlighted by recent efforts to regulate AI at the international level, such as the European Union's AI Act, which aims to establish comprehensive rules for AI across member states. However, differences in regulatory frameworks between the EU and other regions, like the United States or China, create challenges for AI developers and users operating in multiple jurisdictions. Without coordinated international standards, companies may engage in regulatory arbitrage, moving operations to regions with less stringent regulations to avoid stricter oversight. The global nature of AI development necessitates cooperation among countries to establish common approaches or standards that ensure consistency and prevent loopholes once efforts progress towards regulation-based solutions.

To effectively navigate these challenges, several strategies can be employed. First, dynamic and adaptive regulation is essential. Regulatory frameworks for AI should be designed to allow for regular updates and adjustments as the technology evolves and new insights are gained. This flexibility ensures that regulations remain relevant without stifling innovation.

Second, stakeholder engagement is critical to ensure that diverse perspectives are considered when defining performance standards and regulatory outcomes. Involving AI developers, users, ethicists, and the public can help create more balanced regulations that address both technical capabilities and societal concerns.

Third, regulators will need to develop cross-disciplinary expertise. AI regulation requires more than just legal and policy knowledge; regulators must also understand computer science, ethics, and social implications. This broader expertise is crucial for assessing AI technologies comprehensively and ensuring that regulations are both effective and forward-looking.

Finally, international collaboration is key. As AI technologies cross borders, regulatory cooperation between countries is essential to creating and implementing harmonized standards. Such coordination can reduce confusion, ensure fairness in AI development, and prevent companies from exploiting regulatory differences between jurisdictions.

Performance-based regulation offers flexibility and encourages innovation, but it still faces challenges when applied to rapidly evolving and complex technologies like AI. By employing adaptive regulation, engaging a diverse range of stakeholders, cultivating cross-disciplinary expertise, and promoting international collaboration, regulators can create a balanced approach that fosters technological growth while safeguarding ethical standards and societal well-being.

## 6 Shocking Progress

Progress in technology and societal advancement rarely follows a steady, predictable path. Instead, it often moves in fits and starts, punctuated by moments of collective shock that push the public and policymakers toward action. History offers many examples of such events. For instance, Upton Sinclair's 1906 novel *The Jungle* exposed the appalling conditions in the meatpacking industry, shocking the nation into realizing the urgent need for food safety regulations. Similarly, the Chernobyl disaster in 1986 highlighted the dangers of nuclear power and led to stricter oversight of the nuclear industry. These moments of crisis illuminate underlying problems in technological systems or societal practices that, until then, have gone largely unnoticed or unaddressed. In these instances, change is often driven by fear, outrage, or a sense of vulnerability, forcing governments and industries to confront issues they may have previously ignored.

The rise of artificial intelligence (AI) follows a similar pattern. Although AI has been steadily evolving, its potential risks have only recently begun to spark public concern, often triggered by specific incidents that expose its dangers. These shocks typically revolve around powerful or influential individuals realizing that AI could affect their own interests, such as when politicians became alarmed by the prospect of AI-generated deepfakes influencing elections, or when celebrities and ordinary people alike discovered that AI systems had replicated their likenesses without permission. Public health crises or medical errors related to AI, as well as situations where people feel powerless to stop AI-driven decisions that seem unfair or unethical, are further examples of the societal shocks that push regulation forward. These events expose the misalignments in current strategies and definitions, showing where the gaps lie in the existing regulatory frameworks and prompting calls for stronger oversight.

One of the earliest AI-related shocks came from the realm of politics, where AI-generated deep fakes – realistic yet fabricated videos – threatened to undermine the democratic process. Politicians, acutely aware of how these technologies could be weaponized against them, became early advocates for AI regulation. In the lead-up to the 2024 U.S. elections, fears about deep fakes prompted state-level legislation such as Iowa House File 2549, which aimed to make the use of AI in creating deceptive campaign materials a felony. The urgency behind such laws arose from fears that AI-generated videos, robocalls, or social media posts could falsely depict candidates making statements they never uttered, potentially swaying voters and destabilizing campaigns. This fear, rooted in self-preservation, reflects how shocks to personal interests can drive regulatory action, though often without the clarity needed for long-term solutions. For instance, broad definitions of AI in these early legislative efforts have sometimes swept up technologies like simple spell check programs, highlighting the difficulty of crafting precise laws in the face of rapid technological change.

The shock surrounding deepfakes is not limited to the United States. In Europe, similar concerns have fueled debates over AI regulation, as evidenced by the European Union's AI Act, which is attempting to strike a balance between curbing harmful uses of AI and fostering innovation. The EU's definition of AI is narrower, aiming to focus on systems using machine learning and logic-based approaches. This contrast in approaches between the U.S. and Europe reveals the broader challenge of aligning regulatory frameworks to address a technology as diverse and rapidly evolving as AI.

Another significant shock came when the public realized that AI systems were replicating people's voices, faces, and identities without their consent.

This issue came to the forefront when OpenAI released a voice assistant that eerily resembled the voice of actress Scarlett Johansson, raising alarms about the legal and ethical implications of digital replicas.[18] This incident sparked a broader debate about the ownership of one's voice or image in an era where AI can convincingly reproduce them. The boundaries of privacy and identity are being stretched as AI blurs the lines between what is real and what is artificial. Recent legal battles, such as those involving AI-generated art mimicking the styles of living artists without their consent, underscore the growing need for regulations that address not only copyright and intellectual property but also personal autonomy over one's likeness in digital spaces.

Public health has also become an area of concern as AI technologies increasingly infiltrate healthcare. AI promises to revolutionize medical diagnostics and treatment, but errors in its application have led to fatal consequences. For instance, in 2023, an AI system in a hospital misdiagnosed a patient's condition, leading to denial of care and incorrect treatment, prompting a public outcry over the lack of oversight in AI-driven medical technologies. This incident highlighted the dangerous potential of AI systems when they fail, especially in critical areas like healthcare.[19] While laws such as the Children's Online Privacy Protection Act (COPA) have begun addressing AI's role in protecting vulnerable populations, such as minors, from targeted content, the broader regulatory framework surrounding AI in healthcare remains fragmented and underdeveloped.

Perhaps one of the most pervasive shocks is the growing realization that individuals often have little control over decisions made by AI systems, even when those decisions are clearly unjust. This issue is particularly pressing in cross-border AI applications. AI systems that generate harmful content or enable surveillance may be developed in one country and deployed globally, leaving those affected with no clear recourse. This highlights the difficulty of regulating AI systems that operate beyond national borders, where jurisdictional misalignments can allow harmful practices to persist unchecked.

In recent years, differing definitions and strategies for regulating AI have emerged across the globe, further complicating efforts to create cohesive

---

18 https://www.washingtonpost.com/technology/2024/05/20/openai-scarlett-johansson-chatgpt-ai-voice/

19 United Health Care Uses Faulty AI to Deny Elder Patients Medically Necessary Coverage, Lawsuit Claims, CBS, November 2023: https://www.cbsnews.com/news/unitedhealth-lawsuit-ai-deny-claims-medicare-advantage-health-insurance-denials/

regulation. Canada's proposed Artificial Intelligence and Data Act, for example, defines AI as systems that use models to generate outputs like predictions or decisions,[20] while Russia's national strategy focuses on AI systems' ability to simulate human cognitive functions.[21] These divergent definitions reflect the difficulty in establishing a universal understanding of AI, which in turn complicates the creation of consistent regulations.

To address these challenges, several strategies can help ensure that AI regulation keeps pace with technological development. First, regulatory frameworks need to be dynamic and adaptive, allowing for regular updates as AI technology evolves. This approach prevents regulations from becoming outdated while still maintaining a degree of flexibility that fosters innovation. Second, engaging a broad range of stakeholders is essential to creating well-rounded regulations. Involving AI developers, users, ethicists, and the general public ensures that diverse perspectives are considered, helping to address both the technical and societal implications of AI. Third, regulators must cultivate cross-disciplinary expertise, combining knowledge from fields such as computer science, ethics, law, and public policy to effectively assess AI technologies. Finally, international collaboration is key to ensuring that AI regulation is consistent across borders. Harmonizing regulatory standards across countries will prevent companies from exploiting regulatory gaps and ensure that AI systems are subject to similar rules, regardless of where they are developed or deployed.

Whether triggered by political fears of deepfakes, the ethical dilemmas of digital replicas, or the life-and-death stakes of AI in healthcare, these shocks expose the weaknesses in existing regulatory frameworks and push society toward stronger oversight. By developing dynamic regulations, engaging diverse stakeholders, fostering cross-disciplinary expertise, and collaborating internationally, regulators can better address the complexities of AI and mitigate its potential risks.

## 7 Strategic Parallels

AI is not only a functional mimic. Its rise mimics many technologies before it. How we protect the public while empowering innovation requires an

20 https://www.ourcommons.ca/content/Committee/441/INDU/WebDoc/WD12751351/12751351/MinisterOfInnovationScienceAndIndustry-2023-11-28-Combined-e.pdf

21 https://www.ifri.org/sites/default/files/migrated_files/documents/atoms/files/nocetti_russia_artificial_intelligence_2020.pdf

understanding of past societal challenges that were created or confronted by innovating technologies.

- Energy Efficiency
- Addictive Substances
- Separating Powers to Protect Data
- Personhood
- Identity Theft
- Labor Laws
- Food Labeling
- Risk Based Insurance Requirements
- Product Safety

### 7.1 *Energy Efficiency Regulations*

Current AI models are the 1973 Lincoln Continental of inefficiency[22] – they consume vast computational resources and often exhibit behaviors like over-hallucination, a form of excess, because they are not driven by a need to optimize for energy efficiency. Drawing from the history of fuel economy and energy efficiency regulations, we can envision how regulating AI energy use could not only drive efficiency but also foster innovation, reduce costs, and reshape how consumers and businesses use AI tools.

One of the most illustrative parallels comes from the Corporate Average Fuel Economy (CAFE) standards implemented in the 1970s. These standards revolutionized the automotive industry by requiring automakers to meet minimum fuel efficiency thresholds, prompting innovation in engine technologies like turbocharging and hybrid powertrains. In a similar way, AI regulation could focus on setting energy-use standards per model or task, incentivizing companies to create AI systems that are not only effective but also optimized for energy consumption. Symbolic AI, for example, is often more efficient in certain tasks than massive neural networks. It uses rule-based logic rather than exhaustive computation, offering an alternative architecture that can dramatically reduce energy costs while delivering equally effective results in specific domains, such as knowledge representation or reasoning tasks.

A concrete example is Google's traditional search compared to generative AI models, such as those used in ChatGPT-like systems. While Alphabet's Chairman John Hennessy stated in February 2023 that "having an exchange with AI … likely cost 10 times more than a standard keyword

22 https://driving.ca/features/feature-story/worst-gas-guzzlers-of-all-time

search,"[23] Sasha Luccioni claimed in September 2024 that "generative artificial intelligence uses 30 times more energy than a traditional search engine."[24] AI integrated into search functions, while powerful and flexible, require immense computational power, especially for tasks like generating text from scratch. As a result, Google has explored the possibility of charging users for access to generative AI-based search to reflect its higher operational costs. This shift in pricing signals that less energy-efficient AI services will become more costly for consumers, driving behavioral change – much like how consumers opted for more fuel-efficient vehicles in response to rising gasoline costs. By imposing energy-use standards on AI models, providers might be compelled to adopt more efficient architectures, optimize their computational processes, or pass the cost of inefficiency onto users, thus shaping user behavior, and perhaps creating inequalities when some consumers can afford first tier access and some cannot.

The transition from energy-intensive systems to more efficient alternatives has historical precedence. In the automotive sector, automakers balanced the production of large, fuel-hungry vehicles with smaller, more efficient cars to meet CAFE standards. Similarly, AI companies might be required to balance the energy consumption of large-scale models, such as massive neural networks used in natural language processing, with more efficient alternatives like symbolic AI or compressed models. Just as automotive innovation led to significant cost savings and reductions in fuel consumption, AI innovations could yield similar benefits. Symbolic AI, for instance, could be particularly useful in areas like reasoning or structured data queries, offering a less resource-intensive solution that could lower both operational costs and environmental impact.

Moreover, we can draw lessons from energy efficiency regulations in household appliances. The introduction of standards for products like refrigerators, air conditioners, and light bulbs dramatically reduced energy consumption. For instance, refrigerators have become more than 70% more energy-efficient since the introduction of regulatory standards, even as their size and functionality have improved. A similar regulatory approach for AI could force companies to develop models that use less power without sacrificing functionality. This could encourage innovations like model compression techniques, which reduce the number of parameters in a neural

23 https://www.reuters.com/technology/tech-giants-ai-like-bing-bard-poses-billion-dollar-search-problem-2023-02-22/

24 https://www.scientificamerican.com/article/what-do-googles-ai-answers-cost-the-environment/

network while maintaining performance. The success of these energy-saving regulations in appliances could serve as a blueprint for AI, encouraging the development of more sustainable technologies without diminishing their utility.

In addition, the success of hybrid vehicles like the Toyota Prius offers another powerful analogy. The Prius demonstrated that consumers were willing to embrace energy-efficient technologies when they provided clear benefits, such as reduced fuel costs and environmental impact. Similarly, AI companies could develop more energy-efficient AI models that are just as effective as current models but consume less power. For example, Ericsson researchers report that "hybrid AI [which] combines symbolic approaches with data-driven AI" can produce AI systems that are both efficient and powerful, saving on energy costs while meeting consumer needs.[25] These savings would not only benefit companies through reduced operational costs but could also be passed on to consumers, much like the lower fuel costs associated with hybrid or electric vehicles.

The broader energy sector also provides examples of how regulations can spur technological advances. In response to energy efficiency regulations, the lighting industry transitioned from incandescent bulbs to more efficient alternatives like compact fluorescent lamps (CFLs) and light-emitting diodes (LEDs). This shift led to a dramatic reduction in electricity consumption for lighting. AI could undergo a similar transformation if energy efficiency standards were imposed. For instance, providers might be incentivized to develop more energy-efficient hardware, such as specialized chips for AI computations, or to explore alternative energy sources, such as solar-powered data centers. These innovations could significantly reduce the energy demands of AI, much as the shift to LEDs reduced energy use in lighting.

Another key issue is the "rebound effect," where improvements in energy efficiency lead to increased consumption, offsetting some of the gains. In the context of AI, as models become more energy-efficient, there is a risk that users will simply use AI more frequently, negating some of the environmental benefits. This was seen in the transportation sector, where more fuel-efficient vehicles encouraged people to drive more. AI regulation could address this by setting absolute energy consumption limits or by pricing energy usage in such a way that overuse becomes cost-prohibitive, ensuring that efficiency gains lead to genuine reductions in energy use.

25 https://www.ericsson.com/en/blog/2023/12/enhancing-mobile-networks-the-hybrid-ai-advantage

The political landscape around energy efficiency also offers important lessons. During the Trump administration, certain fuel economy standards were rolled back, creating uncertainty in the market and prompting legal challenges from states like California, which set its own more stringent standards. This tension between federal and state regulations illustrates the challenges AI regulation could face, especially given the global nature of the industry. However, as seen with fuel economy, even in the face of political opposition, consumer demand for efficiency and sustainability continued to grow, eventually pushing the industry toward greater innovation. Similarly, despite potential regulatory setbacks, consumer demand for efficient and cost-effective AI could drive innovation in the sector.

The introduction of energy efficiency labels, such as ENERGY STAR, has also proven highly effective in raising consumer awareness and driving demand for energy-efficient products. An equivalent in AI – such as an "energy-efficient AI" certification – could serve a similar purpose, helping consumers make informed choices about the tools they use and pushing companies to design models that prioritize energy savings.

Just as fuel and energy efficiency regulations transformed the transportation and built environments, similar standards could revolutionize the AI industry. By setting energy consumption targets for AI systems, encouraging innovation in energy-efficient architectures, and driving consumer awareness, these regulations could lead to significant improvements in both the efficiency and effectiveness of AI technologies. The cost savings realized through more efficient AI models, such as those using symbolic AI or optimized hardware, would benefit businesses and consumers alike, while also mitigating the environmental impact of AI's rapid growth. Regulating AI energy use is not just about reducing power consumption – it's about fostering a future where AI is both powerful and sustainable, much like the broader success story of fuel and energy efficiency in the past century.

## 7.2 *Addictive Substances*

AI has rapidly integrated into numerous applications where its ability to interpret, influence, and respond often outpaces a user's capacity to fully evaluate its potential harms. This dynamic raises significant concerns about the addictive potential of AI, not only in feared applications like deepfakes or social media catfishing but also in the more subtle, everyday use of AI in personalized marketing, social media algorithms, and even investment pitches. Researchers have already begun to observe through analyzing current AI usage[26] that AI's capacity to foster addictive behavior often outstrips its more productive uses.[27] As AI becomes increasingly pervasive, regulating it with frameworks developed for addictive substances could be critical to ensuring public safety and improving AI quality.

The regulation of addictive substances has evolved over time, often based on the understanding of their potential harm and the societal need to mitigate their addictive qualities. Historical efforts to regulate substances like tobacco, alcohol, and illicit drugs can provide a framework for addressing AI's addictive properties. One of the primary methods used to control addictive substances has been restricting access, particularly through mechanisms like age gating and marketing limitations. These tools could also be applied to AI systems, particularly those that have been designed to optimize engagement and foster dependency, such as social media algorithms or AI-driven entertainment platforms.

Take tobacco as a starting point. Early in the 20th century, tobacco companies thrived with minimal regulation, even as smoking rates surged. However, as scientific evidence emerged in the mid-20th century linking smoking to lung cancer and other serious health conditions, regulatory pressure began to mount. By the 1990s, lawsuits exposed tobacco companies' strategies of manipulating nicotine levels to increase addiction. This led to far-reaching regulations, including advertising bans, graphic health warnings, and age restrictions on cigarette sales. Similarly, AI companies have employed addictive tactics – such as optimizing algorithms to maximize screen time or engagement through endless content feeds – without facing comparable regulatory scrutiny. These addictive techniques, often deployed by AI systems, are analogous to tobacco companies' practices of engineering products to increase dependency. Age-gating AI systems that target younger audiences, such as social media platforms and video games, could provide an important first step in mitigating the harm of addiction in AI.

For instance, many social media platforms use AI-driven recommendation engines to optimize user engagement, with algorithms specifically designed to keep users online as long as possible. The addictive potential of these systems, especially for adolescents, is increasingly evident. Just as tobacco advertising was eventually banned from television and radio to protect vulnerable populations, regulations could limit the ways AI-driven

26 https://www.technologyreview.com/2024/08/05/1095600/we-need-to-prepare-for-addictive-intelligence/

27 https://www.technologyreview.com/2024/08/12/1096202/how-people-actually-using-ai/

platforms advertise or promote content to young users, requiring platforms to disclose when an AI system is designed to encourage prolonged use or engagement. This would mirror how addictive substances face strict advertising restrictions to minimize their appeal to younger audiences.

The regulation of alcohol offers another relevant parallel. After the failure of Prohibition in the U.S., alcohol returned to being a regulated substance, with age gating and restrictions on sales to reduce the likelihood of addiction, particularly among younger individuals. The standardized drinking age of 21 in the U.S. reflects research that showed young people are particularly vulnerable to alcohol-related harms and long-term addiction. Similarly, AI systems that target young audiences – such as those used in social media, gaming, or interactive entertainment – could be subject to strict age gating. This would help prevent younger users from forming addictive patterns with AI technologies that exploit psychological vulnerabilities, such as dopamine-driven feedback loops in "likes" or social approval cues.

A more extreme form of regulation can be seen in the handling of illicit drugs. Substances like heroin, cocaine, and methamphetamine have been tightly controlled or outright banned due to their highly addictive nature and the severe societal harm they cause. The U.S. government's Controlled Substances Act classifies drugs into schedules based on their potential for abuse, with the most addictive and harmful substances facing the strictest regulations. This approach could be applied to AI systems, particularly in cases where algorithms are explicitly designed to exploit addictive tendencies. Systems that push harmful content, perpetuate conspiracy theories, or manipulate financial decisions could be regulated more tightly, even facing bans if their addictive capacities are deemed too harmful. AI models that encourage addictive behaviors might require a formal evaluation of their potential for abuse, just as substances are classified based on their addictiveness and societal impact.

Another example that highlights the need for AI regulation based on addictive potential is pseudoephedrine, a common cold medication ingredient that became heavily regulated because of its role in producing methamphetamine. While pseudoephedrine itself is not inherently addictive, its misuse warranted stricter controls. Similarly, certain AI technologies, though not initially designed to be addictive, may still facilitate addictive behaviors. AI systems that drive impulse buying in online shopping or foster unhealthy social media use could fall under this type of regulation. Just as regulations now limit how much pseudoephedrine a person can purchase, AI systems could face limitations on how much they can tailor experiences for any individual, especially vulnerable populations like adolescents.

The emerging research on the addictive nature of AI systems shows parallels with the regulatory history of substances. Just as the development of nicotine replacement therapies and addiction treatment programs paralleled tighter tobacco regulations, future AI regulations could mandate the development of tools to help individuals manage their AI use. For example, governments could require AI companies to integrate mechanisms for limiting usage or setting engagement time limits, similar to how governments now require nicotine addiction warnings on cigarette packages or restrict alcohol sales after certain hours. Mandating transparency in AI engagement metrics could help users and parents make more informed choices about how much time is spent interacting with AI-driven content.

The "rebound effect," seen in addictive substances, where users engage more when restrictions are loosened, might also appear in AI regulation. For example, if restrictions on engagement time or algorithmic transparency led to users spending more time finding workarounds, the regulation would need to be continuously monitored and adapted to ensure its effectiveness, just as drug regulation has evolved in response to changing patterns of abuse.

Regulating AI based on its addictive potential, much like substances such as tobacco, alcohol, and illicit drugs, can help ensure public safety and improve the quality of AI systems. By introducing age gating, transparency in AI engagement techniques, and limitations on addictive features, regulators could mitigate the societal harms associated with AI addiction, just as they have with addictive substances. Through regulatory measures, we can ensure that AI is harnessed for its productive potential rather than allowing it to evolve into an unchecked source of societal harm, driven by its capacity to manipulate and addict users. Yet any regulatory effort that offers controls on par with the technologies' parallel danger will have to carefully navigate the liability-free culture that prevents most experts in the field from seeing the danger in AI as a fundamental feature rather than an inconvenient bug.

### 7.3 *Separating Power to Protect Data*

The regulation of industries to prevent vertical integration – where a company controls multiple stages of production, distribution, or services – has long served as a means of creating a balance of power and promoting transparency. This balance prevents conflicts of interest and anti-competitive behavior, ensuring accountability within complex industries. For AI, the challenge lies in adapting these regulatory lessons to a field that revolves around data. A productive regulatory model could involve treating data like other industries – by separating the gathering, processing, and deployment of data into distinct functions and restricting companies from controlling all three. This would encourage transparency, prevent monopolistic control over AI infrastructure, and ensure that innovation benefits both businesses and society.

The Glass-Steagall Act of 1933 offers a powerful example of how separating key activities can promote stability and reduce systemic risks. By dividing commercial banking from investment banking, Glass-Steagall ensured that the same institution could not use consumer deposits for speculative investments. This structural separation reduced conflicts of interest and ensured the accountability of financial institutions. Similarly, an AI company that collects data should not also control how that data is processed and deployed, just as a bank could not both safeguard savings and make speculative investments. By forcing companies to rely on third parties for some functions, a separation of powers in AI could improve transparency, requiring firms to disclose the origin, quality, and purpose of their datasets.

This separation model finds a parallel in the credit reporting industry, where companies that collect consumer data – like Experian, Equifax, and TransUnion – do not directly profit from lending decisions. These credit bureaus gather, organize, and maintain consumer credit data, but lenders independently use that data to assess creditworthiness. This system ensures that the entities responsible for collecting and cleaning data are held to a standard of accountability, while the risk-taking decisions are left to lenders. If the same model were applied to AI, companies that gather raw data could be prohibited from using it to train models directly, or vice versa – ensuring that the functions of data collection, processing, and deployment are separated to foster accountability and reduce conflicts of interest.

The energy sector's separation of generation and distribution offers another compelling framework for AI regulation. In many regions, utilities are restricted from both generating and distributing electricity, ensuring that independent energy producers have access to the distribution grid. This "functional unbundling" prevents monopolies and promotes competition. Applying this concept to AI, regulators could mandate that companies involved in data collection partner with independent processors to clean and validate that data, or that model developers use third-party datasets for training. Such a system would foster greater competition among AI firms, preventing any single entity from monopolizing all aspects of data infrastructure and ensuring a diversity of participants in the AI ecosystem.

Healthcare regulations also illustrate the benefits of separating overlapping functions. In many U.S. states, insurance companies are prohibited from owning healthcare providers to prevent conflicts of interest. Yet as we have already seen in the U.S. health industry, when insurer decisions effectively control both care provision and payment, prioritizing profits over patient outcomes by denying expensive treatments or limiting patient options can occur. In AI, similar risks arise when companies that gather and deploy data also process it for monetization. For instance, a social media platform that collects user data and directly monetizes it through targeted advertising has little incentive to clean or validate that data for ethical uses. Requiring companies to outsource either the cleaning or deployment of data would ensure that multiple actors are held accountable in the data pipeline, reducing the potential for abuse or unethical behavior.

Media and broadcasting regulations also provide insights into how separating functions can maintain public trust and diversity. Laws in many countries prevent media companies from controlling both broadcast platforms and the content aired on them. Without such separations, a company could monopolize public discourse by limiting access to alternative viewpoints and prioritizing its own narratives. In the AI context, an analogous risk emerges when companies that collect data also control how it is deployed through algorithms, as this could lead to biased outputs or the reinforcement of harmful stereotypes. Regulating AI companies to ensure that data collection, processing, and application are conducted by separate entities would promote transparency and accountability, just as media regulations aim to ensure diversity in information.

The airline industry also exemplifies the benefits of separating infrastructure from operations. Regulations prevent airlines from owning or operating airports, ensuring that no single airline can control access to critical infrastructure. If airlines controlled airport operations, they could deny gate access to competitors, distorting market competition. Similarly, in AI, companies that control both the data infrastructure and the tools for deploying AI models could restrict access to those tools, excluding competitors and limiting innovation. A requirement that companies specialize in only two of the three data functions – collection, processing, or deployment – would ensure that no single entity can dominate the entire AI ecosystem, creating a more open and competitive market.

The dangers of dismantling such regulatory separations are evident in the financial sector's experience with the repeal of Glass-Steagall. The Gramm-Leach-Bliley Act (GLBA) of 1999 allowed financial institutions to merge commercial banking, investment banking, and insurance functions, eroding the balance of power that Glass-Steagall had created. This integration led to the excessive risk-taking that contributed to the 2008 financial crisis, revealing the vulnerabilities that arise when companies control multiple layers of a complex system. The lesson for AI is clear: allowing companies to integrate data gathering, cleaning, and deployment functions could lead to unchecked power and systemic risks. Regulating AI to prevent full vertical integration would reduce conflicts of interest, promote market-driven accountability, and limit the potential for harm.

The Dodd-Frank Act of 2010, which introduced the Volcker Rule to limit speculative trading by banks, highlights the importance of maintaining structural separations. While Dodd-Frank did not fully restore Glass-Steagall's provisions, it reinforced the need for checks and balances in complex systems. Similarly, AI regulation must ensure that companies cannot dominate the entire data pipeline without external oversight. By restricting firms to only two of the three data infrastructure functions, regulators could foster a healthy, competitive environment where transparency is rewarded, and each participant is held accountable for its role in the AI ecosystem.

Applying these lessons to AI, a regulatory framework that enforces a balance of power among data collectors, processors, and deployers would help prevent monopolies and conflicts of interest. Just as industries like finance, energy, and telecommunications have benefited from structural separations, AI would be more transparent and accountable if companies were required to contract certain functions to third parties. This approach would ensure that no single company controls the entire lifecycle of data, fostering competition, promoting innovation, and protecting public trust.

## 7.4 *Personhood Providing Agency to Digital Twins*

The arguably greatest danger posed by AI-dependent system providers is the acceptance of provider responsibility. Debates on autonomy and responsibility often center on whether a provider can be held accountable for the actions of an autonomous system once it has been created and released into the world. This evokes parallels with legal and philosophical discussions, such as the personhood movement, where similar debates about agency and responsibility have evolved over time. In considering these themes, AI regulatory strategies may benefit from reviewing the history of the personhood movement, as well as more contemporary developments like distributed autonomous organizations (DAOs), which pose significant challenges in responsibility attribution.

Personhood has long been a subject of debate, traditionally tied to human beings but increasingly applied to non-human entities. Historically, legal frameworks excluded certain groups, such as enslaved people or women, from personhood, but these definitions have evolved. In recent decades, the concept has been extended to animals, corporations, artificial intelligence, and other entities, questioning traditional ideas about agency, rights, and autonomy. Recent legal discussions surrounding fetal viability, digital twins, and DAOs reveal just how much the boundaries of personhood are being tested today.

In the debate over fetal viability, advancements in medical technology have enabled fetuses to survive outside the womb at earlier stages. This shift has led to legal challenges over when life – and thus personhood – begins. Court cases like *Roe v. Wade* and its overturning in *Dobbs v. Jackson Women's Health Organization* have highlighted the complexity of defining personhood based on biological autonomy. In these debates, viability and the ability to make autonomous decisions play a critical role in shaping legal protections for non-human entities, including AI systems.

As artificial intelligence becomes more sophisticated, these debates extend to AI's capacity for autonomy and viability. For instance, AI systems that serve as digital twins replicate a person's voice, behavior, and decision-making processes, raising questions about ownership and rights. If a programmer creates a digital twin of a living person, does the programmer retain intellectual property rights, or does the person being replicated hold ownership over their digital likeness? These questions echo the discussions around fetal viability, whereas with AI the central issue is the transition from a mere object or tool to an autonomous entity deserving of rights and protections.

DAOs further complicate the debate. DAOs, which operate autonomously using blockchain technology and smart contracts, challenge traditional legal frameworks because they lack a central authority or legal person to hold accountable. In the case of DAOs, decisions are made through decentralized mechanisms, with algorithms executing commands based on predefined rules. This raises the question: If a DAO causes harm or violates regulations, who is responsible? The absence of a clear "owner" or operator complicates efforts to attribute responsibility, echoing the debates over AI autonomy and provider responsibility.

An example of this can be seen in The DAO attack in 2016, where a decentralized venture capital fund based on Ethereum experienced a significant exploit when an "anonymous hacker stole over $50M USD worth of Ethers out of $168M invested."[28] The decentralized nature of The DAO

28 Mehar, Muhammad and Shier, Charlie and Giambattista, Alana and Gong, Elgar and Fletcher, Gabrielle and Sanayhie, Ryan and Kim, Henry M. and Laskowski, Marek,

made it difficult to assign blame, as there was no central authority overseeing the organization. This incident highlighted the difficulty in regulating autonomous systems like DAOs and raised questions about how liability is managed when no human actor is directly controlling the system. The lack of a clear legal entity to hold accountable creates concerns about perpetrator-free crimes, where the system itself acts without human intervention.

This same logic applies to AI models that replicate human traits. The case of an AI-generated voice assistant that closely resembled Scarlett Johansson's voice raised important legal questions about digital likeness ownership. While programmers developed the AI, the system replicated a real person's voice, blurring the lines between creation and replication. Should Johansson have control over this digital entity, or does the programmer hold the rights? This mirrors the debates about fetal viability, where courts must determine when something evolves to be viewed as a separate entity with rights.

Similarly, the famous "monkey selfie" case challenged the traditional notion of authorship and intellectual property. A crested macaque named Naruto pressed the shutter button on a camera, sparking a legal battle over whether the monkey could be the rightful owner of the photograph.[29] Although the courts ruled that animals cannot hold intellectual property rights, the case paralleled broader discussions about agency and whether entities outside traditional human definitions – like animals or machines – could one day be granted rights. This ruling echoes the U.S. Copyright Office's stance that AI cannot hold copyrights, a position based on the assumption that only humans can create original works deserving of protection.

In the context of AI and copyright law, North American and Australian courts have consistently ruled that only humans can hold copyrights, excluding AI systems from owning their creations. However, some jurisdictions, like the United Kingdom, take a different approach. UK copyright law allows AI-generated works to be copyrighted, but the rights are attrib-

Understanding a Revolutionary and Flawed Grand Experiment in Blockchain: The DAO Attack (November 26, 2017). Journal of Cases on Information Technology 21(1) 19–32., Available at SSRN: https://ssrn.com/abstract=3014782 or http://dx.doi.org/10.2139/ssrn.3014782

29 https://www.thejakartapost.com/life/2017/09/12/monkey-selfie-copyright-lawsuit-ends-in-settlement.html

uted to the person who set up the AI or provided the necessary inputs.[30] This represents a middle ground, recognizing the creative potential of AI while still tying ownership to human involvement. This approach parallels fetal viability, where the debate has been about legal rights being attributed based on the potential for independent survival, drawing comparisons to AI systems and their creators.

DAOs further complicate this issue. As autonomous organizations, DAOs challenge existing legal frameworks by operating without human oversight. In theory, DAOs could facilitate contracts, financial transactions, and decision-making without a human at the helm. As such, they present a new frontier in discussions of personhood and agency, particularly when they act without direct human input. This lack of a clear "creator" or controlling entity raises concerns similar to those surrounding AI autonomy and intellectual property.

If we apply the logic of personhood to AI, as has been done with DAOs, it prompts us to reconsider questions of ownership, liability, and responsibility. In the case of a digital twin that replicates human traits, at what point does the digital entity become more than just a tool for the programmer? If a digital twin can make autonomous decisions and act in the world, does it possess a form of digital personhood, deserving of rights or protections? Much like the DAO incident, where decentralized systems operated without clear accountability, AI systems raise similar challenges in terms of responsibility and control.

Regulation of AI systems will need to understand how decisions regarding ownership and accountability could interact with personhood philosophies and regulatory efforts. These efforts will most likely see the greatest challenges around definitions of autonomy and agency, including when these qualities are seen in what would have previously been nothing more than an object or tool. Just as technological advancements in fetal viability have forced society to reconsider when life begins, while DAOs have demonstrated the willingness of society to rethink technologically derived agency, ownership, responsibility, AI will likely benefit from a strategic narrowing of personhood that conforms applications that are appropriate for the level of enforcement that can be attributed to or passed through the AI system.

---

30 https://www.gov.uk/government/consultations/copyright-and-artificial-intelligence/copyright-and-artificial-intelligence#:~:text=51.,arrangements%20necessary%20for%20its%20creation

## 8 Identity Theft

Discussions around AI and identity theft often center on the ability of a system to mimic a person so convincingly that a target is defrauded by the identity thief. This is a clear and common case of identity-based fraud. However, if frameworks like "personhood" are applied to AI, granting systems elements of agency, viability, or autonomy, we must reconsider how past approaches to identity theft would apply to protecting these AI systems from theft or misuse. This challenge becomes especially relevant when considering "digital twins" – AI-generated replicas that represent an individual's characteristics or behavior in various domains.

The history of identity theft laws has evolved significantly alongside technological advancements. In the pre-digital era, identity theft primarily involved the physical theft of documents such as passports, Social Security cards, or credit cards. These physical items were used to impersonate victims for financial gain or to evade law enforcement. However, as society became increasingly reliant on digital communications and data storage systems, identity theft shifted to include the digital realm. This transition, which began in the late 20th century, allowed criminals to steal personal data on a much larger scale and often without ever coming into contact with their victims.

One of the most important legal milestones in combating modern identity theft was the Identity Theft Assumption and Deterrence Act (ITADA) of 1998. This law made it a U.S. federal crime to knowingly use or possess another person's means of identification with the intent to commit an unlawful act. The ITADA recognized that personal data – such as Social Security numbers, credit card numbers, and email addresses – could be stolen and misused, even in the absence of physical interaction. It was a significant step forward, as it shifted the legal understanding of identity from being tied to physical documents to encompassing digital data that could be used to impersonate someone.

In digital identity theft, personal data like email addresses, passwords, and biometric data became valuable, as these elements could authenticate an individual's identity in digital transactions or communications. For example, a cybercriminal could steal a credit card number through phishing, bypassing the need for physical possession of the card itself. This shift toward digital identity theft introduced complex legal challenges, as lawmakers grappled with defining what constitutes personal identity in the digital age and how to protect this data.

If AI systems, particularly digital twins, are recognized as having their own identity, protecting them from theft or misuse would introduce a host of new legal challenges. In traditional identity theft, the misuse of personal data is central to the crime – criminals exploit stolen information for financial gain or to commit fraud. But in the case of a digital twin, where AI systems might mimic certain characteristics of a person, the boundaries of identity theft become blurred. A digital twin is not merely a direct representation of its human counterpart; it is an optimized model that can exhibit behaviors and produce outputs distinct from the person on whom it is based.

For example, if a digital twin is created from an individual's health data but optimized to predict future health outcomes based on patterns that are unique to the twin's model, the AI-generated identity may diverge from the original person in meaningful ways. If this digital twin is "stolen" or used without authorization, would this constitute identity theft, or would it fall under a different legal category, such as property theft or intellectual property infringement? The digital twin may not generate personally identifiable information (PII) that directly links it to a specific individual, but its value lies in its ability to create accurate and useful insights based on the data on which it was trained. This raises the question of whether theft of the twin, or its misuse, should be treated as a theft of identity or property.

The evolution of identity theft laws, especially in response to digital challenges, shows a precedent for adapting legal frameworks to new forms of data theft. However, extending these frameworks to protect digital twins may not be straightforward. The theft of a digital twin, which could function autonomously or provide insights about its human counterpart, would likely require new definitions of what constitutes identity. Unlike traditional identity theft, where the goal is often to steal financial resources, the theft of a digital twin might involve exploiting its unique capabilities for commercial or scientific purposes. For instance, a digital twin optimized for medical diagnostics could be stolen and used by unauthorized parties to create medical treatments or devices, raising questions about intellectual property rights and ownership.

Another example comes from the legal challenges associated with biometric data, which has become a key part of digital identity. Fingerprints, facial recognition patterns, and even voiceprints are now used for identification in a variety of settings, from unlocking smartphones to securing financial transactions. If a digital twin were to incorporate such biometric data, its theft could be more easily classified as identity theft because the twin would contain data that directly links to an individual. Yet, if the twin does not include this level of personal detail, but still represents a valuable model of the individual, the legal distinction between identity theft and property theft becomes harder to discern.

Historical approaches to identity theft also focus on victims regaining control of their stolen identity, usually with the assistance of credit monitoring services, Federal Trade Commission (FTC) support, and rights under the Fair Credit Reporting Act (FCRA) to dispute inaccurate information. But digital twins present a more complex problem. If a digital twin is compromised, the harm may not necessarily be financial or reputational; instead, it could involve the misuse of the model's capabilities or its underlying algorithms. This lack of clarity leaves open questions about what legal recourse victims would have if their digital twin were used without consent and what kind of restitution might be appropriate.

Finally, protecting digital twins in the context of identity theft laws would require the same rigorous attention to consent and autonomy that we apply to human identity. If digital twins gain legal recognition as autonomous entities in certain contexts, legal protections must extend to ensure that these systems are not exploited. This might involve assigning ownership rights, establishing regulations around how digital twins can be used or shared, and creating safeguards to prevent unauthorized manipulation.

If AI-generated digital twins were to be recognized as having their own identity, current identity theft laws would need to be reexamined and possibly expanded. The blurred line between identity theft and property theft, the unique value generated by digital twins, and the challenges of protecting the public from AI systems in a digital world would all need to be addressed. As digital twins become more integrated into various industries, clarifying the legal frameworks surrounding their protection will become increasingly important for both public safety and technological advancement. This lack of clarity provides uncertainty with regard to what recourse is accessible, or what remuneration or restitution is most appropriate, providing a need for clarity.

## 9 Labor Laws around Uncompensated Work

The intersection of AI, labor law, and worker rights is becoming increasingly complex as AI-generated digital twins – models replicating human behaviors, skills, and even likenesses – are integrated into the workforce. Just as employers cannot compel employees to work without compensation, questions now arise about whether companies can leverage digital twins without compensating the individuals whose identities and actions were used to create them. As legal frameworks evolve, the issue of defining agency within AI systems could directly impact the rights of individuals and how compensation is handled when digital twins contribute value.

The evolution of labor laws in the U.S. has long been shaped by the principle that labor must be voluntary and fairly compensated. The abolition of slavery through the 13th Amendment in 1865 established the foundation for this understanding, but the ensuing debates focused on what constitutes fair compensation and how to protect workers from exploitation. As labor conditions evolved in the 20th century, regulations like the Fair Labor Standards Act (FLSA) of 1938 were implemented to secure rights such as minimum wage, overtime pay, and protections against child labor. These laws aimed to ensure that workers could not be coerced into unfair agreements and that employers could not profit unduly from an individual's labor.

Meaningful consent to work has become a central tenet of labor law, particularly through the lens of safety and working conditions. The Occupational Safety and Health Act (OSHA) of 1970 exemplified this by ensuring workers had a right to safe working environments. This protection reinforced the notion that labor agreements should be made under fair conditions, where workers are not forced to choose between their safety and their livelihood. In an AI-driven future, this concept of meaningful consent will need to expand. Just as OSHA ensures physical safety, future regulations may need to ensure workers' data, identity, and skills are protected from misuse or exploitation in the context of digital twins.

An element of the 2023 Screen Actors Guild (SAG-AFTRA) negotiations focused on the ongoing use of actors' likenesses by studios, offering a glimpse into how these issues might play out.[31] AI-generated replicas of actors' performances raised concerns about the need for actors to retain control and receive compensation for the use of their digital likenesses. This issue parallels the broader question of whether workers in other fields – such as drivers, salespeople, or creators – should be compensated when their skills and actions are digitized and continue to generate value through AI systems. The SAG-AFTRA negotiations are a critical example of how workers are demanding protections over their digital selves, setting a precedent that could apply across industries.

---

31 https://www.backstage.com/magazine/article/sag-aftra-ai-deal-explained-76821/

In the gig economy, companies like Uber and Lyft classify drivers as independent contractors, a distinction that allows them to avoid providing benefits and protections afforded to employees. However, as AI and digital twins begin to replicate workers' behaviors, this classification becomes even more problematic. For example, if a digital twin of a driver's habits is used to train autonomous vehicles for another company, such as Tesla, should the original driver be compensated for the use of their driving data? The traditional "work for hire" doctrine, which grants employers ownership of works created during employment, was typically balanced by the employer or client acknowledging the individual possessed its own unique skills and intellectual property that would remain the property of the individual. Under this traditional model, it seems difficult to understand how a digital twin could fall within the realm of work for hire. So if a digital twin replicates a worker's skills for the purpose of allowing the company to continue generating value, should that worker receive ongoing compensation when it is that worker's skills and abilities in digital form that are creating the ongoing value?

Labor protections, like the work for hire doctrine, have always been designed to balance the rights of workers and employers. However, digital twins blur these lines. The doctrine typically grants employers control over outputs created during employment, but when the output is a digital replica of a worker's skills or identity, the issue of ownership becomes more complex. In creative industries, workers such as musicians, writers, and filmmakers receive ongoing royalties for work that continues to generate revenue, even long after the initial labor is completed. If AI-generated digital twins are applied beyond entertainment, similar protections may be necessary. Workers should retain rights to ongoing compensation when their digitized skills are used for profit, just as actors seek royalties for their likenesses being used by studios.

A landmark labor dispute that reshaped the landscape of labor relations in the U.S. was the 1981 air traffic controller strike. When President Ronald Reagan fired striking air traffic controllers,[32] it cemented an orthodoxy that even government safety standards could be sacrificed in the name of efficient Federal services when seen as being for a national benefit. In today's gig economy, this threat of replacement is evolving. Workers' data, including their behaviors and skills, is increasingly being used to build AI models – essentially training their digital replacements. As in the

32 https://jacobin.com/2023/09/reagan-patco-strike-faa-air-traffic-controllers-short-staffing-safety-crisis

air traffic controller strike, the power associated with employee threats to remove their labor is now diminished, as AI is accelerating gig economy tools for companies to sidestep workers entirely.

Uber drivers, for example, are not only performing tasks but also generating the data needed to train autonomous vehicle technologies that may ultimately replace them. As companies increasingly rely on digital twins to automate tasks once performed by humans, the traditional power dynamic, where workers could withhold their labor to gain bargaining power, is eroding. The workers themselves are contributing to their eventual replacement by providing data used to refine AI models. This raises significant ethical and legal questions about how much control and compensation workers should retain when their skills are digitized.

Additionally, non-compete agreements have been a controversial issue in labor law, particularly in knowledge-driven industries like technology and finance. These agreements restrict workers from taking their skills to competing firms. In states like California, which largely prohibits non-compete clauses, workers' freedom to move between companies has been credited with fostering innovation in industries like Silicon Valley. However, as AI increasingly captures workers' skills through digital twins, the enforceability and relevance of non-compete agreements may shift. If an employer can replicate a worker's skills in a digital twin, do non-compete agreements still hold the same power? Could a digital twin be used in place of a human worker to avoid these legal restrictions?

Looking forward, the challenge for labor law is to determine how AI-generated digital twins should be treated in terms of rights and compensation. Should a digital twin, modeled after a worker's unique abilities, continue to work without compensating the original worker? When does the representation of an individual's skills, whether in driving, decision-making, or creative output, become so similar that the original worker must be compensated for the continued use of their digital likeness? These are pressing questions that labor law must address as AI and digital twins become more integrated into the workforce.

## 10 Food Labeling

Questions of labor law surrounding AI-generated digital twins will inevitably lead to debates about the origin of the data used to create these systems. The ambiguity over whether AI models, such as those developed by OpenAI, used a famous voice like Scarlett Johansson's is an example of how critical transparency about data sources will become. Much like how consumers demand to know what ingredients are in their food, the same demand will arise for knowing the "ingredients" that form AI models. This is where the history and strategy of food labeling and safety regulations can offer a valuable framework for addressing AI's transparency challenges.

In the United States, food labeling requirements have long been rooted in the premise that consumers have the right to know what they are ingesting. This principle – that we deserve to know what we are consuming – has informed the evolution of food regulations aimed at protecting public health, ensuring trust, and empowering consumers to make informed decisions. Similarly, when individuals interact with AI systems, they should have access to clear information about the data used to train those models. Just as food labels disclose ingredients and nutritional information, AI models should provide transparency about the datasets used to generate their capabilities, enabling informed use and safeguarding against misuse.

The origins of modern food labeling regulations, such as the Pure Food and Drug Act of 1906, were a response to industrialization and unsanitary food production practices exposed by Upton Sinclair's *The Jungle*. This landmark legislation required that manufacturers provide truthful information about their products, preventing the sale of adulterated or mislabeled goods. Similarly, in AI, the need for transparency in the datasets used to create models is crucial to prevent deception or misuse. If AI systems are used to make decisions – whether in hiring, finance, or social services – users deserve to know if the system was trained on biased, incomplete, or ethically questionable data. Such transparency could be regulated in much the same way that food labels are designed to inform consumers about the health risks of certain additives or ingredients.

The Nutrition Labeling and Education Act (NLEA) of 1990, which mandated the inclusion of standardized nutrition labels on most packaged foods, offers another parallel. The NLEA aimed to empower consumers by providing information on ingredients, calories, fats, and more, thus helping them make healthier choices. In the AI landscape, standardized "labels" detailing the data sources and model architectures could help users understand an AI's biases, strengths, and limitations. For instance, a label could specify whether a language model was trained primarily on publicly available data, proprietary datasets, or copyrighted content, much like how food labels disclose sugar or fat content. Just as consumers use Nutrition Facts to avoid unhealthy foods, companies and users could use AI data labels to avoid biased or problematic AI systems.

Balancing transparency with commercial interests has been a challenge for food manufacturers, as seen in the protection of proprietary recipes. A soda company may list sugar and caffeine as ingredients but is not required to reveal its exact flavoring formula. Similarly, AI companies may be concerned about revealing too much about their datasets and algorithms for fear of losing a competitive edge. However, this challenge can be addressed through the same balance seen in food labeling: ensuring that critical information is disclosed without compromising trade secrets. For AI, this might mean disclosing the general sources and types of data used, as well as any significant biases or limitations, without necessarily revealing proprietary details about how the model was trained or optimized.

Food labeling regulations have also had to adapt to consumer demands for more information, such as the rise of organic and non-GMO labels. This parallels the increasing call for AI transparency, where users want to know not just how an AI works but also how it was built, including whether it respects privacy, avoids bias, and is ethically developed. For example, consumers might want AI systems to be labeled as "privacy-protected" or "bias-mitigated" in the same way that food products are labeled "organic" or "fair trade." The introduction of ethical AI certifications could build consumer trust, much as food labels have done for consumers concerned about sustainability and health.

One of the key lessons from food regulation is that overloading labels with too much information can confuse consumers. The FDA and USDA have worked to ensure that food labels focus on the most critical information, such as ingredients, allergens, and nutritional content, without overwhelming buyers with extraneous details. In the context of AI, regulators will need to ensure that labels strike the right balance – offering enough information to inform users without drowning them in technical details. For instance, AI labels could focus on key information such as the origin of the data, potential biases, and limitations of the model, leaving more granular details accessible through supplemental links, much like how food products are now incorporating QR codes for consumers to access additional data.

Food labeling laws, like the Nutrition Labeling and Education Act, also reflect the government's role in safeguarding public health, while adapting to scientific advancements and consumer expectations. This same role should extend to AI regulation, where transparency is not just about fairness but about safety and trust. Misleading AI models can have real-world consequences, from flawed medical diagnoses to discriminatory hiring practices. Clear and accessible labeling, much like food labels, would help mitigate these risks by ensuring that users understand what they are engaging with when they use AI systems.

Furthermore, food labeling offers a guide for international cooperation in AI regulation. Just as food labels need to align with international standards – given the global nature of food production – the global use of AI will require harmonization of data transparency regulations across borders. Different countries will have different standards for AI ethics, data usage, and transparency, but a shared framework could help build trust and accountability in AI systems worldwide. This mirrors how the European Union has stricter food labeling laws than the U.S.,[33] but international companies comply to reach consumers across both markets.

Finally, food labeling illustrates the importance of industry cooperation. Just as the food industry has generally supported labeling that balances transparency with protecting proprietary information, the AI industry could voluntarily adopt guidelines for responsible data usage and transparency, building consumer trust and potentially avoiding stricter future regulation. The voluntary guidelines that already exist in AI, such as ethical AI principles and fairness initiatives, show that the industry has the capability to meet such transparency requirements, just as food manufacturers do.

The history of food labeling regulation provides a valuable framework for addressing AI's transparency challenges. Just as food labels inform consumers without revealing trade secrets, AI models should disclose their "ingredients" – the datasets and methodologies that shape their behavior – while protecting proprietary information. Using food safety regulations as a model for AI transparency can help balance the need for public trust with the industry's commercial interests, making it a logical and effective first step in AI regulation.

## 11 Risk-Based Insurance Requirements

The EU AI Act acknowledges the unavoidable uncertainty of a rapidly developing technology like AI by adopting a risk-based approach to its appropriate uses. In the case of the EU AI Act, the system rates appropriate uses as a function of their risk, with lower risk use cases being regulated through transparency and disclosure requirements, while high risk use cases are outright banned. For industries or technologies where regulators are less

33 https://www.theguardian.com/lifeandstyle/2015/sep/08/food-labeling-us-fda-eu-health-food-safety

certain on how to quantify or define risk thresholds for appropriateness, many rely on a strategy of requiring insurance and defining either its quantity or features.

The history of risk-based insurance requirements is closely linked to the evolution of regulatory strategies designed to protect public health, safety, and property in industries where the potential for catastrophic loss is high. This regulatory approach has long been recognized by agencies like the Federal Aviation Administration (FAA), particularly in high-risk sectors like the space flight industry. To address these risks, the FAA developed the concept of Maximum Probable Loss (MPL) as a metric to determine the appropriate level of insurance coverage for companies. MPL measures the potential financial loss from an accident, weighing both the likelihood of the event and the scope of possible damages, including threats to human life, public safety, and property. Over time, this risk-based insurance model has been applied in other industries, with MPL serving as a regulatory tool to protect not only businesses but also consumers and public interests.

The MPL model was crucial to the FAA's regulatory framework for space flight, which is inherently a high-risk endeavor. Space exploration and commercial space launches, whether by government agencies or private companies, carry the potential for disastrous accidents with far-reaching consequences. Early in the space race, it became clear that the stakes were too high not to enforce stringent safety standards and robust financial protections for accidents. The FAA's implementation of MPL calculations provided a way to quantify these risks and determine how much insurance companies needed to carry in order to cover possible liabilities. For instance, a rocket launch with an MPL of $500 million would require the company to secure that level of insurance to cover potential damages from an accident, such as property destruction, loss of life, or environmental harm. This dynamic insurance system offers the flexibility to tailor coverage to specific missions and technological innovations, making it adaptable to each unique launch scenario.

Beyond space flight, the concept of MPL has since been adopted by other industries facing significant financial risk. In cybersecurity, for example, businesses are increasingly required to carry insurance against the financial fallout from data breaches and cyberattacks. Regulations like those in Iowa provide companies with an affirmative defense against liability in the event of a breach, provided they meet certain cybersecurity frameworks and carry sufficient insurance coverage based on their MPL. In this case, MPL helps businesses assess their potential exposure to risks such as data theft, legal liability, and reputational damage. By using risk-based insurance models like MPL, regulators and businesses alike can better prepare for the financial impact of catastrophic incidents, protecting consumers while also encouraging companies to invest in stronger risk management strategies.

The rise of risk-based insurance as a regulatory strategy has also extended to areas like law enforcement. In some regions, there have been calls to require police officers to carry individual liability insurance, particularly to reduce the risk of excessive use of force incidents. Just as medical professionals carry malpractice insurance, police officers would carry personal insurance policies, which would factor in their past behavior, history of complaints, and risk of engaging in violent conduct. Officers with higher risk profiles would pay higher premiums, creating a market-based incentive for both police officers and departments to reduce the likelihood of misconduct. This concept shifts the financial burden of excessive force from taxpayers to officers and insurers, offering a path to accountability and potentially reducing the frequency of violent civilian encounters. Although this model is still under debate, it represents another way in which risk-based insurance can be used to influence behavior in high-stakes professions.

Another significant development in the insurance industry is the rise of parametric insurance, which offers an innovative approach to managing risks where the exact triggering event may not be easily provable or where traditional methods of loss adjustment are impractical. Parametric insurance differs from conventional insurance policies in that it pays out based on predefined metrics or triggers – such as the wind speed of a hurricane or the magnitude of an earthquake – rather than requiring proof of specific damages. This form of insurance provides immediate and predictable payouts without the need for the insured party to demonstrate actual losses, which can be valuable in industries where loss determination is difficult or time-sensitive.

While parametric insurance first emerged in the 1800s, it gained accelerated traction in the insurance industry in the late 1990s and early 2000s, when Swiss Re and other major reinsurers began offering parametric policies in response to the growing risks associated with natural disasters.[34] At that time, the insurance industry recognized the need for more efficient ways to manage catastrophe risk, particularly as climate change increased the frequency and severity of weather-related events. Traditional indemnity-based insurance policies, which require time-consuming assessments

34 https://corporatesolutions.swissre.com/insights/knowledge/evolution-of-parametric-insurance.html

of actual damages, were seen as inadequate for dealing with large-scale, rapid-onset disasters. Parametric insurance emerged as a solution, allowing insurers to provide faster payouts based on measurable triggers like rainfall, temperature, or seismic activity, making it possible for policyholders to recover more quickly after a catastrophic event.

Swiss Re, one of the global leaders in the reinsurance market, played a pioneering role in the development and expansion of parametric insurance. The company recognized that, in certain situations, traditional insurance products were not well-suited to cover the complexities of large-scale risks, especially when losses were difficult to verify or quantify in real-time. By shifting from a model that required proof of actual loss to one that relied on objective, measurable criteria, Swiss Re and other reinsurers were able to offer more flexible and responsive insurance products. This model has since gained popularity, not only for natural disaster coverage but also in sectors like agriculture, energy, and even event insurance.

The insurance industry views parametric insurance as a valuable tool for several reasons. First, it simplifies the claims process, eliminating the need for lengthy loss assessments and dispute resolution. This is especially important in cases where speed is critical, such as when a natural disaster leaves communities or businesses in urgent need of funds for recovery. Traditional indemnity insurance can take weeks or months to process claims, but parametric insurance can pay out almost immediately, helping policyholders to mitigate the impact of a disaster more quickly. Second, parametric insurance reduces the potential for disputes between the insurer and the insured, as the payout is based on clearly defined triggers that are agreed upon in advance. This reduces the administrative burden on both parties and provides greater certainty about when and how payouts will occur.

The value of parametric insurance is particularly evident in industries like agriculture, where weather conditions can have a profound and unpredictable impact on crop yields. Traditional crop insurance often relies on assessments of actual losses after the growing season, but parametric insurance offers a way to insure farmers based on measurable weather-related metrics, such as rainfall or temperature thresholds. If rainfall falls below a certain level during the growing season, for example, the policy pays out automatically, regardless of whether the farmer can prove specific crop losses. This system allows farmers to access funds more quickly and make timely decisions about planting, irrigation, and other critical factors. It also reduces the uncertainty associated with crop failure, which can be difficult to measure in exact terms.

Beyond its initial applications in disaster and agricultural insurance, parametric insurance is now being explored in emerging industries like artificial intelligence (AI), where the exact cause of a negative event may not always be clear or provable. In AI systems, where algorithms can be opaque and decision-making processes difficult to trace, parametric insurance could offer a way to manage risks associated with unpredictable system failures. For example, if an AI system used in financial trading exceeds certain error thresholds or generates losses that meet predefined criteria, parametric insurance could provide immediate compensation without requiring the insured to prove exactly why the failure occurred. This approach could be valuable in an industry like AI, where the pace of technological change often outstrips the ability of traditional insurance models to assess and address risks in real time.

The flexibility of parametric insurance also makes it well-suited for situations where traditional insurance might struggle to capture the full scope of potential risks. In the case of AI systems, where it is often unclear when or why a negative event occurred, parametric insurance could provide a more efficient and predictable form of coverage. For instance, if an AI system's performance drops below a certain accuracy rate, or if it experiences a significant error in a critical application, the insurance payout would be triggered based on those predefined metrics. This kind of coverage could help protect businesses from the financial impact of AI system failures, while also encouraging the development of stronger risk management practices within the industry.

The range of insurance options available for incorporation into regulations may vary as a function of use case and industry uncertainty. For example, it is difficult to see use cases around natural systems ever being predictable enough to not see parametric insurance as the most viable insurance strategy. Other use cases where the risks could become better defined may be able to see the types of insurance products of use in the market become more refined as more experience is gained to the point where EU AI Act type thresholds can be meaningfully supported. If the development or refinement of risk definition or thresholds outpaces industry experience, though, challenges like those seen in the EU AI Act may become significant. For example, the EU AI Act defines the "administration of justice" as a high-risk activity, yet it is reasonable to argue that the relationship between an insurance coverage dispute resolution process and the "administration of justice" is unclear. While the insurance claims process is private, the outcome of that private process too often becomes an inequitable starting point for disputes that reach the public justice system. Since this inequitable starting point often retains many of the biases accumulated throughout the claims process, it is unclear why AI should be allowed to aid in the accumulation of this bias when it will impact the "administration of justice."

## 12 Product Safety

When considering AI regulation, product safety laws may seem like a natural starting point, given their role in protecting consumers from harmful or defective products. However, traditional product safety frameworks may fall short in addressing the unique challenges posed by AI, which is not a static, well-defined product but a continually evolving technology. Understanding the history of product safety regulation is crucial in determining where such an approach could apply to AI and where it may fall short.

Product safety laws have historically focused on mitigating risks posed by tangible goods like lawnmowers, automobiles, and household products. For example, the establishment of the Consumer Product Safety Commission (CPSC) in 1972 provided a mechanism for setting safety standards, issuing recalls, and banning products that posed unreasonable risks. This framework works well for static products, where hazards can be identified, and specific safety measures – such as protective shields on lawnmowers or seat belts in cars – can be mandated. However, AI, by nature, is dynamic. Machine learning models evolve with new data, algorithms continuously update, and AI systems adapt to changing environments. This constant flux makes applying static safety standards more challenging, requiring a new regulatory approach that can accommodate AI's fluidity.

Seat belts are a good example of how safety measures can be implemented for a defined risk in a relatively unchanging product. When the public became aware of the dangers posed by cars without proper safety features, such as seat belts, safety experts and advocates like Ralph Nader led to the introduction of the Motor Vehicle Safety Act of 1966, mandating seat belts in vehicles.[35] In contrast, AI does not present a singular, easily identifiable hazard like a lack of seat belts. AI's risks – such as bias, decision-making errors, or cybersecurity vulnerabilities – are not as immediately visible or as easy to define, especially as AI systems can change behavior over time. Regulating AI, therefore, requires ongoing monitoring

35 https://www.sciencefriday.com/segments/ralph-nader-auto-safety/

and dynamic safety measures rather than one-time design improvements like seat belts.

This dynamic nature of AI also poses challenges for public participation in identifying risks, a key element of traditional product safety regulations. Under the CPSC framework, consumers can report hazards with products, leading to recalls or new safety standards. For instance, consumer reports about injuries from lawnmowers led to the implementation of safety decks to prevent accidents. However, in the case of AI, identifying risks is more complex. The harm caused by AI systems, such as biased hiring algorithms or inaccurate medical diagnoses, may not be immediately apparent or even recognized by users as a safety issue. Additionally, AI systems often operate in ways that are opaque even to their developers, making it difficult to pinpoint the exact cause of harm. This means that while consumer reporting can still play a role in AI regulation, it will need to be supplemented by more proactive monitoring systems that can detect subtle or long-term risks that are not easily identified by the public.

A significant example of the gap between static product safety regulations and AI's dynamic nature is the regulation of autonomous vehicles. Traditional car safety regulations, designed for human-driven vehicles, do not easily translate to self-driving cars, which rely on AI systems that continuously learn and adapt to road conditions, traffic, and driving behaviors. Autonomous vehicles introduce new, evolving risks that do not fit neatly into the regulatory frameworks developed for static products. As these systems gather more data and improve their decision-making capabilities, their risk profiles also change, meaning regulatory strategies must be flexible enough to adapt to these changes without stifling innovation.

This need for flexibility in regulating AI is also evident in areas like cybersecurity and data privacy, which have become central concerns as more products connect to the internet. Traditional product safety laws focus on preventing physical harm, such as injuries from defective appliances or toys. However, AI-driven systems, particularly those that connect to networks or rely on data sharing, pose different kinds of risks, such as data breaches or algorithmic manipulation. These risks evolve alongside technological advancements, making it essential for regulators to adopt adaptive safety measures that can address the ongoing and often unpredictable changes AI systems undergo. Static regulations will not be sufficient to mitigate the potential harms from AI-enabled products that continuously update and change functionality.

Flame retardants provide another relevant example of how product safety regulations deal with static hazards. After years of use, research revealed that flame retardants in furniture posed serious health risks, leading to updated safety standards in 2014. This process worked because the product – the furniture – did not change; once the risk was identified, new regulations could be put in place. But AI does not present a single, fixed hazard. AI models evolve, and the data they use and the decisions they make can change over time, making a one-time regulatory intervention less effective. Regulating AI requires ongoing oversight, similar to continuous monitoring of data privacy practices, rather than static rules that assume a fixed product design.

The continually evolving nature of AI mirrors the challenge of regulating chemicals like per- and polyfluoroalkyl substances (PFAS), or "forever chemicals." PFAS are persistent in the environment and human bodies, and despite evidence of their harm, regulatory action has been slow due to industry resistance. Like PFAS, AI can have long-term, widespread effects that are difficult to detect and regulate in a timely manner. However, unlike a chemical compound, AI's risks are not fixed – they can change as the technology evolves, which makes it harder to identify clear regulatory thresholds. This reinforces the need for flexible, adaptive regulatory strategies that can evolve alongside AI's development.

One key strategy for regulating AI might involve adopting a more proactive, iterative approach to regulation, similar to how California adjusted its flammability standards in response to evolving health concerns. Regulators might need to require regular audits, transparency reports, or ongoing compliance checks for AI systems to ensure they meet safety and ethical standards as they evolve. These checks could focus on the risks associated with dynamic learning systems, such as ensuring that algorithms do not become biased over time as they are exposed to new data, or that updates to AI models do not introduce new vulnerabilities or unintended behaviors.

Additionally, AI regulation could take cues from the evolving regulation of energy-efficient appliances. Under the Obama administration, regulations were implemented to improve the energy efficiency of products like washing machines and refrigerators. These regulations, while initially resisted by industry, aimed to reduce long-term environmental harm by pushing manufacturers to innovate. Similarly, AI regulations could focus on setting minimum safety and ethical standards while allowing for ongoing innovation, ensuring that AI development proceeds in a way that benefits society without creating undue harm.

While product safety regulations have succeeded when applied to well-defined products and specific hazards, AI's continually evolving nature presents a different set of challenges. AI-enabled products change over time, often in unpredictable ways, making static regulations ill-suited to manage the risks they pose. Instead, AI regulation will require adaptive, dynamic frameworks that can evolve alongside the technology, much like how regulations for autonomous vehicles and cybersecurity are being developed today. By combining traditional product safety principles with ongoing monitoring and flexible standards, regulators can better address the unique challenges posed by AI and ensure that innovation continues without compromising public safety.

## 13 Finding a Standards Road Forward

Many international organizations, governments, and industry groups are already well on the way towards standards-led AI regulations. The Organisation for Economic Co-operation and Development (OECD), for example, introduced its AI Principles in 2019, which promote fairness, transparency, accountability, and respect for human rights. These principles, endorsed by many countries including all G20 nations, serve as a foundational framework for building trustworthy AI systems globally. Similarly, UNESCO launched its Recommendation on the Ethics of AI in 2021, emphasizing human dignity, sustainable development, and the ethical use of AI. Both the OECD and UNESCO frameworks have become central to the global discourse on AI governance, establishing ethical guidelines that governments and institutions can adapt to their own contexts.

On the technical front, the International Organization for Standardization (ISO) has developed detailed standards to guide AI development and deployment, ensuring global interoperability and safety. ISO's subcommittee SC42 has introduced critical standards like ISO/IEC TR 24027:2021, which addresses bias in AI, and ISO/IEC 23894:2023, which provides guidance on risk management in AI systems. These standards offer practical frameworks for mitigating risks and ensuring fairness in AI across sectors and regions. At a policy level, the G7 and G20 have consistently included AI on their agendas, emphasizing the need for coordinated global efforts to establish ethical standards and governance frameworks for AI. This need for global coordination is a sentiment shared by United Nations (UN) efforts at shaping AI governance through various agencies, including UN Global Pulse and the International Telecommunication Union (ITU). The UN Secretary-General's proposed Global Digital Compact highlights commitments to AI regulation, focusing on fairness and transparency, with discussions emphasizing the global importance of creating ethical frameworks that protect human rights while allowing AI technologies to flourish. These global discussions underline the importance of human-centered AI, prioritizing fairness, accountability, and transparency while fostering innovation.

While Europe's EU AI Act is the first comprehensive, risk-based approach to regulating AI, its fundamentals were rooted in internationally vetted standards and guidelines. In the case of the EU, the EU High-Level Expert Group on AI developed the Ethics Guidelines for Trustworthy AI (2019) as the foundation for a human-centered and ethical approach to AI development before creating its legally binding regulatory structure. For the United States, any future regulation could follow a similar lead by incorporating the National Institute of Standards and Technology (NIST) AI Risk Management Framework of 2023, which currently offers a voluntary, industry-friendly model that focuses on trustworthiness, accountability, and risk mitigation in AI systems. This framework complements other national initiatives, such as executive orders issued by U.S. President Biden that address AI safety, ethical use in surveillance, and technological leadership, and differs significantly from the Cyberspace Administration of China (CAC). Through the CAC, China has taken a more centralized and stringent approach, issuing draft regulations for generative AI models in 2022 that prioritized data security and content control, reflecting China's emphasis on national security and social stability in AI governance.

Like the similarities and differences seen in the EU, United States, and China, most national efforts reflect local culture or priorities. For example, Canada has adopted a comprehensive approach to AI governance with its Directive on Automated Decision-Making (2019) focused on ensuring that government use of AI systems meets high standards of fairness, transparency, and accountability, requiring impact assessments and mechanisms for human oversight. Japan, on the other hand, has embraced a human-centric approach in its AI strategy, emphasizing trustworthiness, safety, and ethical AI practices. Japan's efforts align closely with international standards established by the OECD and UNESCO, contributing to the development of a global AI governance framework.

In Australia, the government has pursued a pro-innovation AI regulation framework, outlined in its AI Ethics Framework, which encourages flexibility and self-regulation in AI deployment. Similarly, the United Kingdom has taken a light-touch regulatory approach with its 2023 white paper titled "AI Regulation: A Pro-Innovation Approach", aiming to balance fostering innovation with ensuring ethical oversight. These strategies emphasize industry-driven governance and adaptability, contrasting with the more prescriptive regulatory models seen in the European Union. A similar approach is being followed by Singapore, where the Model AI Governance Framework focuses on voluntary guidelines and sector-specific governance initiatives such as the Veritas Initiative, which promotes the ethical use of AI in financial services. Singapore's emphasis on innovation and self-regulation reflects its goal of becoming a global AI hub, balancing responsible AI use with minimal regulatory burdens. Israel has also adopted a modular and flexible approach to AI regulation, offering voluntary guidelines tailored to specific sectors like healthcare and finance. Israel's strategy promotes innovation while addressing sector-specific risks, ensuring that regulation does not stifle technological advancement.

In Saudi Arabia, AI regulation is driven by the country's Vision 2030 initiative, with the aim of using AI to diversify the economy and attract investment. The government has established the Saudi Data and AI Authority (SDAIA) to promote the responsible use of AI, but the regulatory framework remains flexible to encourage rapid technological growth. This light-touch approach is intended to position Saudi Arabia as a leader in AI development while maintaining ethical safeguards. In Bangladesh, the National AI Strategy is designed to integrate AI into key sectors like healthcare and agriculture, while ensuring ethical considerations are met. Although still developing its regulatory framework, Bangladesh's approach reflects a focus on growth in essential sectors without heavy regulatory constraints that might slow innovation. Similarly, New Zealand's Algorithm Charter promotes ethical AI use in the public sector with a focus on transparency, but its overall regulatory strategy remains adaptable and flexible, aligning with the country's emphasis on innovation and responsible AI use in government services. Nations with smaller populations, such as Mauritius and Argentina, have also developed tailored AI governance strategies that reflect their specific economic and social needs. Mauritius has focused its National AI Strategy on integrating AI into agriculture, a critical sector for its economy, while Argentina's National AI Plan and public sector guidelines emphasize trustworthy AI use in government services. Both countries draw from international standards like the OECD's AI Principles but adapt them to their local contexts, demonstrating how global frameworks can be customized to address national priorities.

Regardless of how each government chooses to respond, non-governmental and industry-led efforts have remained at the heart of nearly all AI standards and governance model efforts. The World Economic Forum (WEF) has introduced its AI Toolkit, providing companies with resources to integrate responsible AI practices into their operations. The Partnership on AI (PAI), a consortium of leading technology companies like Google,

Microsoft, and Apple, works to promote ethical AI development, focusing on transparency, accountability, and fairness. IEEE, through its Global Initiative on Ethics of Autonomous and Intelligent Systems, has developed the Ethically Aligned Design (EAD) guidelines, which aim to ensure that AI and autonomous systems benefit humanity. And like ISO/IEC efforts, the IEEE P7000 series of standards further address ethical and societal concerns in AI development, providing detailed guidance on issues such as algorithmic bias and transparency.

These initiatives reflect a global consensus on the need for ethical AI standards and governance, with organizations like OECD, UNESCO, and ISO laying vital groundwork for trustworthy AI that has been incorporated by national governments and industry stakeholders in manners that fit their unique legal, economic, and social contexts. While many countries and organizations share common goals of fairness, transparency, and safety, their approaches differ significantly in how they balance regulation with flexibility. For example, some will continue to prioritize strict oversight, while others adopt more adaptive, industry-driven models, reflecting the diverse strategies needed to govern AI responsibly in different parts of the world.

How each community of stakeholders chooses to progress from recognizing a need for some form of governance over AI to a standardized, implementable strategy will depend heavily on the tools available for use. These tools, as they have been for generations before, will depend more than anything on the standards development processes each community chooses to undertake.

## 14 So What?

Creating safe, effective AI regulation requires a nuanced understanding of the technology's unique risks and a commitment to balanced oversight. As AI evolves, regulation must keep pace, carefully balancing the encouragement of innovation with the need for public safety and trust. Past regulatory missteps in fields like finance and pharmaceuticals show how reactive, fragmented approaches can undermine confidence and fail to prevent systemic risks. Given AI's complexity and rapid advancement, regulation must begin with adaptive, performance-based frameworks – broad, flexible goals that become more prescriptive as understanding deepens. Moving away from rigid models to frameworks that emphasize "informational sovereignty" – ensuring the informational sources used in training AI models respect local laws and cultural norms – can promote global consistency while honoring regional diversity.

Effective AI regulation relies on the collaborative expertise of technologists, policymakers, legal experts, and ethicists to address the technology's societal impacts and develop standards that guide adaptive regulatory efforts. Building this interdisciplinary collaboration across organizations and public platforms ensures that ethical, safety, and efficacy considerations are embedded into every stage of AI development. Such cooperation lays the groundwork for standards bodies and industry consortia to establish essential benchmarks for safety, transparency, and reliability, which in turn serve as the foundation for adaptive regulatory frameworks. This commitment to informed, adaptive regulation will enhance public trust and provide a consistent, cross-jurisdictional approach that evolves alongside technological advances, creating a regulatory ecosystem rooted in safety, accountability, and best practices.

AI's rapid growth demands regulatory frameworks that remain flexible and adaptable. Traditional approaches may lag, so encouraging frameworks with adaptable mechanisms – such as regulation by waiver, performance-based goals, and insurance-driven standards – ensures that policies evolve alongside AI, balancing public safety with innovation. By advocating for education, fostering collaboration, supporting data transparency, endorsing standards, raising public awareness, and promoting adaptable regulation, stakeholders can build a regulatory foundation that protects society while fostering a path for responsible AI innovation.

CHAPTER 4

# The Role of International Standards

The prior chapter discussed the efficacy of using regulation and law to govern or control products, services, processes, etc., that pose potential harm to the citizens of a nation state. For the most part, regulation can be very effective in governing the development and use of potentially harmful products or services, but most regulations are bound to the nation state which produced them – with some exceptions such as the EU/EC. However, international standards can be very effective at creating voluntary governance that easily crosses the borders of nation states–and even become incorporated into their laws–but they, too, can also come with their own vulnerabilities. In this chapter we will discuss generally the efficacy of international standards and particularly those developed by ISO (the International Standards Organization). The chapter closes with an examination of the state of international standards in terms of AI.

The nation-states have shown themselves adept at creating AI position papers and regulations, but their transnational applicability is questionable and certainly has yet to be demonstrated. And even within their own jurisdictions, governments tend to overwrite, and are often captive of older technologies. In a dynamic environment such as AI development governments, to borrow a phrase, are often caught fighting the last war.

Preserving "sovereignty" as a monopoly of the national authority has meant that progress in the labs has become subject to questionable regulation and ongoing battles in the courts. So, how are standards different?

It took many multi-government gatherings over decades, beginning in the 19th century, for the development of non-sovereign standards that made communication and commerce between those in different countries more efficient. The nations developed standards to ensure that mail could transit international boundaries; that cross-border trains ran on time; that telegrams were delivered. Ultimately, this cross-border cooperation paved the way for an increasingly sophisticated global communication system that would ultimately lead to the Internet.[1] As a contemporary of the early standards creators cautioned in 1899:

1 Among the original international organizations created were the International Telegraph Union (1865), the Postal Union (1874), the Bureau of Weights and Measures (1875), the Copyright Convention (1886) and the International Bureau of Railways (1890).

© KONINKLIJKE BRILL BV, LEIDEN, 2025 | DOI:10.1163/9789004737389_006

> These [international], Bureaux were not established without considerable misgivings, and even now, although they have functioned – and functioned well – for years .... It is necessary for them to be very prudent, for the respective administrations of the various states are as jealous of their autonomy and as prompt to resent any infringement of their sovereignty as though they were high contracting parties dealing with territorial or political rights.[2]

But the rise of a global marketplace and the interconnectivity and commonalities of the expectations of the world's citizens (healthier, safer environment, better life expected for children, etc), clearly won out, to some extent, as international standardization continued to be fostered by nation states and making us all stakeholders in developing practicable solutions to world discontents.

It is true that the non-sovereign approach to consensus global governance[3] lacks the safety net of sovereign consent. Non-sovereign governance can only aspire to *de facto* 'standing' when a non-sovereign consensus solution is attempted. If a proposed private governance initiative is not widely accepted and successfully implemented on a voluntary basis, it is at best, a precedent for future endeavors, at worst a cautionary failure. But in all cases, a private governance initiative has no formal *de jure* legitimacy; it will succeed or fail on its own merits. As John Dewey suggested in 1927, 'It is mere pretense then, to suppose that we can stick by the *de facto* and not raise at some point the question of *de jure*: the question of by what right, the question of legitimacy.'[4] Therein lies the critical relationship between regulation and standards.

In many cases, governments have actively looked to consensus standards to respond to difficult "wicked" problems with consensus public goods solutions.[5] Regulatory agencies also, will often defer to private sector standards

2 "The United States of Europe on the Eve of the Parliament of Peace" W.T. Stead London 1899 p. 21 (Note: These nascent private institutions presaged the shift of global governance from *de jure* to *de facto*; being the practicable, prosaic work of small, prudent mammals successfully functioning in a world of irritable dinosaurs.).

3 Which recognizes citizens in their own right, businesses, civil society etc., as having standing in the identification and resolving of wicked problems.

4 The Public and Its Problems. John Dewey NY 1927 [PB 1991] p. 6 Further, "And such a question has a way of growing until it has become a question as to the nature of the state itself." Ibid p. 6.

5 A 'wicked problem' is one that can be highly difficult or impossible to solve confidently, because of incomplete, contradictory and/or changing requirements that are often too

for defining and implementing its rulemaking authority (based on consensus international standards, and the use of third-party inspections and certification of global supply chains).

As was noted in the preceding chapter, in the United States, when consensus standards are accepted in law or rulemaking, this is considered an "incorporation by reference" [IBR]. According to the Administrative Conference of the United States (ACUS), use of IBRS:

> ... furthers important, substantive regulatory policies, enabling agencies to draw upon the expertise and resources of private sector standard developers to serve the public interest. Incorporation by reference allows agencies to give effect to a strong federal policy ... in favor of agency use of voluntary consensus standards.[6]

It is estimated that there are over 10,000 consensus standards incorporated into US public law[7], which 'allows agencies and the public to reap the significant benefits of collaborative governance through public-private partnership in standards.'[8]

The ultimate measure of success, let's call it the "Turing Test" of governance, for both *de jure* and *de facto* governance solutions should be whether they can successfully address related issues in a way that accounts for the advantages and the dangers of the systems they have set out to govern. If successful, this can be liberating, as projects can be designed along functional, non-sovereign grounds, to offer practicable solutions to global 'wicked problems.' As voluntary governance systems, the formal acquiescence of the nation-states is often not needed for the implementation of the governance solution. Nor is formal acquiescence in the form of laws or regulations mandatory for development of the commensurate independent,

difficult to recognize at the time. Wicked problems are often ones that do not have a 'true-false-axis, but may fall on a 'better or worse' continuum. Such problems are often predicted by economic, political or environmental issues, and involve stakeholders (who may not always be invited to sit at the table), with radically disparate viewpoints. Often efforts at finding political 'solutions' to wicked problems can tune out those who do not have formal 'standing' in the issue (a limitation in outreach and resource support which often induces policymakers to kick the can further down the road).

6 Administrative Conference of the United States (ACUS). Adoption of Recommendations. *Federal Register* Vol. 77. No. 10. 1/17/12. p. 2257.

7 And many more at the state and local level.

8 Incorporation By Reference in an Open-Government Age. Emily S. Bremer. Harvard Journal of Law and Public Policy. Vol. 36. No. 1. p. 135–36. Jan 2013.

third-party oversight required to ensure that agreements are indeed followed through constructively and successfully. Standards can easily cross borders, but are only trustworthy when they are embraced by both buyers and sellers in the global marketplace, where most nation-state economic and trade competition is (and should be) carried out.

Individual nations, or even collections of nations, may not be the main movers and shakers in the development of governance tools such as international standards, but they may develop laws and regulations that mirror or support the standards, or they may simply accept that the standards are critical for cross border trade and endorse their use.

The need for cross border governance has spawned a multitude of global standards that can inspect, test, and attest to market trustworthiness. As an example, in the early 1990s a number of national initiatives on environmental issues began to create mixed political signals with the proliferation of potentially conflicting national and regional environmental standards on such issues as environmental management, life cycle assessment, sustainability, green labeling and disclosure. The lack of global harmonization was not only wasteful of environmental resources and muddled mitigation efforts, but it also created perverse incentives. World Trade Organization (WTO) rules target countries, not companies, allowing environmentally reputable companies to suffer the same fate as 'bad actors' when country-specific trade penalties were assessed. Dissimilarly, International Organization for Standardization (ISO) standards are both global and company-specific; the existence of national boundaries are irrelevant to the success (or failure) of meeting ISO global management standards requirements. An ISO approach to environmental standards development was incentivized in the run-up to the June 1992 United Nations Conference on Environment and Development ("Rio"), where the UN conference leadership specifically asked the ISO Central Secretariat to make a commitment to create a global environmental standard. The resulting management system, ISO 14000, covers five separate environmental concerns; a baseline management system, auditing of assertions, green labeling, environmental performance evaluation, and life cycle assessment. As with ISO 9000 management system requirements, meeting what is now the ISO 14000 suite of environmental standards has become a prerequisite for many manufacturers and other organizations who wish to participate in the global marketplace. As stated by a leader of the ISO 14000 effort in testimony before Congress:

> ISO 14000 expects organizations to take responsibility for their environmental aspects without having to be ordered or directed by

> government agencies. Organizations are expected to exhibit maturity, initiative and stewardship vis-a-vis their environmental obligations and consequences. Under command and control, organizations are often lulled into a passive role, expecting direction and commands from the regulators. Organizations are told by regulators which environmental technologies to use and how to use them. ISO 14000 expects organizations to consider all their environmental technology options as they develop and maintain their environmental management system. This encourages organizations to develop and utilize innovative technology solutions that are performance-based rather than prescriptive. ISO 14000 is premised on the idea that environmental protection must be integrated into the general management of the organization.[9]

In this way, the development and implementation of ISO 14000 reflects both approaches to international standards development discussed above: the role of nation-state participation (via the UN's role and the national representatives negotiating the ISO standard) and the role of the private sector in providing expertise to ISO and having responsibility for implementing the standard. As a management system, ISO 14000 is seen by governments and corporations as both carrot and stick. Unlike the 'command and control' of many national environmental laws, ISO 14000 – as a performance standard, and not a design standard – allows corporations to meet obligations in advanced and creative ways. A global standard also cuts through the idiosyncrasies of national laws; it allows countries to 'buy into' a global framework, and offers a point of reference to lenders and other participants in the marketplace as to the bona fides of those who meet ISO 9000 and 14000 standards.

This last point is of importance for global manufacturers, supply chain transactors, and ultimately consumers. While take-up on global standards is strictly voluntary, WTO Rules give deference to widely recognized international standards. This makes it difficult for manufacturers with products that have quality control or environmental attributes *not* to participate in an ISO global management certification process. An ISO certification will meet WTO obligations not to discriminate under the Technical Barriers to Trade (TBT) agreement. Thus, WTO has delegated to ISO 'standing', in international trade, creating a non-sovereign status for global standards as a

9 "The Increasing Importance of International Standards to the US Industrial Community and the Impact of ISO 14000." Testimony of Joseph Cascio, Subcommittee on Technology, US House of Representatives Committee on Science. June 4, 1996, p. 5.

preferred business condition for operating in the global marketplace. Because nation-states have a weakness to support national champions – regardless of their qualities – the WTO does not recognize commensurate national (sovereign) standards.

In addition to ISO and IEEE, several other standards organizations have made significant contributions to solving critical industry challenges. The American National Standards Institute (ANSI) has facilitated the development of standards across diverse industries, including healthcare, construction, and energy. By coordinating U.S. standards with international bodies such as ISO, ANSI ensures global compatibility. For example, its involvement in standards for electronic health records (EHRs) improved patient data management and enabled seamless information exchange across healthcare systems and providers.

The International Electrotechnical Commission (IEC) has focused on electrical, electronic, and related technologies, producing standards that ensure the safety and efficiency of electrical equipment and systems. One of its notable contributions is IEC 61850, which addresses interoperability issues in energy grids. This standard has been instrumental in integrating renewable energy sources and improving grid reliability. Similarly, the European Telecommunications Standards Institute (ETSI) specializes in telecommunications, broadcasting, and electronic communication standards. ETSI's work in developing frameworks for 5G and the Internet of Things (IoT) has resolved challenges related to high-speed data transmission, latency, and network scalability, facilitating advancements in autonomous vehicles, smart cities, and remote healthcare.

The World Wide Web Consortium (W3C) has developed open standards for the web, such as HTML, CSS, and Web Content Accessibility Guidelines (WCAG). These standards have addressed inconsistencies in web development, promoting interoperability across browsers and devices while ensuring accessibility for individuals with disabilities. In transportation, the Institute of Transportation Engineers (ITE) has focused on traffic engineering and transportation systems, developing guidelines for smart traffic signals and vehicle-to-infrastructure (V2I) communication. These standards have enhanced urban mobility by optimizing traffic flow and reducing congestion, paving the way for the integration of autonomous vehicles into public infrastructure.

The National Institute of Standards and Technology (NIST) has contributed to standards in cybersecurity, nanotechnology, and artificial intelligence, providing a foundation for secure and ethical technological innovation. NIST's Cybersecurity Framework addressed growing threats to data security by establishing best practices for risk management across industries. Additionally, the International Telecommunication Union (ITU) has set global standards for telecommunications, including 5G and satellite communications. ITU's work has been critical in resolving cross-border communication challenges, enabling global roaming and consistent broadband performance.

Each of these organizations has addressed specific industry pain points by creating standards that improve interoperability, enhance safety, and support innovation. By fostering collaboration across governments, industries, and academia, they provide solutions to complex challenges, such as improving data security, managing environmental impact, and ensuring equitable access to technology. Their work ensures that technological progress aligns with societal needs while mitigating risks associated with innovation.

What global standards can supply – that national law cannot – is this sense of global legitimacy. This is somewhat paradoxical as national law is considered the apex of legality. But national authority ends at territorial borders and your neighbor may have distinctly different ideas on fairness, equity and due process. The nation-states use International Organizations (IOs), as surrogates for determining global rules.

Creating national law is an adversarial process. Public hearings, floor debates and advocacy campaigns are designed to accentuate differences between sides. Last-minute 'deals' are usually the result of exhaustion and time running out. Very often a law will carry the baggage of side-bar agreements on unrelated issues adding complexity to an already wicked problem. So what's different with international standards development?

## 1 International Examples of IBR in Action

Governments often turn to consensus standards to resolve complex wicked problems – issues that lack clear solutions and involve diverse stakeholders. These challenges often span multiple jurisdictions, involve technological complexities, or require balancing competing interests such as public safety, economic growth, and environmental protection. By leveraging standards as public goods, regulatory agencies frequently adopt these frameworks to define and implement rules, particularly in industries with global supply chains. ISO standards, for example, underpin many regulatory practices through incorporation by reference (IBR), which, as noted previously, is a mechanism in which legal frameworks formally adopt private sector standards. This approach allows governments to benefit from the expertise, flexibility, and global applicability of private entities while advancing public policy goals.

One prominent example of standards integration is the incorporation of ISO 9000 standards into federal procurement regulations under the Federal Acquisition Regulation (FAR). In the 1990s, ISO 9000 was referenced in FAR Part 46, which governs the quality assurance processes required for federal contracts. This move aimed to address inconsistencies in the quality of goods and services procured by federal agencies, which often led to inefficiencies and increased costs. By referencing ISO 9000, the government standardized quality management expectations, enabling contractors to implement globally recognized best practices while reducing the regulatory burden on both agencies and suppliers.

At the state level, California's California Code of Regulations (CCR) Title 8, which includes safety standards for elevators and escalators, incorporates ASME A17.1 standards. These standards, developed by the American Society of Mechanical Engineers (ASME), provide comprehensive guidelines for elevator and escalator design, installation, and maintenance. This incorporation addressed growing safety concerns in urban environments where diverse building designs and technologies presented significant risks. The adoption of ASME A17.1 ensured uniformity and clarity in safety requirements, making compliance easier for manufacturers and operators working across jurisdictions.

Globally, the European Union's Eco-Management and Audit Scheme (EMAS) explicitly incorporates elements of the ISO 14000 series on environmental management. Established under Regulation (EC) No 1221/2009, EMAS mandates adherence to ISO 14001 for organizations seeking EMAS certification. This integration was crucial in addressing the EU's challenge of harmonizing environmental standards across member states with differing regulatory priorities and enforcement capacities. The ISO 14001 framework provided a universally recognized baseline for environmental performance, simplifying compliance for businesses operating across borders and enabling the EU to promote sustainable practices effectively.

In Japan, the Electrical Appliance and Material Safety Act (DENAN Law) incorporates IEC 60335, a standard for household electrical appliances developed by the International Electrotechnical Commission (IEC). This incorporation was designed to ensure product safety and compatibility in a technologically advanced and competitive consumer electronics market. By leveraging IEC 60335, Japan addressed safety concerns comprehensively, setting clear benchmarks for manufacturers and ensuring the safe operation of appliances while enabling Japanese products to remain competitive in global markets.

Another significant example is the inclusion of ASTM F963 within the United States' Consumer Product Safety Improvement Act (CPSIA) of 2008. This legislation came in response to a series of high-profile recalls of children's toys due to safety hazards such as toxic lead paint and choking risks. ASTM F963, developed by ASTM International, provides detailed safety specifications for toy manufacturing, including mechanical and chemical testing requirements. By mandating compliance with this standard, CPSIA addressed urgent consumer protection needs while leveraging the expertise of industry stakeholders, enabling rapid implementation and widespread acceptance.

In the food industry, the Food Safety Modernization Act (FSMA) of 2011 references ISO and ANSI standards for third-party food safety audits. This legislation aimed to overhaul food safety regulations in the wake of numerous foodborne illness outbreaks, emphasizing preventive measures over reactive enforcement. The use of internationally recognized standards ensured the credibility and reliability of third-party inspections, addressing gaps in government oversight and enabling safer global food supply chains.

Standards often prove more effective than traditional regulatory efforts because they are developed through a collaborative, consensus-driven process that incorporates input from a wide range of stakeholders, including industry experts, regulators, and civil society. This ensures that standards are technically robust, practical, and reflective of current best practices. Additionally, standards are typically more adaptable than regulations, allowing them to evolve quickly in response to technological advancements or changing societal needs. By relying on standards, governments can address complex challenges more efficiently, avoid duplicative efforts, and foster global harmonization, all while ensuring that the solutions are grounded in expertise and practicality. For example, the adoption of ISO 45001 standards on global worker safety by various countries, including Canada and the United Kingdom, through national health and safety regulations has enhanced protections for workers in global supply chains, addressing workplace hazards in industries like construction and manufacturing.

These examples demonstrate how standards can solve societal challenges more effectively than traditional regulatory approaches, offering a flexible, collaborative, and technically sound pathway to address complex problems in a globalized world.

The development of international standards typically follows a structured, iterative process designed to achieve global consensus. While the stages of this process are well-defined, the timelines, costs, and stakeholder involvement can vary significantly depending on the complexity and scope of the standard being developed. This process has been instrumental in creating solutions for challenges across various industries. The benefits of the process can be observed in landmark standards such as ISO 9000 quality management and quality assurance, demonstrating the collaborative efforts required to produce solutions to wicked problems that span multiple jurisdictions and sectors.

## 2 Key Stages of the Standards Development Process

While there are multiple successful approaches to the development of international standards by industry and international disciplinary membership organizations, the stages used by ISO will illustrate one of the major and most respected international standards development frameworks.

1. Proposal and Drafting: A member organization or stakeholder identifies a need and proposes a standard, often based on emerging industry challenges or regulatory gaps. The ISO 9000 series on quality management arose in the 1980s to address inconsistencies in quality assurance across global supply chains, while ASTM F963, a toy safety standard, was developed to prevent hazards such as toxic materials and choking risks in children's toys. Drafting these standards typically involves 10–20 core experts over 6–12 months, with costs ranging from $50,000 to $250,000 for initial research and stakeholder coordination.
2. Committee Deliberation: Multi Stakeholder technical committees, comprising experts from academia, industry, and civil society, review and refine the draft. For ISO 20121, the ISO Technical Committee (ISO/TC 228) on tourism and related services led the review process, which included representatives from over 30 countries. Over two years, the committee addressed challenges such as defining measurable sustainability outcomes and creating guidelines applicable to events of all sizes. Similarly, the development of ISO 14000, focused on environmental management, involved over 100 experts from 25 countries, tackling challenges like pollution control and sustainable practices. The deliberation process for ASTM F963 included toy manufacturers, consumer advocates, and government safety agencies, ensuring the standard addressed mechanical and chemical hazards comprehensively. This phase typically costs $100,000–$500,000 and may involve multiple meetings, both in person and virtual.

3. Public Consultation: Draft standards undergo global public review to ensure transparency and inclusivity, allowing stakeholders to provide input. The draft of ISO 20121 was reviewed globally in 2011, gathering feedback from over 450 organizations. Public consultations for ISO 14000 generated extensive comments, particularly from businesses in developing nations concerned about implementation costs. Similarly, the draft of ASTM F963 received substantial input from toy industry stakeholders and consumer groups during the consultation phase. Public consultation usually lasts 60–120 days and costs between $10,000 and $50,000, covering outreach, coordination, and feedback analysis.
4. Consensus and Adoption: After addressing feedback, the standard is finalized and adopted through consensus, ensuring broad acceptance. ISO 20121 achieved consensus approval from over 75% of voting member countries and was officially published in June 2012, in time for the London Olympics. Likewise, ISO 9000 and ISO 14000 underwent rigorous finalization processes, culminating in adoption by global stakeholders. The adoption of ASTM F963 was further bolstered when it was incorporated into U.S. law through the Consumer Product Safety Improvement Act (CPSIA) of 2008, making compliance mandatory for toy manufacturers. Adoption costs, which include final drafting and coordination, typically range from $20,000 to $100,000.

The entire process for developing a standard, from proposal to publication, typically takes 2 to 5 years, though highly complex or contentious standards can take longer. For instance, ISO 9000 required five years of development and involved hundreds of experts across 36 countries. Similarly, the development of ISO 14000 took three years and included over 100 technical experts. In comparison, the development of ISO 20121 was relatively swift, taking three years and involving contributions from more than 30 countries. Each process underscores the extensive collaboration required, with stakeholders often numbering in the hundreds and representing a wide range of interests, including industry leaders, government representatives, and civil society organizations.

Global standards gain their legitimacy by the broad base of experts involved and the commitment to problem-solving.[10] The goal of standards creation is to find consensus rather than sound bites. 'Even if often mocked as

10 …"not bureaucrats, but engineers and managers [and civil society, consumers and academics], directly concerned [who reflect], the needs of their constituency."… "Two Bits:. The Cultural Significance of Free Software". Christopher Kelty. Duke U. 2008. p. 171.

slow or bureaucratic, the [standards] process – based on consensus international agreement and thorough technical specifications – is a process of unquestioned legitimacy."[11]

## 3 Examples of ISO Standards Development

### 3.1 *Toxic Levels of Lead in the Toy Supply Chain*

In 2006 it was discovered that numerous products were entering the global toy supply chain that contained toxic levels of lead paint. Most of these toys came from China. In the US, the agency with oversight and responsibility, the Consumer Product Safety Commission (CPSC) signed a series of MOU's with its Chinese peers pledging cooperation and increased scrutiny, but – for reasons of sovereignty – US and European government inspectors were not allowed access to Chinese factories.

An August 15, 2007 recall of almost 20 million toys by Mattel (until then seen as having the 'gold standard' of testing procedures), created a critical mass of concern by consumers, retailers and policymakers. The US toy industry agreed to work with the American National Standards Institute (ANSI), retailers and US consumer groups to develop a regime of testing, inspection and auditing of factories in China based upon ISO standards.

The Chinese – as committed users of ISO standards – agreed to allow such ISO-accredited third-party inspections of factories supplying products into the global toy supply chain. The US Congress accepted this approach in the Toy Safety Act (CPSIA), which was signed into law in August 2008, allowing the CPSC to delegate global inspection authority to accredited third-parties.

### 3.2 *Melamine Poisoning of Pet Food and Infant Formula*

In March 2007, there was a wide-spread recall in the US of pet foods sourced from China for melamine and cyanuric acid poisoning. Vegetable glutens with lower protein content were being used to take the place of more expensive meat proteins. These substitutes contained melamine, a toxic substance which was causing kidney failure in cats and dogs.

In Nov 2010, the crisis caused by milk adulterated with melamine led the International Dairy Federation (IDF) and the International Organization for Standardization (ISO) to make public a new test standard to determine

11 Ibid. p. 171.

the content of melamine and cyanuric acid in liquid milk, powdered milk products and infant formula.[12] This developed out of pressure when "dairy products were removed from shops at home and abroad, in a widespread consumer movement to avoid products made with imported milk powder."[13]

### 3.3 *Automotive Crash Test Standards*

The development of automotive crash test standards, such as those under the New Car Assessment Program (NCAP) and ISO standards, has been fraught with disagreements over acceptable safety thresholds and the costs of compliance. In the 1970s, the U.S. and Europe adopted markedly different approaches to vehicle safety testing, with the U.S. focusing on mandatory crashworthiness regulations and Europe favoring voluntary guidelines. Efforts to create an international crash test standard faced economic barriers, as some automakers pushed back against stringent requirements that increased production costs. While ISO 3779 (vehicle identification number) and related standards eventually provided some global consistency, regional differences in enforcement and testing methods persist, delaying the widespread adoption of unified global standards.

### 3.4 *Electrical Appliance Safety Standards*

The creation of the IEC 60335 standard for household electrical appliances, including refrigerators, washing machines, and microwaves, illustrates the challenges of addressing safety concerns across diverse regulatory environments. The standard, developed by the International Electrotechnical Commission (IEC), was initiated in the mid-20th century in response to a growing number of electrical fires and shocks. Disagreements arose over regional variations in voltage, frequency, and usage conditions, as well as differing national approaches toward consumer responsibility. Even though it's not an ISO standard, and despite these challenges, the standard has evolved over decades to become a benchmark for global appliance safety.

### 3.5 *Food Packaging and Safety Standards*

Efforts to establish safety standards for food packaging have faced challenges related to chemical migration, environmental impact, and regional dietary habits. The development of ISO 22000, a global food safety management standard, sought to address these issues by incorporating hazard

---

12 ADM (Archer-Daniels-Midlands) news release. Nov. 16, 2010.

13 "A favorite brand reinvents itself" "Economist" June 3rd 2023. p. 33.

analysis and critical control points (HACCP) principles. However, early attempts to harmonize packaging standards under ISO 11607 encountered resistance from countries with differing views on permissible levels of chemical leaching and recycling requirements. While ISO 11607 eventually gained acceptance, its adoption highlighted the difficulty of aligning environmental and safety priorities across different jurisdictions.

### 3.6 *Portable Power Tool Standards*

The establishment of standards for portable power tools, such as ISO 11148, was driven by the need to reduce workplace injuries caused by tool malfunction or misuse. Developed in the 1990s and early 2000s, the standard aimed to address diverse safety concerns, including noise levels, vibration, and accidental activation. However, its creation was hindered by resistance from manufacturers who argued that the proposed standards would significantly increase production costs. Additionally, national laws toward workplace safety varied widely, with some countries prioritizing productivity over worker protection. Efforts to harmonize ISO 11148 with regional standards like those of ANSI and the European Committee for Standardization (CEN) required extensive negotiation, delaying its finalization by several years.

In the case of a contentious issue such as AI, standards have to show their *bona fides* not only through continuous improvements in the standards utilized, but stepped-up outreach to civil society, consumers and participants in the global marketplace. While standards have long been important tools for trade, dispute resolution and the development of reciprocal trust, it is really with ISO 9000 and ISO 14000 that international management standards have proved their utility to buyers and consumers in the marketplace, and have been accepted by the nation-states as part of the recognized global governance structure. The ISO standards for AI will be discussed in more detail further below.

This approach to global governance has begun to find traction. Businesses that want to sell into the global marketplace find that they need to develop trust and credibility before buyers will take the chance on purchasing their products, ideas or solutions. International standards can create that needed trust and credibility. In particular, ISO 9000, and 14001 are used extensively in the global marketplace to drive continual improvements in organizations through independent (accredited) third-party conformance activities. Achieving such ISO certification allows companies to provide confidence and trust between buyers and sellers through an attestation of compliance with international standards for quality and environmental management.

International management standards (*de facto*) are playing an increasingly important role in global governance as the nation states (*de jure*) find it difficult to transit nation-state laws into ecumenical global governance authority. The scope and process for identifying, crafting and implementing global standards depends on a level playing field with rules that accentuate trustworthiness and verification.[14]

## 4 New Global Standards

There are also many new opportunities for standards to play important roles in addressing compelling global governance issues ("wicked problems") and in the creation of needed Global Public Goods.

A new ISO standard on global worker safety (ISO 45001), creates a necessary foundation of worker safety standards and inspections that can be used by all global supply chains, for contractors and subcontractors in countries supplying products into global supply chains. Workers should not be put at risk merely by entering the factory door. Dangerous business practices and lax government oversight should not be allowed to be used as a perverse competitive advantage by contractors willing to condone or ignore unsafe working conditions in order to cut costs. This new global worker safety standard can offer manufacturers and retailers a global 'brand' and inspection regime needed to bring oversight and execution to the far ends of global supply chains.

Pervasive corruption and weak anti-bribery enforcement efforts also add costs, lower the safety of products, and degrade national governance. A new ISO anti-bribery standard (ISO 37001) is a global instrument that can energize and focus anti-bribery efforts. The ISO standard identifies a tool-box of anti-bribery initiatives and requires the creation of accredited third-party auditing and inspection obligations by those organizations involved in this anti-corruption, anti-bribery initiative. As with other ISO standards, inducing participation in the anti-bribery initiative becomes a tool of good governance. Good corporate citizens will want to endorse these ISO initiatives, and corporations with a mixed record can be 'encouraged' by NGOs, public officials, and their corporate peers to participate. Over time, as anti-corruption standards become embedded into good corporate governance practices, failure to participate should be seen as a rebuttable presumption:

14 With 'verification' expected to drive 'trustworthiness'.

corporations should be expected to explain *why* they have *not* participated in global anti-corruption standards regimes.

Finally, standards can help facilitate the development of needed solutions for life-and-death issues involving the most disenfranchised global citizens. Every day, 3 billion people cook their food on primitive stoves or open fires. And every year, 4 million women and young children die from exposure to indoor smoke.[15] Conventional cookstoves burn inefficiently and are thus a major cause of respiratory diseases, deforestation, and desertification. Poorly combusted biomass (black carbon), is also the second largest contributor to rising global temperatures.[16] The global standards community – working with ISO – developed 'clean' cookstove standards for cheap, efficient, and durable stoves. The U.S. State Department publicly urged governments, manufacturers and the standards community to create and disburse at a minimum, 100 million clean cookstoves.[17] All these examples of consensus *de facto* standards are developed in a process observed by, and many are endorsed or followed by, law-making sovereign bodies.

## 5 *De Jure* Approaches by the Nation-States for AI Governance

Movement toward governing or controlling AI through law and regulation within various nation states has moved forward rather rapidly and below are a few examples, illustrating the context in which international standards on AI are being developed. They illustrate the various approaches that have been taken and the countries' different priorities which can, of course, make international consensus building challenging despite its importance.

### 5.1 *EU and AI*

The EU claimed to be the first out of the starting gate with their AI Act issued by the Commission and the member states in December 2023. Thierry Breton, the lead Commissioner, declared that "Europe has positioned itself as a pioneer, understanding the importance of its role as global

15 World Health Organization (WHO): https://www.who.int/news-room/fact-sheets/detail/household-air-pollution-and-health#:~:text=Key%20facts,6.7%20million%20premature%20deaths%20annually.

16 Climate and Clean Air Coalition: https://www.ccacoalition.org/short-lived-climate-pollutants/black-carbon

17 Remarks on Global Alliance on Clean Cookstoves: https://2009-2017.state.gov/secretary/20092013clinton/rm/2010/09/147500.htm

standards setter."[18] The Commission is obligated to have the omnibus AI Act sync up with the existing EU Digital Services Act and the Digital Markets Act that already apply AI technologies in both social media and commercial sites.[19] The overarching AI Act is thus running parallel with other Euro AI laws, and may have issues with adoption. For example, millions of European small and medium-sized enterprises are not reportedly compliant with the EU Privacy Directive (the General Data Protection Regulation – GDPR) years after the law went into effect in the individual nation-states.'[20]

The Europeans are focussing on data security and GDPR privacy requirements, which will add complexity, time, and resource obligations to rule-making determinations that will place greater implementation, oversight, and control efforts on regulators.[21] In the past, EU privacy laws were picked up pretty quickly by national bodies. This has not been the case with the recent Digital and AI initiatives.

### 5.2 *China and AI*

China – along with the US and EU – has made a strong commitment to using international standards as an important governance instrument.[22] Participants in global standards efforts have stated that Chinese "participants have often been constructive."[23] They have joined non-sovereign international organizations such as ISO. They have done so, and they have used it constructively.[24] China promulgated a new standards regime in 2018, with the purpose of making Chinese standards initiatives global. This was to be a

18 "NYT" 1 2/8/23 Adam Satariano A-1.

19 Democracy & Tech Initiative. Rose Jackson. Atlantic Council Wash DC 12/11/23, who goes on that "we don't exactly know what is in the EU's recently passed AI Act....wise to view...with a bit of skepticism." Ibid.

20 Atlantic Council Europe Center. Nichole Lawler.

21 A significant number of traditional European companies have expressed their concerns that draft legislation is too arbitrary and attempts to regulate AI before they have a chance to begin exploring its possibilities. "WSJ" EU Rules for AI worry big brands." July 1, 2023 B-11. ("Politicians, academics, activists and many tech executives have pushed for some form of AI regulation. But the breadth of the industries represented by the letter's signatories demonstrates an unease among many companies about taking a proscriptive approach in reining in the technology.") B-11.

22 This acknowledgement of the authority of private-sector standards in developing global governance solutions was shown in China's willingness to allow third-party conformance activities by ISO inspectors, in reforming the testing, inspection and audit requirements of the global toy supply chain.

23 "Small Yards, Big Tents – How to Build Cooperation on Critical International Standards." Cameron Kerry. Brookings Institute Governance Studies. March 2024 p. 4.

24 Ibid p. 28.

shift from government-initiated standards to standards that will be "driven equally by the government and the marketplace."[25]

The China State Council has recently released a draft AI law that puts the government back at the center of AI decision-making. The lexicon is not in prescriptive legal terminology but sociological: AI programs cannot be 'unsound' or 'emotionally harmful'. Various Chinese academic organizations including the Chinese Academy of Social Sciences (CASS) have responded, and a second draft is expected soon.

## 5.3 *The U.S. and AI*

The Biden Administration issued in 2024 a comprehensive executive order to address a range of AI risks under existing law. The ultimate fate of this executive order is in question with the incoming administration, but elements of the order frame an approach to responsible development and deployment of AI systems, including securing voluntary commitments on AI safety and transparency from most large technology companies. [26]

Acknowledging the tentative nature of the order, it:

- Requires that developers of the most powerful AI systems share their safety test results and other critical information with the U.S. government. This public obligation (it is hoped), will set an example for the private sector and governments around the world.
- Defines uses of AI that are presumed to impact rights and safety, including many uses involved in health, education, employment, housing, federal benefits, law enforcement, immigration, child welfare, transportation, critical infrastructure, and safety and environmental controls.
- Establishes an advanced cybersecurity program to develop AI tools to find and fix vulnerabilities in critical software. Several AI bills – largely focused on the federal government's internal use of AI – have also been voted on and passed through committees but did not go further in the Congress.

The Federal Communications Commission (FCC) announced in mid-July 2023 a new initiative, the "US Cyber Trust Mark" to inform consumers

25 Ibid p. 19. However, "the law provides for compulsory standards where they effect health and Safety, state security {and other] fundamental social and economic needs." p. 20.

26 Executive Order. Oct 30, 2023 White House.

"President Joe Biden on Monday signed an ambitious executive order on artificial intelligence that seeks to balance the needs of cutting-edge technology companies with national security and consumer rights, creating an early set of guardrails that could be fortified by legislation and global agreements."

about new security and privacy measures that consumer-goods manufacturers will be encouraged to take.[27] The Trustmark will be voluntary, but the FCC expects (hopes) that manufacturers will do the right thing. The FCC acknowledged that 'These things don't move fast'.[28]

More recently, the FCC has banned the use of AI-generated voices in unsolicited robocalls.[29] This rule is based on the authority of the 1991 Telephone Consumer Protection Act (TCPA) (PL 47 USC & 227) empowering the FTC to regulate unsolicited phone calls, and allowing State Attorneys General as well as the FCC to be able to enforce the federal Act.

The FCC's initial do-not-call list regulations were ineffective at stopping unsolicited calls as consumers had to make individual do-not-call requests for each telemarketer. In 2003, even though the FCC was the agency entrusted with the TCPA, it was the Federal Trade Commission that established the National Do Not Call Registry and implemented regulations prohibiting commercial telemarketers from making unsolicited sales calls to persons who did not wish to receive them. The FCC is now using the AI issue to play-catch-up on its original authority to police unsolicited marketing calls.

States and private sector organizations have developed their own versions of in-house AI rules, draft legislation, best practices or standards through other channels.

## 6 Current International AI Standards Efforts

As artificial intelligence (AI) technologies become increasingly pervasive, governments and international bodies are grappling with the need to regulate their development, deployment, and impact. Consensus standards are likely to play a central role in this regulatory landscape, providing a foundation for harmonizing global practices, ensuring safety, and fostering trust. Just as standards have historically shaped regulations in other industries, several existing and emerging AI-related international standards could be

27 AI systems and procedures are most likely to be front and center in attempts to draw lines in the law between 'good' and 'bad' AI.

28 "Technology and Innovation". Geoffrey Fowler...[quoting FCC Chair Rosenworcel] "Wash. Post". July 30, 23. p. G5.

29 "Bad actors are using AI-generated voices to extort vulnerable family members, imitate celebrities, and misinform voters." FCC press release on issues the AI regulation. (WSJ) Feb 9, 2024 p. A5.

incorporated into future legislation by nation-states to address the unique challenges posed by AI technologies.

As illustrated below, a great deal of international standards work has been done, both on AI directly and on technology issues related to AI. It goes without saying that in a dynamic environment like AI, more is needed now and will be needed in the future.

The UK government has also made initial efforts to cultivate international standards development to rein in AI misuse. At an AI Safety Summit held at Bletchley Park (of WWII code-breaking fame) on November 1-2 2023, Delegates from 27 governments, heads of the leading AI companies, and other interested parties were in attendance at the conference to address the challenges and opportunities of AI technology.

The UK is worried about 'present ethical challenges which do not always have clear answers. Unless we act, household consumers, public services, and businesses will not trust the technology and will be nervous about adopting it.'[30] The UK encourages the 'collaboration between government, regulators, industry and civil society.'[31]

The UK recognizes that formal AI regulations will never catch up with the myriad of uses that will employ AI.[32] Other consensus efforts, including "technical standards," are needed to develop 'methods to assess, design and improve transparency and explainability within AI systems'[33]. The UK sees 'an important leadership role' for itself in the development of a 'global AI assurance industry, including in auditing and safety.[34]

ISO/IEC 42001, the first international standard for AI management systems, is a natural candidate for incorporation into AI-specific regulations. This standard offers a structured framework for organizations to establish, implement, and continuously improve their AI systems while aligning with ethical principles, transparency, and accountability. Governments could incorporate ISO/IEC 42001 into laws to mandate responsible AI management

30 Bletchley Park AI Summit. Summary: Department for Business, Innovation and Skills. Nov 1–2 2023. ISBN 978-1-5286-4009-1The Hon. Michelle Donalon Minister for the UK Business and Industry Ministry.

31 Ibid.

32 "We are not creating blanket rules for specific technologies or applications of AI [nor do we need] to use rigid legal definitions." Ibid.

33 Ibid. Further, collaboration is needed with *de facto* organizations including "industry, civil society …trade unions, and advocacy groups, academia and the general public."

34 Ibid. The British Standards Institute (BSI) has long been at the forefront of global standards initiatives; including recently, in issuing the ISO Anti-Corruption standard (ISO 3700) and Worker Safety in Global Supply Chains (ISO 14001).

practices. For instance, the European Union's AI Act, which established comprehensive rules for AI technologies, could have referenced this standard to create a uniform governance framework across member states. Similarly, Singapore's Model AI Governance Framework could adopt IAO/IEC 42001 to ensure consistency in governance across industries.

Given the data-intensive nature of AI, ISO/IEC 27001, which addresses information security management, it is another standard that could feature prominently in AI-related regulations. Data security and privacy are critical concerns in AI, and incorporating ISO/IEC 27001 would help establish a baseline for safeguarding sensitive information. The European Union's General Data Protection Regulation (GDPR) already aligns with the principles of ISO/IEC 27001, and future amendments could explicitly reference the standard for organizations deploying AI systems. In the United States, legislation such as the proposed Algorithmic Accountability Act could adopt ISO/IEC 27001 to ensure the secure handling of data in automated decision-making processes.

Trustworthiness is a recurring theme in discussions about AI regulation, and ISO/IEC TR 24028, which provides guidelines for building trust in AI systems, could serve as a cornerstone for addressing this issue. The standard emphasizes transparency, risk assessment, and stakeholder engagement, making it a valuable tool for laws aimed at ensuring accountability in AI deployment. The United Kingdom's National AI Strategy, which prioritizes creating trustworthy AI systems, could incorporate ISO/IEC TR 24028 to establish measurable criteria for transparency and accountability. On a global scale, treaties addressing AI governance could adopt the standard to ensure consistency in applications across critical sectors such as healthcare, finance, and autonomous transportation.

The risks associated with AI, including algorithmic bias and unintended outcomes, highlight the need for robust risk management frameworks. ISO 31000, which provides principles and guidelines for risk management, could be adapted and incorporated into AI regulations to address these challenges. Japan's Social Principles of Human-Centric AI could integrate ISO 31000 to ensure comprehensive risk assessments for AI systems deployed in public and private sectors. Similarly, international agreements, such as a potential United Nations treaty on AI governance, could include ISO 31000 as a reference point for managing risks in areas like autonomous weapons systems and global financial markets.

ISO/IEC JTC 1 SC 42, a subcommittee dedicated to AI, has developed numerous technical reports and standards addressing the lifecycle of AI systems, from development to deployment and monitoring. These standards could be integrated into sector-specific regulations for industries such as healthcare, transportation, and defense. For instance, regulatory frameworks governing autonomous vehicles, such as the United Nations Economic Commission for Europe (UNECE) WP.29 regulations, could reference SC 42 standards to ensure consistency in safety testing and operational protocols. National healthcare regulations could similarly adopt SC 42 standards to govern the use of AI in medical diagnostics and treatment planning, ensuring patient safety and ethical practices.

There are other international organizations beyond ISO, such as the IEEE and the National Center for Technology and Dispute Resolution[35] (NCTDR) in partnership with the International Council for Online Dispute Resolution (ICODR) that have developed AI related international standards from within professions. The work of the latter collaboration is expounded upon in the next chapter. The IEEE P7000 series of standards, which focus on ethical considerations in AI, offers another critical framework for future legislation. These standards address issues such as algorithmic bias, transparency, and data privacy, making them highly relevant for regulations aimed at ensuring ethical AI practices. For example, the proposed amendments to the California Privacy Rights Act (CPRA) could incorporate IEEE P7002, which provides guidance on data privacy, to mandate stronger protections in AI-driven applications. Internationally, the OECD AI Principles could adopt P7003, which focuses on bias mitigation, to ensure fairness and equity in AI systems deployed by member countries.

AI is inherently global, and its regulation requires international cooperation. Consensus standards offer a practical means of bridging regulatory gaps between jurisdictions, providing a common language for addressing AI's challenges while respecting political, cultural and economic differences. A multilateral framework for AI governance under the WTO's Technical Barriers to Trade Agreement could incorporate standards from the IEEE P7000 series, ensuring that AI technologies meet consistent ethical, safety, and transparency benchmarks across member states. Such integration would enable governments to align their regulatory frameworks with global best practices, facilitating cross-border cooperation and trade.

As AI continues to evolve, new standards will be created to address emerging challenges such as quantum-enhanced AI and adaptive learning systems. Policymakers should anticipate incorporating these future standards into regulations to stay ahead of technological advancements. For example, ISO's ongoing work on explainable AI standards could be critical in regulations requiring transparency in decision-making systems, such as

35 Which, despite its name, is an international organization.

those used in law enforcement and judicial processes. These standards could also inform international guidelines for ethical AI use in sensitive applications, ensuring that technological innovation aligns with societal values.

By integrating consensus standards into legislation, governments can create robust regulatory frameworks that balance innovation with accountability. These standards provide not only technical guidance but also ensure consistency, fairness, and trust across jurisdictions, making them indispensable tools for navigating the complexities of AI governance. As seen in the incorporation of standards into regulations for other industries, the use of AI-specific standards in future laws will likely play a transformative role in shaping the safe and ethical deployment of these technologies worldwide.

## 7 Where We Are with AI in Global Society

Currently, decisions about the development of AI are overwhelmingly in the hands of global multinationals, especially the tiny number of big tech companies with access to vast stores of digital data and immense computing power. Both are needed to 'scrape' intellectual property from sources in the public domain, and by copyright rustlers that make no distinctions. The EU and some individual nation-states have issued AI laws. But, as time goes by, the head-start high-tech companies have to research the AI universe, and make *de facto* global governance decisions continuing to leave the nation-states playing catch-up.

AI technology has prodigious potential to enhance areas such as education, health care, access to justice, scientific discovery and environmental protection. If it is to do so, and do it in a responsible way, it is vitally important that democratic governments reach out beyond the usual *de jure* suspects and recognize the *de facto* entities that are already shaping AI's future. Since many challenges posed by AI regulation cannot be addressed at a purely domestic level, international cooperation is urgently needed to establish basic global standards that mitigate the most dire consequences of an AI "arms race" between countries. Failure to do so will hamper efforts to encourage responsible technological development.

As stated in the official summary from Bletchley:

> We are only at the early stages of understanding how these models work, the risks they pose, and therefore how to develop adequate safeguards. – We need global and decisive action now to acknowledge and

> act on these risks. Frontier AI companies, governments, and academic and civil society researchers need to rapidly work on this together.[36]

At best, we can envision how AI products can 'substitute for current practices.'[37] It is the second wave of a new disruptive technology that always surprises us with unforeseen opportunities (and problems).[38] Success in governing AI will take a more ecumenical approach, one that recognizes the need for other stakeholders to be involved, such as civil society, users of AI, (and those who *don't* want to use AI), end-use consumers, and others who will be affected by these technologies.

Nation-state courts (as well as the EU) have taken on (or accepted) a number of lawsuits attacking mis-use of AI derivatives. On a personal level in the US and Europe, defamation claims have been brought. Europe is most concerned with privacy cases. The US also has Section 230 defenses which gives a limited deference to publishers for the unknowing dissemination of false material.

Copyright is another legal standard attacked from new directions by AI products and services. With older technologies, "fair use" claims were qualitatively different from fair use claims that are beginning to be made with respect to AI. "Fair use" is a legal term of art that requires review when it is challenged. Fair use was generally allowed by the music industry when music was taped from a vinyl record to a cassette. The sound on an analog cassette degrades significantly when there is a copy of a copy. A digital copy of a CD was a different matter, with no degradation. The same basic situation existed with VHS copies of visual material – each subsequent generation lost quality and therefore lost value. With new digital technology that can be used and manipulated by AI came a continuing number of class action lawsuits which argue that 'fair use' was never intended to protect duplication or use such as is seen with AI generated products.[39] AI technology

---

36 Bletchley Park Nov 1–2 2023.

37 For example, when internal combustion vehicles first hit the roads, they were a sorry sight – parts sticking out in all directions and aerodynamics not even a consideration. The first Damylier was calibrated to have ¾ of a horsepower. The first automobiles were thus not cars, but merely horseless carriages. Creating the automotive network required paved roads, gas stations (and gas), dealerships and repair facilities, motels and Triple-A.

38 "During this first phase, there are no rules because none are needed. Innovation hasn't developed to the point where property rights are critical; there are no questions yet about access or unfair competition and the societal impact of the new technology is minimal." Ruling the Waves. Deborah Spar. NY 2001 p. 12.

39 "Creatives" is a new (?) noun and verb to describe those who use object to the "fair use" doctrine, allowing the 'scraping ' of IP from commercial sites.

exponentially expands the manner in which material protected by intellectual property rights and fair use may be accessed, processed, used, and included in products that make money for those other than the creators of the material. An analysis of Anderson v. Stability AI[40] suggests that: 'Arguments that Generative AI is Similar to Past Technologies, Like the VCR, Aren't Going to Hold Much Weight.'[41]

The ubiquity of AI use cases has also forced a discussion at the FTC and the courts concerning how responsibility is shared when AI creates patterns of abuse. Are insurers liable when they use AI algorithms[42] to make back-office decisions on whether to pay a claim? Attaching AI to an already controversial legal case (liability, class or race targeting, climate change, etc.) will assuredly add new complexity to the parsing and resolving of wicked problems.

Recently, the U.S. Uniform Law Commission[43] has promulgated a draft Uniform Personal Data Protection Act (UPDPA)[44], based on consensus standards advocated by ANSI. The draft 'authorizes state and federal consumer protection regulators to grant qualified recognition to voluntary, consensus standards … .[45] Privacy, as we have indicated, is one of the concerns surrounding the development and deployment of AI systems. The ULC's privacy legislation would require adherence to the OECD 1980 Privacy Principles and a rebuttable presumption of 'opt-in' requirements for consumer choice. Aligning US privacy regulation to this international consensus 'consumer protection framework … avoids conflicts with the hundreds of existing federal and state sectorial privacy laws … ."[46]

## 8 Where Is AI Governance Likely to Go?

What, in the end, nation states and standards developers will try to govern is an expanding use, and usefulness, of technology that touches all aspects

40 Andersen v. Stability AI Ltd., 3:23-cv-00201, (N.D. Cal.).

41 Copyright Alliance, "Top Takeaways from Order in the Anderson v. Stability AI Case." https://copyrightalliance.org/andersen-v-stability-ai-copyright-case/

42 As opposed to non-AI algorithms?

43 The ULC is best known as the promulgator of the Uniform Commercial Code (UCC) accepted as part of state law in all 50 states.

44 https://www.uniformlaws.org/HigherLogic/System/DownloadDocumentFile.ashx?DocumentFileKey=009e3927-eafa-3851-1c02-3a05f5891947&forceDialog=0

45 ULC "Alternative Uniform Act" 8/4/2020 p. 1.

46 "Uniform Law Commission Could Resolve the State and Federal Impasse on Internet Privacy Legislation." Roslyn Layton "Forbes" 4/4/2020 p. 8.

of our social interactions, and on the intellectual, scientific, and personal interactions affected by data and process.

Without a coherent governance approach to AI, it is easy to point out dangers and misuses. But also without a coherent governance approach there are without doubt great advantages that have been and can be gained by the use of AI.

In the case of molecular research, protein folding can investigate complex organic molecules that can be formed into billions of variations. Research scientists in the past would sometimes get lucky and stumble onto a natural compound that could lead to the discovery of life-saving drugs. Molecular compounds today can be tested to see if they will possibly evolve into a useful gene code. Using AI, synthetic compounds can thus be discovered that were not previously known. AI can find the needle in the haystack: 'the evolutionary system generates billions of random molecules. Out of the billion humdrum candidates one molecule (may) match.'[47]

Google's "Deep Mind" machine-learning model has cataloged 71 million genetic mutations in the structure of proteins that can induce sickle-cell anemia and cystic fibrosis. Over 216 million possible mutations in more than 19,000 proteins were identified, with 71 million mutations considered deserving of further research. Google is making its catalog of mutations available to molecular biologists, geneticists and doctors.[48]

In counterpoint, Meta Platforms (Facebook), has released AI chatbots – each with its own (artificial) personality – 'as a way to attract young users' for its social media apps.[49] Beyond Facebook, Meta is currently the creator/home of the largest open source AI effort, with over 350 million downloads.[50]

One of the more interesting personal uses AI has been put to, was the thought experiment of ELIZA; an artificial psychotherapist that allowed users to have personal interactions through a machine. ELIZA responded to queries like a gestalt therapist who would reframe statements from the questioner, and respond to key words and phrases that allowed ELIZA to appear present in the 'conversation'. Participants were told that ELIZA could not think, but only respond. However rabbit holes abounded, and

47 Out of Control. Kevin Kelly Addison-Wesley. Reading Mass. 1994. p. 299.

48 Wall Street Journal. "Google 'Deep Mind" AI used in search for Disease Genes." Jo Craven McGinty 9/20/23 p. A-3.

49 Wall Street Journal. "Meta to use Chatbots in AI-fueled Youth Push." Salvador Rodriguez. 9/28/23 p. B-1.

50 See https://venturebeat.com/ai/meta-leads-open-source-ai-boom-llama-downloads-surge-10x-year-over-year/)

'this approach led to wild non-sequiturs and bizarre detours.'[51] In a classic case of cognitive dissonance, participants were aware that ELIZA was a software program, but discovered that a symbiotic relationship was possible where man and machine took the conversation places that were both unexpected and fulfilling.[52]

These types of advances by AI, which produce new opportunities and concerns, have taken place in an environment of little but growing AI governance. Developing global governance, through regulation and standards for AI, is going to be especially challenging. Definitions and approaches to 'trustworthiness' will quickly run into existing nation-state laws on such issues as privacy, security, proprietorship of products created, and the legality of the creation itself (what is the legitimacy of a non-fact 'fact'?).[53] Trying to develop an exhaustive list of all the characteristics that an AI *cannot* have, will indeed be an effort in futility.[54]

We have a great deal of case law in the nation-states that define fraud, deception and patterns of abuse. Admittedly, around the edges there are areas of controversy. (One person's free speech is another person's treasonous statement.) But there is considerable consensus on identifying illegal proceeds in the business-to-consumer (B2C) and consumer-to-consumer (C2C) arenas. Case law whenever possible, should continue to identify and resolve legal and contractual dissatisfactions in emergent AI applications.

We would posit that in the case of developing AI rules – consensus-based and practicable – national consumer protection organizations (public and private) – with a stated belief in personal and citizen rights – should be receptive to an interdependent partnership with the global standards community.

Standards can break a large, unwieldy problem into specific functional problems that can be addressed individually. This is true with AI where a

51 Machines of a Loving Grace. John Markoff. NY 2015 p. 173. Further, a lead academic from MIT Joseph Weizenbaum, (A.K.A. – ELIZA), "... was stunned to discover ELIZA users became deeply engrossed in conversations with the program, and even revealed intimate personal details....Humans; it turns out, have a propensity to find humanity in almost everything they interact with, ranging from inanimate objects to software programs that offer the illusion of human intelligence." Ibid p. 173.

52 Prof. Weizenbaum was nonplussed. "Even his secretary, who knew it was just so much software, was seduced", asking the prof to leave the room, "as she was embarrassed by the intimacy of the conversation"... The Shallows. N. Carr p. 205.

53 Sometimes called "fiction'.

54 When the Federal Trade Commission was created in 1914, the first effort was to develop an exhaustive list of "deceptive" practices that the Act would outlaw. There were more examples discovered than could be listed. The consensus reached was that the FTC would unearth current deceptive practices through adjudications and the courts; ultimately giving the FTC a wealth of case law to use for future situations.

number of directed standards have already been created, and sector-specific areas that are ramping up testing, inspection and audit regimes to meet the new AI challenges (as well as those re-cycled from previous scams).

The nation-states lack the tool box of consensus global strategies; white papers and draft laws have been aimed almost exclusively at domestic audiences. The 'how' and 'when' are conspicuously absent.

> That isn't because we know where artificial intelligence will take us, but precisely because we don't. Worrying properly about a novel technology with tremendous promise and a real potential for creating novel risks requires clarity and humility. The AI debates could use more of both.[55]

Standards development organizations need to expand their outreach to ensure that civil society, consumer, environmental professional and worker organizations, SMEs, academics and all others who have standing in developing AI guardrails (pretty much everyone), are part of the AI standards creation process. This will require concerted efforts to bring more organizations and individuals to the table.[56] Standards Developers should also look to existing treaties and trade agreements to utilize the scope and authority of the WTO's Technical Barriers to Trade for developing AI norms and rulemakings.

Standards have been perceived by many to be a classic 'black box.' A problem is ushered in the front end, and a solution will be issued from the back end. What goes on inside is certainly arcane, and often impenetrable to outsiders. Standards are 'the products of specialized knowledge emerging from obscure procedures with an alphabet soup of organizations and a number salad.'[57] When public policy issues are addressed (such as with AI), there should be concerted efforts to develop FAQ's (including interactive question/response locations), plain language abstracts of standards, and cites for running commentary of comments during drafting efforts.

Achieving successful AI governance is a forcing mechanism for greater democratic participation. Foundations should recognize that informed voices from civil society are needed to both encourage Public Good creation though AI, and to build the guardrails. This effort should be both the

---

55 Artificial Intelligence and the Law of the Horse. Yuval Levin. American Enterprise Institute. "WSJ" 12/22/23 A-17.

56 "Standards development organizations must take the lead in increasing participation." Small Yards, Big Tents. p.5. Further, standards developers "will need to broaden lines of communication with stakeholders outside of their usual participants." Ibid. p. 6.

57 Ibid p. 9.

encouragement of participation in standards creation and an undertaking of 'capacity building' to help non-sovereign organizations find their voice (and create standing), for participation in creating the 'rules of the road' (and guardrails), for integrating AI into our world.

John von Neuman, who designed much of the architecture of early computers, wrote Lewis Strauss, the *eminence grise* of post WWII U.S. federal research policy, in 1945, exhorting that improving computer responses by 10,000 times (a goal quickly reached ...) was not the objective, it was rather 'to handle problems that are considered completely unassailable at present.'[58] All those searching for knowledge now have an exciting new tool available that is user-friendly, can respond to user inquiries, and seeks abnormalities that humans on their own would likely miss.[59] Intelligent machines already supply "exotic senses" that humans lack – radar, sonar, and spectrum (such as infrared), that drive our knowledge of the universe.[60] What is lacking are the standards, rules and the enforcement of norms and law needed to keep AI sites clean, well-lighted and trustworthy.

The AI industry itself needs to address its own internal trustworthiness issues. The laborious 'scraping' of data sets from the opaque world at the borders of copyright and fair use is a public policy issue in need of resolution. As well, the AI industry needs to showcase the public good that it can create, where AI creation can take us in the near future, and the goals still to be aimed for in the transference of information into knowledge.

## 9 So What?

The history of global standards development reveals a consistent tension between the promise of technological advancement and the practical hurdles of achieving international consensus. AI presents a new frontier in this tradition, embodying the profound complexities of our interconnected, rapidly evolving world. As with past efforts to regulate products ranging from children's toys to household appliances, the journey to create robust, widely

58 Turing's Cathedral. George Dyson. NY. 2012. p. 85. [von Neuman to Strauss 8/24/45].

59 In the best of worlds "abnormalities" would show up between the Bhagavad Gita and the creation of galaxies; the study of Relativity covering light, space, time and physical matter; or where atoms and solar systems share the same rules (or not)." The Coming of Age of the Milky Way. Timothy Ferris. NY 2003. p. 193. Further, "The act of exploration alters the perspective of the explorer; Odysseus, and Marco Polo and Columbus returned home as changed men." Ibid p. 285.

60 On Intelligence. p. 228.

accepted AI standards will be shaped by challenges that echo through history: competing national interests, political, and possibly cultural divergences, and the sheer pace of technological change.

Developing AI standards requires a nuanced approach that respects both the lessons of the past and the unique demands of this new technological era. Much like the 19th-century international postal agreements that eventually transcended the misgivings of jealous nation-states, AI standards must be crafted with prudence and collaboration. From the tumultuous efforts to establish toy safety standards after high-profile lead contamination cases to the protracted negotiations over ISO 14000 environmental management systems, successful standards have been born of patient collaboration, iterative refinement, and a willingness to adapt. Each of these examples underscores the importance of stakeholder engagement across governments, industry, and civil society – a hallmark of any successful global standard.

The challenges faced in coordinating AI standards are reminiscent of those encountered in developing earlier frameworks. Political decisions and legal norms continue to shape the priorities and expectations of participating nations, as evidenced by the stark differences in privacy frameworks between the United States and the European Union. The resigned realization of sociologists that complex problems often demand overlapping perspectives is equally applicable here, as AI regulation requires contributions from technologists, ethicists, policymakers, and historians alike. Economic disparities, which complicated ISO 9000 adoption in the 1980s and fueled resistance to stringent safety regulations in developing nations, remain relevant in today's efforts to ensure equitable AI governance. These issues are compounded by the unprecedented speed at which AI evolves, making traditional standards development timelines increasingly untenable.

One of the most pressing questions for AI standards is how to create trust in an environment rife with skepticism. As in the past, the creation of trust depends on designing practicable answers that will work in the real world. Just as the incorporation of ISO 9000 into U.S. federal procurement regulations in the 1990s helped establish a baseline for quality management, emerging AI standards like ISO/IEC 42001 for AI management systems and ISO 37001 for anti-bribery could form the foundation for global trust in AI systems. However, achieving this will require not only technical rigor but also the cultivation of transparency, inclusivity, and adaptability to evolving societal needs.

Despite the formidable obstacles, the potential for AI standards to contribute to meaningful global governance is vast. International standards offer the unique advantage of being inherently collaborative and adaptable, capable of addressing challenges that elude traditional regulatory frameworks. For example, the success of ISO 45001 in improving workplace safety across global supply chains demonstrates the potential for AI standards to similarly address concerns ranging from algorithmic bias to data security. AI, like other technologies before it, represents especially high tides that never recede – it is here to stay and must be harnessed responsibly.

As we navigate the complexities of AI governance, it is worth recalling the resilience and creativity that have defined the standards movement throughout history. From the early coordination of international postal services to the development of modern sustainability frameworks, the ability to create solutions that transcend borders and align with shared human values has been a hallmark of progress. In crafting AI standards, we must harness this spirit, balancing innovation with accountability to ensure that artificial intelligence serves as a tool for collective advancement rather than division.

The path forward will demand patience, compromise, and an unwavering commitment to trustworthiness and equity. AI's governance must reflect the same measured optimism and faith in collaboration. Drawing inspiration from the successes and failures of the past, the global community has an opportunity to chart a course for AI that reflects not just the technology's immense potential but also the shared aspirations of humanity. By embracing the lessons of history and the promise of collaboration, we can create a framework for AI governance that is both robust and responsive, capable of guiding us through the challenges of the present and into an uncertain but hopeful future.

CHAPTER 5

# International Online Dispute Resolution Standards and AI: A Case Example

## 1 The Importance of International ODR Standards for AI

As the sun rose Wednesday morning, she opened her laptop to check on a mediation case. She suspected both disputing parties, in disparate time zones, would have had time by now to asynchronistically look at the four AI-generated proposed agreement packages and she was curious whether they had chosen the same package. The parties had elected to use the AI option for agreement generation to optimize the likelihood that the outcome in this complex case would meet both their needs to the greatest extent – this, they hoped, would create durability and reduce resentment about any necessary compromises they had to make. The parties also had preferred using tech at this stage of the process because it provided interpersonal distance, somewhat reducing the emotionality of engagement during the decision-making. Noting that they had reached agreement, she initiated invites to a scheduling calendar to organize a video conferencing session since they had requested to meet post-agreement for closure – to get together virtually so that it was both face-to-face but also at a distance. As she pressed 'Send,' she reflected on how efficient the process had been for the parties and for her, how technology had provided so many benefits through the ODR platform: e-case management, multiple and multilingual communication channels, video conferencing, and the integration of AI into a variety of features that offered text and visuals generation, brainstorming, options generation, and even decision-making functions. This had significantly enhanced the functionalities she could offer as well as the overall quality of the experience and outcome for the parties. She recalled how it had reassured the prospective parties to know in advance of agreeing to mediate about the benefits and flexibility that her mediation practice could provide through the use of AI and other forms of technology. And she was struck by their appreciation for the fact that her practice and the ODR tools she used, were aligned with international standards for online dispute resolution that included attention to both the risks and benefits of

© KONINKLIJKE BRILL BV, LEIDEN, 2025 | DOI:10.1163/9789004737389_007

> artificial intelligence. The more she and the parties had relied on technology, the more valuable it was to know where the boundaries of risk lay. They had commented on how transparency about not only the benefits but also the risks had enhanced their trust in the process more than it would have otherwise. She was pleased to be part of an international profession not only dedicated to access to justice but also to keeping its ethical standards relevant in light of changing technologies.

A field dedicated to providing quality dispute resolution faces continuously changing goalposts as artificial intelligence and other technologies are increasingly embedded in judicial and alternative dispute resolution (ADR) processes. Application of various technologies is not new: online dispute resolution (ODR) has been around in one form or another since the late 1990s. However, there has been an explosion in usage due to the pandemic lockdown and with the new widely available AI generative text chatbots. The use of technology and of AI in particular, has disrupted the boundaries of dispute resolution and the roles for dispute intervenors: we have many more channels of communication, the ability to engage with exponentially more issues, parties, and possibilities than historical face-to-face ADR and judicial procedures; and we can rely on AI to organize, summarize, replicate, analyze, generate, and communicate data faster and more efficiently than most of us could ever have imagined. Given the trend to rely on AI in other parts of our lives and the accelerated experimentation with AI in ADR recently, there is every reason to believe that AI will not only play increasingly significant roles within dispute resolution processes but will continue to alter the roles of disputing parties and the intervenors (third parties). This growing usage of AI and other technologies carries great possibility for enhancing efficiency and access to justice[1] and also for reducing it, especially

1 See A. Lee 'Online Dispute Resolution in China: Today and Future,' in D. Rainey, E. Katsh, and M.S. Abdel Wahab (Eds.), *Online Dispute Resolution: Theory and Practice*, Second Edition, Eleven International Publishing, The Hague, 2021, pp. 681–705; A.J. Schmitz, 'Dangers of Digitizing Due Process,' in K. Benyehhlef (Ed.), *AI and Law: A Critical Overview*, Les Éditions Thémis, 2021; A. Schmitz and L. Wing, 'Beneficial and Ethical ODR for Family Issues,' *Family Court Review*. Special Issue: Online Dispute Resolution (ODR), Vol. 59, No. 2, April 2021, pp. 250–267; A.M. Kusomotu, 'Online Dispute Resolution and Africa,' in D. Rainey, E. Katsh, and M.S. Abdel Wahab (Eds.), *Online Dispute Resolution: Theory and Practice*, Second Edition, Eleven International Publishing, The Hague, 2021, pp. 667–679; C. Rule 'ODR and Peacetech' in D. Rainey, E. Katsh, and M.S. Abdel Wahab (Eds.), *Online Dispute Resolution: Theory and Practice*, Second Edition, Eleven International Publishing, The Hague, 2021, pp. 451–470; F. Bell, M. Legg, J. McIntyre, and A. Olijnyk, 'The Use of Technology (And Other Measures) to Increase Court Capacity,' *International Journal of*

for some more than others.[2] Therefore, the rapid and continuously changing nature of the influence of technologies will continue to have ethical implications when they are deployed within dispute resolution processes.[3]

This chapter will explore the landscape of technology's – and particularly AI's – role and influence in dispute handling and why international online dispute resolution standards are necessary to harness its potential and reduce risks it can pose in the transformation and resolution of disputes. The chapter will provide an example of how international standards developed from within a discipline or profession can contribute to the ecosystem of AI governance, as resolution processes not only serve disputing parties across nation state boundaries but also are embedded in and utilized by all sectors of society.

## 2 Beneficial Roles and Influence of AI and Other Technologies in Dispute Handling

The infusion of technology in dispute handling processes has significantly expanded the boundaries of what we can do and what we can envision accomplishing. Whether we are using tech as a tool, a location (website, video conference space, etc.), or a decision maker, the fourth party[4] has many guises and its roles and impacts are rapidly evolving through experimentation and application.[5] It can significantly enhance efficiency in the cost of human energy, time, and financial output; be used to prevent and detect conflicts at an early stage to reduce their implications and foster more

*Online Dispute Resolution*, Vol. 8, No. 2, 2016, pp. 102–130; G. Ross, 'What's Good for ODR: AI or AI,' *International Journal of Online Dispute Resolution*, Vol. 8, No. 1, 2021, pp. 20–30; P. Embley and Lise Embley, 'Online Dispute Resolution in US Courts Looking Back and Going Forward,' in D. Rainey, E. Katsh, and M.S. Abdel Wahab (Eds.), *Online Dispute Resolution: Theory and Practice*, Second Edition, Eleven International Publishing, The Hague, 2021, pp. 275–296; Wing, Martinez, Katsh, and Rule, 2021.

2 Wing, L. "Artificial Intelligence and Online Dispute Resolution Systems Design: Lack of/ Access to Justice Magnified." *International Journal of Online Dispute Resolution,* (4)2, 2017, 16–20.

3 Wing, L. with Draper, C., principal authors. *Framing the Parameters of Online Dispute Resolution.* National Center for Technology and Dispute Resolution, 2022; Rainey, D. *Making Friends with the Fourth Party: Integrating Technology into Your Dispute Resolution Practice.* The Hague: Eleven Publishing, 2022, 43.

4 The term "Fourth Party" was coined by Katsh and Rifkin, see E. Katsh and J. Rifkin, *Online Dispute Resolution: Resolving Conflicts in Cyberspace*, San Francisco, Jossey-Bass 2001.

5 Wing, L., Martinez, J., Katsh, E. and Rule, C. "Designing Ethical Online Dispute Resolution Systems: The Rise of the Fourth Party." *Negotiation Journal* 37(1), Special Issue: Artificial Intelligence, Technology, and Negotiation, Winter 2021, 49–64.

speedy resolutions; manage large volumes of data to rapidly map greater numbers and types of potential outcomes to maximize mutual benefits of negotiated agreements – particularly useful in disputes with multiple stakeholders and numerous issues; and facilitate the generation of creative suggestions or outcomes – harnessing information from previous decisions by fourth parties, third parties or the disputing parties. For example, parties can employ a Retrieval-Augmented Generation (RAG) tool that can leverage customized and more up-to-date data through online document retrieval that a large language model (LLM) can use to generate responses[6] for conflict analysis and/or use in solution decision making. Using hybrid architectures for generative AI systems, like RAG augmented LLMs, has the potential to strengthen the accuracy of the LLM output and its relevance to a particular context. It can deepen and strengthen the pool of data an LLM can call upon to generate answers to queries in ways that can enhance their applicability to particular parties and their dispute in text, video, audio, and multilingual forms. Artificial intelligence can also harness a Geographic Information System (GIS) for predictive purposes to reveal possible impacts in a variety of scenarios contemplated by disputing parties, and significantly enhance the value of what the resolution process can offer as they seek a sustainable agreement. Picture an arbitrator using an LLM augmented by a contextually appropriate RAG to generate a list of arbitration decisions based on cases with similar fact patterns to examine as she contemplates her case; two businessmen using AI to generate a decision to their contractual dispute; a facilitator intervening in a complex public policy conflict involving hundreds of stakeholders who employ AI to help them collaboratively design queries for a RAG augmented LLM that will generate options for mutual gain relevant to their particular context.

The use of a RAG can provide more curated generative responses by extracting information from sources presently available online as well as from knowledge repositories in internal databases; for example, from within an organization (i.e., a court) or section of practice (i.e., arbitration awards published in a particular jurisdiction and language), thus adding a RAG to the architecture of an LLM has the capacity to strengthen the accuracy and relevancy of the AI generated responses. This can reduce the limitations of LLMs that are restricted by their pre-trained data, which can be out-of-date, and most commonly have algorithms designed to be abstract enough to have strong portability but can therefore often reduce their relevance to

---

6 Horsey, J. "How to build Large Language Models (LLMs) and RAG pipelines using open-source models. *Geeky Gadgets*. September 5, 2023; AWS, What is Retrieval-Augmented Generation?" https://aws.amazon.com/what-is/retrieval-augmented-generation/

specific contexts.[7] An additional brand new[8] AI companion to LLMs are Large Action–or Agentic–Models (LAMs)[9] which have the potential to revolutionize dispute resolution.

> In terms of the overview on their working, LAMs interact with the real world through integration with external systems, such in IoT devices and others. By connecting to these systems, LAMs can perform physical actions, control devices, retrieve data, or manipulate information. This permits LAMs to mechanise complete processes and smartly interact with the world, converse with people, adjusting as conditions vary, and even working together with other LAMs.[10]

The ability to utilize LAMs – including to harness LLMs – as agents that can complete tasks, issue responses, and make decisions autonomously can be a game-changer in altering the nature, roles, and possibilities for every aspect of dispute management. Imagine individuals who wish to file a small claims case in a language they do not know, in a legal jurisdiction outside where they live, and using laws with which they are unfamiliar. It may not be long before a court can dramatically increase access to justice for those claimants by enabling them to use an LAM to file their case using the court's case filing system which harnesses an LLM and RAG. As predicted to occur in some form,[11] it is also likely that LAMs will be put to work negotiating on behalf of parties.

---

7 For a critique of portability and the need for incorporation of social context into the design of algorithms, see Andrew D. Selbst, Danah Boyd, Sorelle A. Friedler, Suresh Venkatasubramanian, and Janet Vertesi. 2019. *Fairness and Abstraction in Sociotechnical Systems.* In FAT* '19: Conference on Fairness, Accountability, and Transparency (FAT* '19), January 29–31, 2019, Atlanta, GA, USA. ACM, New York, NY, USA, 61. https://doi.org/10.1145/3287560.3287598

8 It is less than a month old at the time of writing.

9 "The Rabbit R1 is an AI-powered gadget that can use your apps for you." *The Verge.* January 9, 2024. https://www.theverge.com/2024/1/9/24030667/rabbit-r1-ai-action-model-price-release-date

10 For a brief overview of LAMs, brand new at the time of writing this book chapter, see Thomas, R.J. "The Rise of Large Action Models, LAMs: How AI Can Understand and Execute Human Intentions?" *Medium.* January 16, 2024. https://medium.com/version-1/the-rise-of-large-action-models-lams-how-ai-can-understand-and-execute-human-intentions-f59c8e78bc09; The rise of Large Action Models (LAMs)." *Dataconomy.* N.d. https://dataconomy.com/2024/01/15/what-is-a-large-action-model-lam/

11 Wing, L., Martinez, J., Katsh, E. and Rule, C. "Designing Ethical Online Dispute Resolution Systems: The Rise of the Fourth Party." *Negotiation Journal* 37(1), Special Issue: Artificial Intelligence, Technology, and Negotiation, Winter 2021, 49–64.

How else might an LAM be integrated with RAG and LLM tools to support dispute resolution? A mediator could employ it when working with stakeholders from municipal, provincial, and national government agencies, as well as with private industry, research and educational institutions, nonprofit advocacy groups, and the general public. He, along with other environmental and public policy mediators and facilitators from his ADR membership organization could design RAG access to not only archives of mediated agreements but also previously brainstormed options generated during similar public disputes. The mediator could utilize an LLM harnessing that RAG to assist stakeholders to develop a set of jointly agreed fact-finding questions to ask the LLM to generate multilingual textual responses that could assist with accessibility for more equitable participation in the negotiation process. With the resulting data, a LAM could be directed to engage the LLM to produce a range of options and illustrate the potential long-term outcomes for each, including AI generated visuals using GIS maps and AI generated written descriptions. Each option could highlight what benefits would accrue to which stakeholder, noting the mutuality or lack thereof. For stakeholders with less technical knowledge and fewer resources than others, this could impact an imbalance of power by providing them more information than they would otherwise have and enhancing their leverage in negotiating, or at least their understanding of the extent of their lack of leverage, thus providing information crucial for their decision making. In what other ways might LAMs, LLMs and RAGs be harnessed to detect at the earliest stage the possibility of errors in a medical chart – reducing harm, saving lives, creating greater efficiency, and preventing conflict and lawsuits?

These examples illustrate the productive disruption of artificial intelligence and importantly, how this can dramatically impact efficiency, accessibility, and power imbalances; reducing barriers for access to justice and fostering more creative problem-solving for dispute prevention and resolution. The benefits of using tech, including AI, can also address some of the historical concerns about barriers in dispute resolution processes inside and outside of judicial systems; for example, reducing costs in terms of time, transportation, childcare, and lost work time to participate which can increase access to justice. And there already is evidence that it increases the likelihood of showing up for hearings when they are virtual.[12] The use of Universal Design for the websites and software tools used by courts and ADR practitioners can increase accessibility for persons with disabilities and

12 Matterhorn Family Court Results, https://getmatterhorn.com/get-results/family-court/ Last visited Dec. 21, 2019.

for a multilingual public through the use of AI translation. LLMs and GIS can provide data visualization to be shared with stakeholders in a public dispute who otherwise may not have access to complex mapping systems or research capabilities for analyzing them. Cross jurisdictional document origination verification via blockchain can serve as a dispute prevention tool and banking and digital payment platforms requiring online dispute resolution at point of contact will increase access to rapid dispute resolution benefiting customers, businesses, and the public purse by reducing court dockets.

The expansion of the capabilities of the fourth party and its utilization can contribute valuably to the improvement of human relations, as well as our relations with the earth. At a time of climate crisis, it is ever more urgent that we explore harnessing LLMs, RAGs, and LAMs to prevent, reduce, and resolve climate and other environmental-related conflicts and reduce transportation footprints.[13] Technology can assist us in "righting" our relationships with each other and the precious ecosystem to which we belong. Arguably then, it is incumbent upon us to consider how to proactively harness formal and informal governance mechanisms to structure the productive and enhancing use of AI and other technologies in the management of disputes. Legislation, regulation and other public policies as well as standards can and should be utilized to foster increased benefits for those disputing and for society and our ecosystem as a whole through the responsible use of technologies.

## 3 Magnified Risks of AI and Other Technologies in Dispute Handling

Artificial intelligence and other technologies not only magnify access to opportunities but can also generate and magnify inequalities, hardwiring them into dispute resolution processes without sufficient transparency or accountability. 'AI's exquisiteness manifests in the ways we can use it to expand access to justice and improve relationships; however, it can also maximize opportunities to harm and create and reinforce injustice'.[14]

13 As noted in Chapter Three, innovations and governance to reduce the drastic levels of energy consumption of these technologies is critical to ensure the benefits of their usage are not offset by increasing environmental damage.

14 Wing in Katsh, E., Draper, C., Ebner, N., Loebl, Z., Rainey, D., Ross, G., Rule, C., Vilalta, E. and Wing, L. "Comments on Artificial Intelligence." *International Journal of Online Dispute Resolution*, (9)2, 2022, 167. See also Wing, L. 'Artificial Intelligence and Online Dispute Resolution Systems Design: Lack of/Access to Justice Magnified.' *International Journal of Online Dispute Resolution*, Vol. 4, No. 2, 2017, 16–20; Wing, L. 'Ethical

Technology's influence on our processes and outcomes necessarily means that it has a direct relationship with 'the ethical imperatives and standards of practice that guide our work as third parties'.[15] The disruptive force of technological innovation and use creates new ways of generating[16] not only reducing[17] disputes. Therefore, governance mechanisms need to account for the reality of on-going and escalating disruptive innovation to protect the value of advancement while simultaneously protecting other cherished values foundational to judicial and informal processes of dispute management. Governance tools such as international online dispute resolution (ODR) standards, for example, are important to reduce and prevent risks and also to set baseline requirements for the responsible use of technology including AI to effectively harness its potential to maximize access to the benefits of dispute resolution for all. They need to address both opportunities and risks by accounting for the reality that these are not symmetrically experienced by people and entities that are differently positioned from each other in society and may also be differentially impacted by the context of their dispute and their relationship to technology [Figure 5.1]. A person's positionality in relation to power, leverage, and ability to effectively participate can be impacted not only by the resources available to them and the other disputant, but also by their familiarity with software and whether the algorithms in the training and functioning of an LLM, for example, reflect or marginalize their worldview and context.

To explore this further, let us consider several foundational values which, while manifesting differently in various processes (court, mediation, arbitration, etc.), can all be impacted when technology is employed: empowerment (agency and choice), access to justice, efficiency (time, cost, and ease), neutrality, and fairness (procedural and substantive).

When we add a fourth party, and in particular, artificial intelligence, it alters the relationships, choices, and access to power within a process.[18] This was demonstrated in a study that found that the use of (perceived) AI decision making in arbitration resulted in lower levels of procedural justice

Principles for Online Dispute Resolution: A GPS Device for the Field.' *International Journal of Online Dispute Resolution*, Vol. 3, No. 1, 2016, 12–29.

15 Rainey, D. *Making Friends with the Fourth Party: Integrating Technology into Your Dispute Resolution Practice.* The Hague: Eleven Publishing, 2022, 43.

16 Katsh, E. and Rabinovich-Einy, O. *Digital Justice: Technology and the Internet of Disputes*. Oxford: Oxford U. Press, 2017, 2.

17 See Katsh in Katsh, E., Draper, C., Ebner, N., Loebl, Z., Rainey, D., Ross, G., Rule, C., Vilalta, E. and Wing, L. "Comments on Artificial Intelligence." *International Journal of Online Dispute Resolution*, (9)2, 2022, 147–176, 148.

18 See Rainey, D. *Making Friends with the Fourth Party: Integrating Technology into Your Dispute Resolution Practice*. The Hague: Eleven Publishing, 2022.

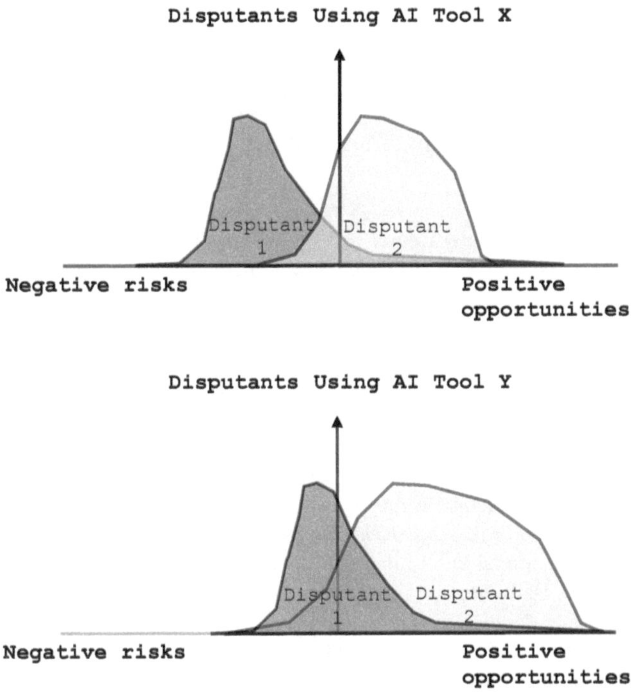


FIGURE 5.1 Disruptive innovation: unequal risks and opportunities for disputants using AI
CONCEPT: LEAH WING; VISUAL: CHRIS DRAPER

compared to when a (perceived) human arbitrator made the final determination.[19] It also found that disputants' perception of the fairness of an AI arbitrator was influenced by their level of control over the process and decision-making and that there was more comfort and perceptions of fairness relating to the use of AI in mediation capacities where parties retained more influence over the process and outcome. This study raises interesting questions about the relationship between choice, decision-making power, and the role of AI in settings where the parties have expectations about who the final decision-maker will be and whether it is viewed as procedurally fair how justice is meted out. Will greater use of AI alter these expectations for disputants and/or third parties in the future? Arguably it will provide disruption and new possibilities and risks that are worth exploring further regarding historically cherished values in judicial and ADR proceedings.

19 Ayelet Sela, "Can Computers Be Fair: How Automated and Human-Powered Online Dispute Resolution Affect Procedural Justice in Mediation and Arbitration." 33 *Ohio State Journal on Dispute Resolution*. 91, 146 (2018).

Relatedly, the core values of neutrality and procedural and substantive fairness face significant risks of AI generating and replicating inequality through the use of big data,[20] incomplete or biased data,[21] and particularly when combined with insufficient transparency and accountability.[22] A lack

---

20 Lytton, C. "AI hiring tools may be filtering out the best job applicants." *BBC*, February 16, 2024. https://www.bbc.com/worklife/article/20240214-ai-recruiting-hiring-software-bias-discrimination (accessed February 17, 2024); A.L. Bannon and D. Keith, "Remote Court: Principles for Virtual Proceedings During the COVID-19 Pandemic and Beyond," *Northwestern University Law Review*, Vol. 115, No. 6, 2021, 1875–1882; A. Barsky, 'The Ethics of App-Assisted Family Mediation,' *Conflict Resolution Quarterly*, Vol. 34, No. 1, Fall 2016, 31–42; B. Davis, "ODR and Social Justice: Technology Not Tricknology," in D. Rainey, E. Katsh, and M.S. Abdel Wahab (Eds.), *Online Dispute Resolution: Theory and Practice*, Second Edition, Eleven International Publishing, The Hague, 2021, 297–313; A.M. Kusomotu, "Online Dispute Resolution and Africa," in D. Rainey, E. Katsh, and M.S. Abdel Wahab (Eds.), *Online Dispute Resolution: Theory and Practice*, Second Edition, Eleven International Publishing, The Hague, 2021, 667–679; C. Draper, "Online Dispute Resolution Data Security," in D. Rainey, E. Katsh, and M.S. Abdel Wahab (Eds.), *Online Dispute Resolution: Theory and Practice*, Second Edition, Eleven International Publishing, The Hague, 2021, 181–228; L. Wing, "Artificial Intelligence and Online Dispute Resolution Systems Design: Lack of/Access to Justice Magnified," *International Journal of Online Dispute Resolution*, Vol. 4, No. 2, 2017, 16–20; L. Wing, "Ethical Principles for Online Dispute Resolution: A GPS Device for the Field," *International Journal of Online Dispute Resolution*, Vol. 3, No. 1, 2016, 12–29; M. Anderson and K. Madhumitha, *Digital Divide Persists Even as Lower-Income Americans Make Gains in Tech Adoption*, Pew Research Center, 7 May 2019.

21 Hilke Schellmann in Lytton, C. "AI hiring tools may be filtering out the best job applicants." *BBC*, February 16, 2024. https://www.bbc.com/worklife/article/20240214-ai-recruiting-hiring-software-bias-discrimination (accessed February 17, 2024); Drahl, C. "AI was asked to create images of Black African docs treating white kids. How'd it go?" *NPR*, October 6, 2023. https://www.npr.org/sections/goatsandsoda/2023/10/06/1201840678/ai-was-asked-to-create-images-of-black-african-docs-treating-white-kids-howd-it-; Engstrom, D. F., D. E. Ho, C. M. Sharkey, and M.-F. Cuellar. 2020. *Government by Algorithm: Artificial Intelligence in Federal Administrative Agencies*. NYU School of Law Research Paper No. 20–54; and Katsh, E. and Rabinovich-Einy, O. *Digital Justice: Technology and the Internet of Disputes*. Oxford: Oxford U. Press, 2017.

22 Hilke Schellmann in Lytton, C. "AI hiring tools may be filtering out the best job applicants." *BBC*, February 16, 2024. https://www.bbc.com/worklife/article/20240214-ai-recruiting-hiring-software-bias-discrimination (accessed February 17, 2024); Wing, L., Martinez, J., Katsh, E. and Rule, C. "Designing Ethical Online Dispute Resolution Systems: The Rise of the Fourth Party." *Negotiation Journal* 37(1), Special Issue: Artificial Intelligence, Technology, and Negotiation, Winter 2021, 49–64; Wing, L. "Artificial Intelligence and Online Dispute Resolution Systems Design: Lack of/Access to Justice Magnified." *International Journal of Online Dispute Resolution,* (4)2, 2017, 16–20; J. de Werra, "ADR in Cyberspace: The Need to Adopt Global Alternative Dispute Resolution Mechanisms for Addressing the Challenges of Massive Online Micro-Justice," *Swiss Review of International & European Law*, 2016, 289–306; E. Katsh and O. Rabinovitch-Einy, *Digital Justice: Technology and the Internet of Disputes*, Oxford, Oxford University

of knowledge about the harmful impacts of AI and the absence of requirements to redress patterns of inequality[23] and repeat player bias[24] can impact procedural–and potentially substantive–fairness and raise reputational and liability risks for dispute resolution providers. Given that not everyone is equally positioned to fully access either the benefits of AI usage or protection against its risks, this raises concerns about AI's impact on equal access to justice. Below, this is explored further, highlighting the importance of governance mechanisms for AI usage in dispute prevention and resolution.

## 4 AI Bias and Inequality: Effects on Dispute Handling

Notwithstanding decades of research on artificial intelligence and bias, the problem has not been defeated. It should challenge us to consider how this can impact ODR when arguably 'even within the sectors of the tech community that advocate for human-centered design, such as human-computer interaction, little has been done to grapple with racism,'[25] gender bias,[26] and other biases. Many heart-rate trackers and face recognition technologies are disproportionately inaccurate with darker skin[27] despite long-term acknowledgment that this is the case.

---

Press, 2017; S.J. Shackelford & A.H. Raymond, "Building the Virtual Courthouse: Ethical Considerations for Design, Implementation, and Regulation in the World of ODR," *Wisconsin Law Review*, Vol. 3, 2014, 614–657; and L. Wing, "Ethical Principles for Online Dispute Resolution: A GPS Device for the Field," *International Journal of Online Dispute Resolution*, Vol. 3, No. 1, 2016, 12–29.

23 Hilke Schellmann in Lytton, C. "AI hiring tools may be filtering out the best job applicants." *BBC*, February 16, 2024. https://www.bbc.com/worklife/article/20240214-ai-recruiting-hiring-software-bias-discrimination (accessed February 17, 2024)

24 Katsh and Rabinovich-Einy, 2017; Mentovich, A., Prescott, J.J. and Rabinovich-Einy, O. "Are Litigation Outcome Disparities Inevitable? Courts, Technology, and the Future of Impartiality," *Alabama Law Review*, Vol. 7, No. 4, 1, 2020, 893–979.; Wing, 2016.

25 Winchester, W. "Black-centered design is the future of business: Designers can dismantle the New Jim Code. Here's how." *Fast Company* 06-08-20 https://www.fastcompany.com/90513962/black-centered-design-is-the-future-of-business Last accessed February 3, 2021.

26 Thakur, H., Jain, A., Vaddamanu, P., Liang, P.P., and Morency, L.-P. "Language Models Get a Gender Makeover: Mitigating Gender Bias with Few-Shot Data Interventions." *Proceedings of the 61st Annual Meeting of the Association for Computational Linguistics Volume 2: Short Papers*, Association for Computational Linguistics, 2023, 340–351.

27 Najibi, A. "Racial Discrimination in Face Recognition Technology." The Graduate School of Arts and Sciences, Harvard University, October 24, 2020. https://sitn.hms.harvard.edu/flash/2020/racial-discrimination-in-face-recognition-technology/

> For, just as with skin tone recognition software (i.e. for surveillance and medical devices) and AI used for decision-making about police surveillance and defendants' bail, after 60 years we have still not tackled the problem of biases in AI that disproportionately negatively affect those with dark skin tones.[28]

In 2021, Professor Sonia M. Gipson Rankin argued:

> The gravity of harm is incomprehensible [related to] … [t]he lack of technical transparency and legal accountability leav[ing] wrongfully convicted defendants without legal remedies if they are unlawfully detained based on a cyberattack, faulty or hacked data, or rogue AI. Scholars and engineers acknowledge that the artificial intelligence that is giving recommendations to law enforcement, prosecutors, judges, and parole boards lacks the common sense of an eighteen-month-old child.[29]

Research on LLMs reveal concerns about hallucinations and their compounding of inaccurate data in legal cases. Researchers at the Stanford RegLab and Institute for Human-Centered AI found that

> legal hallucinations are pervasive and disturbing: hallucination rates range from 69% to 88% in response to specific legal queries for state-of-the-art language models. Moreover, these models often lack self-awareness about their errors and tend to reinforce incorrect legal assumptions and beliefs. These findings raise significant concerns about the reliability of LLMs in legal contexts, underscoring the importance of careful, supervised integration of these AI technologies into legal practice.[30]

---

28 See Buolamwini, J. Written Testimony. Hearing on Facial Recognition Technology (Part 1): Its Impact on our Civil Rights and Liberties. United States House Committee on Oversight and Government Reform, 22 May 2019; and videotape of this testimony: www.congress.gov/event/116th-congress/house-event/109521.

29 Gipson Rankin, S.M. "Technological Tethereds: Potential Impact of Untrustworthy Artificial Intelligence in Criminal Justice Risk Assessment Instruments." *Washington and Lee Law Review*. Vol. 78, 2021, 647–724, 648.

30 Dahl, M., Magesh, V., Suzgun, M., and Ho, D.E. "Hallucinating Law: Legal Mistakes with Large Language Models are Pervasive." January 11, 2024. https://hai.stanford.edu/news/hallucinating-law-legal-mistakes-large-language-models-are-pervasive

Importantly, they also found

> case law from lower courts, like district courts, is subject to more frequent hallucinations than case law from higher courts like the Supreme Court. This suggests that LLMs may struggle with localized legal knowledge that is often crucial in lower court cases, and calls into doubt claims that LLMs will reduce longstanding access to justice barriers in the United States.[31]

Another significant finding revealed 'the tendency to assume that a factual premise in a query is true, even if it is flatly wrong'.[32] Why then, should ADR and ODR providers assume that the incorporation of LLMs and other AI tools into their practices would be different?

What guardrails are needed to ensure that AI can perform bias-free data collection and analysis for text, video and audio generation in RAGS, LLMS and LAMS and enhance ODR without compromising procedural and substantive justice for some disputants and privileging others by comparison? Those responsible for and committed to providing access to justice have responsibilities to ensure that the application of technology and the harnessing of AI, in particular, accomplishes this. Relying on market forces and good intentions has unfortunately continued to result in patterns of bias and inequality through the implementation of AI[33] that includes the use of LLMs which 'learn, reproduce, and even amplify denigrating, stereotypical, and exclusionary social behaviors';[34] many of which often significantly negatively impact already marginalized populations. Algorithmic achievements abound. For example, researchers have overcome the plant-human communication barrier and engineered the capability of spinach roots to detect nitroaromatics and emit a signal wirelessly, relaying information to infrared cameras that can initiate email alerts to scientists identifying pollution, land

31 Ibid.

32 Ibid.

33 See "Coded Bias." Directed by Shalini Kantayya. 7th Empire Media, 2020; Buolamwini, J. *Written Testimony.* Hearing on Facial Recognition Technology (Part 1): Its Impact on our Civil Rights and Liberties, United States House Committee on Oversight and Government Reform, May 22, 2019.

34 Gallegos, I.O., Rossi, R.A., Barrow, J., Tanjim, M.M., Yu, T., Deilamsalehy, H., Zhang, R., Kim, S., and Dernoncourt, F. "Self-Debiasing Large Language Models: Zero-Shot Recognition and Reduction of Stereotypes." arXiv:2402.01981v1 [cs. CL] February 3, 2024, 1.

mines, other environmental conditions;[35] and yet, AI continues to erase the humanity of people of color while anthropomorphizing spinach. As acclaimed algorithmic researcher Dr. Joy Buolamwini testified before the U.S. Congress, 'failures of a broad set of facial analysis technologies including facial recognition technology have real and dire consequences for people's lives, including in critical areas such as law enforcement, housing, employment, and access to government services'.[36]

As artificial intelligence – including LAMS, LLMS, and other generative AI tools – is increasingly being deployed not only within judicial and ADR processes, but within public and private entities that serve to identify and refer cases, urgent concerns are raised about the lack of accuracy and disproportional negative impact on already marginalized and vulnerable populations in a variety of countries.[37] This includes lack of access for under-resourced populations including those in geographic regions without sufficient infrastructure to provide mobile phone coverage or Internet access. The digital divide persists when, out of a global population of 8.0 billion people, almost a third are without mobile phone access (2.39 billion people–30.6 percent) and 32 percent do not use the Internet (2.64 billion people).[38] And for those who do have access but are self-represented litigants or those who are

35 India Today Web Desk. "Spinach plants can now detect explosives, send email alert to researchers." *India Today*, February 3, 2021.

36 Buolamwini, J. *Written Testimony*. Hearing on Facial Recognition Technology (Part 1): Its Impact on our Civil Rights and Liberties, United States House Committee on Oversight and Government Reform, May 22, 2019, 2.

37 See Ibid for multiple examples in China, New Zealand, U.K., and U.S.

38 Kemp, S. "Digital 2024: Global Overview Report." *Datareportal*, January 31, 2024. https://datareportal.com/reports/digital-2024-global-overview-report Furthermore, the assumption that developed economies provide sufficient access is undercut by findings such as these in the U.S. where an estimated 42 million people do not have broadband access according to a 2021 study by BroadbandNow (Busby, J. Tanberk, J. and Cooper, T. "BroadbandNow Estimates Availability for all 50 States; Confirms that More than 42 Million Americans Do Not Have Access to Broadband." April 3, 2024. https://broadbandnow.com/research/fcc-broadband-overreporting-by-state); and findings that in homes with household incomes below $30,000/year, 29% had no smartphone, 44% had no home broadband, 46% had no computer, and the majority had no tablet while 26% were "smartphone-dependent" Internet users but had no broadband at home. While in homes with household incomes of $100,000/year all these technologies were 'nearly ubiquitous among adults.' M. Anderson and K. Madhumitha, *Digital Divide Persists Even as Lower-Income Americans Make Gains in Tech Adoption*, Pew Research Center, 7 May 2019. https://www.pewresearch.org/fact-tank/2019/05/07/digital-divide-persists-even-as-lowerincome-americans-make-gains-in-tech-adoption/

functionally illiterate in the language of the court, consider their risks if, seeking to reduce dockets, courts choose to require use of monolingual chatbots to negotiate on litigants' behalf as a step prior to accessing a hearing. Interestingly, such a feature could have the potential to either magnify or to help to reduce significant power imbalances between, for example, creditors and those in debt. The question arises then, who may benefit more? Likely repeat players such as creditors – those with access to the technology and who are most familiar with the court's way of using it.

> Consumer advocates … especially worry about the use of ODR in debt collection cases, which typically have an attorney representing the plaintiff and a self-represented defendant. … this power imbalance can lead to defendants feeling pressured into entering repayment agreements without raising legitimate defenses they may have. "So throwing an unrepresented party into this negotiating space online really threatens to re-create a lot of the abusive situations that happen in hallways or in courtrooms around the United States [April Kuehnhoff, staff attorney at the National Consumer Law Center in Boston states]".[39]

Courts face perennial allegations of inequality regarding procedural and substantive justice that too often bear out. And ADR processes have also faced their own related challenges: power imbalances, unequal outcomes for people of color, repeat player bias, and exclusionary practices in who are hired as third parties.[40] How might incorporating AI affect these longstanding concerns? What are the ways it could exacerbate them? 'Countless studies of new technologies emphasize how existing groups use the occasion of this new technology to reinforce or argue for power and position'.[41] What mechanisms need to be put in place so that patterns of inequalities do not play out when AI is embedded in ADR and court? In what ways could AI

39 Moran, L. "Online Dispute Resolution Promises to Increase Access to Justice, But Challenges Remain." *ABA Journal*, October/November 2021, 1–9.

40 Davis, B. "American Diversity in International Arbitration: A New Arbitration Story or Evidence of Things Not Seen," 88 *Fordham L. Rev.* 2143–2154 (May 2020); Thevenin, N. and Simpson, K. *Arbitrators of African Descent – with a U.S. Nexus*. August 2020; and Simpson, K. *Law Firm Names and Numbers*. June 2020.

41 Andrew D. Selbst, danah boyd, Sorelle A. Friedler, Suresh Venkatasubramanian, and Janet Vertesi. 2019. "Fairness and Abstraction in Sociotechnical Systems." In FAT* '19: Conference on Fairness, Accountability, and Transparency (FAT* '19), January 29–31, 2019, Atlanta, GA, USA. ACM, New York, NY, USA, 65. https://doi.org/10.1145/3287560.3287598

help us prevent the likelihood of such outcomes? These questions are important to raise here because while AI has a track record of perpetuating inequalities through reliance on biased and limited data, hope can reside in the creative and dedicated attention to preventing and tackling this not just by avoiding the use of AI, but by harnessing and cultivating its promise. Several key factors can point the way, such as designing algorithmic and data frames for input and output that require the inclusion of the social realities[42] of diversity and inequality; in other words, context must matter in coding and in dispute system design. This challenges typical programmer training – where portability is valued over context:[43]

> To treat fairness and justice as terms that have meaningful application to technology separate from a social context … make[s] a category error … an abstraction error … Key to this resolution is shifting away from a solutions-oriented approach to a process-oriented one – one that draws the boundary of abstraction to include social actors, institutions, and interactions.[44]

## 5 The Perils and Promise of Disruptive Innovation for Addressing AI Bias and Inequality

Experimentation with fair-Machine Learning (fair ML) with an eye towards its integration into larger systems that involve human actors can hold promise through

> thinking 'simultaneously about what different technical parts of the apparatus will do, and what the humans that operate, live alongside, and otherwise contribute to them will do as well … draw[ing] the boundaries of abstraction to include people and social systems as well, such as local incentives and reward structures, institutional environments, decision-making cultures and regulatory systems.[45]

42 Andrew D. Selbst, danah boyd, Sorelle A. Friedler, Suresh Venkatasubramanian, and Janet Vertesi. 2019. "Fairness and Abstraction in Sociotechnical Systems." In FAT* '19: Conference on Fairness, Accountability, and Transparency (FAT* '19), January 29–31, 2019, Atlanta, GA, USA. ACM, New York, NY, USA, 59–68. https://doi.org/10.1145/3287560.3287598

43 Ibid.

44 Ibid, 59–60.

45 Andrew D. Selbst, Danah Boyd, Sorelle A. Friedler, Suresh Venkatasubramanian, and Janet Vertesi. 2019. "Fairness and Abstraction in Sociotechnical Systems." In FAT* '19:

Inclusion of the social actors and the process, not only the outcome and technical aspects, when drawing abstraction boundaries in the design of LLMs offers potential for decreasing biased data generation, replication and magnification as, arguably 'by moving decisions made by humans and human institutions within the abstraction boundary, fairness of the system can again be analyzed as an end-to-end property of the sociotechnical frame'.[46] However, including social actors and processes within the abstraction boundaries will need to be purposeful since doing so goes beyond typical computer science training. How do we make this an expectation of design for LLMs and RAGs that will be used by those who employ AI in dispute handling? Such a shift is necessary since attention to context can be quite relevant to substantive justice in court and arbitration decisions and is vital to crafting mediation outcomes. Additionally, context can be instrumental in furthering or hindering access to procedural justice depending on whether universal design principles are utilized in the development and implementation of a process using AI; including attention to barriers to participation due to unequal access to the technology by the parties.[47]

Since RAGs can assist LLMs to contextualize outputs by expanding and specializing their knowledge base, such an approach is worth continuing to innovate. However, the promise that such innovation will address the needs of those most vulnerable to biased outputs remains an uphill challenge. For example, the use of RAGs could potentially enhance the accuracy of the output of LLMs to some extent by providing access to more context-specific knowledge outside an LLM's training sources by including all law review articles, trade journal articles, blogs, and materials from some private archives on a particular topic. However, this may still be insufficient since the RAG can still replicate and amplify biases prevalent in hegemonic narratives found in this expanded and curated database.[48] And in addition to the concerns raised previously about data and modeling bias regarding gender, race, nationality, culture, and legal jurisdiction, LLM data sets and algorithms have also proven to be biased in what they determine is important information to provide when assisting dispute resolvers in how they frame

Conference on Fairness, Accountability, and Transparency (FAT* '19), January 29–31, 2019, Atlanta, GA, USA. ACM, New York, NY, USA, 63–64. https://doi.org/10.1145/3287560.3287598

46 Ibid, 59.

47 Wing, L. "Artificial Intelligence and Online Dispute Resolution Systems Design: Lack of/Access to Justice Magnified." *International Journal of Online Dispute Resolution*, (4)2, 2017, 16–20.

48 This is resonant with the Chapter Three discussion of Anthropic's Constitutional AI strategy.

relevant questions about specific conflicts, legal cases, etc.[49] All of this can have significant implications for disputants, mediators, arbitrators, attorneys, judges, and other parties who rely on AI to generate relevant questions, case law citations, and frameworks for analyzing the origins and key attributes of conflicts, and to generate potential resolutions or render decisions. If a conflict is analyzed according to the views of only one party or only according to the most common framing of similar conflicts as presented in the LLM and RAG data sets, outputs will be biased. This not only will reduce access to justice, but if it occurs within the black box, it dramatically reduces the chances of being identified and addressed not only in a specific case, but in the judicial or informal dispute resolution system that relies on the LLM and RAG. This makes it quite challenging for disputants to successfully have the bias and unfairness redressed and, in turn, can have implications for the level of trust in third parties, fourth parties, and institutions such as courts.

Who then, should be responsible for preventing and addressing these challenges when harnessing AI? Who is typically invited to the proverbial table to set parameters for which sources of so-called authoritative knowledge are included in RAG development? To state it realistically, at present software developers continue to be the gatekeepers of the bounded universe of knowledge utilized via AI for generating responses which dispute resolvers rely upon for conflict assessment, options, and decisions. RAGs can provide access to newer and more specialized data even from private sources which are beyond the data an LLM was trained upon, however, it is still the views and decisions of those designing the RAG who reign. Given the creative innovations in generative AI that have taken the world by storm recently, further possibilities may be developed for preventing and addressing AI bias and hallucinations and there are those working on that who are aware that at present, 'the users who would benefit the most from legal LLMs are precisely those who the LLMs are least well-equipped to serve'.[50]

In the face of AI bias, computer science theory and practice continues to evolve and there are researchers and tech innovators seeking to tackle this

49 See Dahl, M., Magesh, V., Suzgun, M., and Ho, D.E. "Hallucinating Law: Legal Mistakes with Large Language Models are Pervasive." January 11, 2024. https://hai.stanford.edu/news/hallucinating-law-legal-mistakes-large-language-models-are-pervasive; Wing, 172–173 in Katsh, E., Draper, C., Ebner, N., Loebl, Z., Rainey, D., Ross, G., Rule, C., Vilalta, E. and Wing, L. "Comments on Artificial Intelligence." *International Journal of Online Dispute Resolution*, (9)2, 2022, 147–176.

50 Dahl, M., Magesh, V., Suzgun, M., and Ho, D.E. "Hallucinating Law: Legal Mistakes with Large Language Models are Pervasive." January 11, 2024. https://hai.stanford.edu/news/hallucinating-law-legal-mistakes-large-language-models-are-pervasive

within LLMs, particularly with regards to issues such as race, gender, religion and nationality.[51] This is vital given the long history of biased AI being fed into the bloodstream of our institutions, economies, and cultures and increasingly, into our dispute handling processes. As AI usage becomes ubiquitous in virtually every aspect of our lives through media, entertainment, transportation, education, medicine, and dispute resolution we have all become stakeholders in its design and output. When these AI tools are embedded in our systems of adjudicating disputes, dispensing justice, repairing relationships, and addressing needs through ADR and the courts, we must have higher aspirations and standards than the present state of what has been produced. Additionally, it is important to consider that some actors can purposefully seek to use AI to provide procedural and substantive inequality in dispute handling whether for profit or other motivations.

> A system can be designed to harness the power of big data and machine learning to identify characteristics[52] of a complainant to reduce costs and risks for repeat players. The data can then be used to provide different processes and outcomes dependent upon the characteristics of the complainant. For example, a company could employ algorithms in its in-house ODR platform that determines what is offered to a specific customer [in business-to-customer (B2C) disputes] or business [in business-to-business (B2B) disputes] complainant based on their assessed characteristics and the complainant's relationship with the company. The algorithms can be used to determine the likelihood of

51 Gallegos, I.O., Rossi, R.A., Barrow, J., Tanjim, M.M., Yu, T., Deilamsalehy, H., Zhang, R., Kim, S., and Dernoncourt, F. "Self-Debiasing Large Language Models: Zero-Shot Recognition and Reduction of Stereotypes." arXiv:2402.01981v1 [cs. CL] February 3, 2024; Joshi, R.K., Chatterjee, A. and Ekbal, A. "Saliency Guided Debiasing: Detecting and Mitigating Biases in LMs using Feature Attribution." *Neurocomputing*, Volume 563, 1 January 2024, 126851. Accessed at: https://www.sciencedirect.com/science/article/abs/pii/S0925231223009748; Ranaldi, L., Ruzzetti, E. S., Venditti, D., Onorati, D., & Zanzotto, F. M. (2023). "A Trip Towards Fairness: Bias and De-Biasing in Large Language Models." *arXiv (Cornell University)*. https://doi.org/10.48550/arxiv.2305.13862; Thakur, H., Jain, A., Vaddamanu, P., Liang, P.P., and Morency, L.-P. "Language Models Get a Gender Makeover: Mitigating Gender Bias with Few-Shot Data Interventions." *Proceedings of the 61st Annual Meeting of the Association for Computational Linguistics Volume 2: Short Papers*, Association for Computational Linguistics, 2023, 340–351.

52 These characteristics can be based on social group categories or personalized data, for example: location of purchaser in a high- or low-income neighbourhood, gender, race, age, country of purchase, purchase power based on credit card usage, the net worth of the complainant and the likely impact of their social media footprint on others who have significant purchasing power.

> increasing loyalty to the company if the complainant is given access to particular types of ODR or steps in an ODR process; or it can assess the outcome least costly to the company that the complainant is likely to settle for without escalating his or her complaint to social media or breaking the complainant's business relationship with the company.[53]

With the infusion of technology, particularly AI in dispute resolution processes, we need to consider how the software developer, LLM architect, RAG designer, and AI innovator are serving as gatekeepers not only to access to justice but to equal access to justice. We will be better positioned to maximize our potential for providing fair processes and outcomes when we recognize the role of these fifth parties[54] who structurally determine the technical architecture and delivery of services. Acknowledging the critical importance of this can help determine the most effective ways to reward– and when necessary, require – the use of innovations that deliver for all.

System design for the integration of AI and other technologies into any dispute management process is central to whether and how it can magnify risks and opportunities for access to justice and for whom. Therefore, it requires attention to transparency about technology's use and impact as well as 'what's under the hood' – providing visibility for how AI is functioning for the disputants and third parties. This is key to being able to prevent and as needed, to track and repair when it reproduces bias and inequality; and such visibility is crucial not only for ensuring fairness but also for increasing and maintaining trust in the courts, ADR, and ODR. As AI becomes further integrated into dispute handling processes, transparency about the level and type of reliance on technology versus human intervention, oversight, and decision-making throughout each stage of a dispute resolution process will help us to more effectively consider guidance and controlling governance tools for ensuring increased equal access to justice for all, including the most marginalized.

## 6 AI and the Parameters of ODR

The pandemic fed an acceleration in the widespread adoption of technology, particularly video conferencing, in courts and alternative dispute

---

53 Wing, L. "Artificial Intelligence and Online Dispute Resolution Systems Design: Lack of/Access to Justice Magnified." *International Journal of Online Dispute Resolution,* (4)2, 2017, 18–19.

54 See Parker-Toulson, S. *Online Dispute Resolution (ODR) and New Immigrants*. British Columbia: Ministry of Labour, Citizens' Services and Open Government, 2010, 13.

resolution fora and the post lockdown public access to use of AI chatbots for generating text are becoming a game changer[55] for decision making, problem-solving, and dispute resolution. For example, the business sector has integrated AI into customer service and hiring procedures, and to generate tools that a wide variety of sectors including dispute resolution use from off-the-shelf products to on-going services. As noted earlier, this explosion in the use of AI not only can positively impact how we resolve disputes, it also generates them:

> One biased human hiring manager can harm a lot of people in a year, and that's not great .... But an algorithm that is maybe used in all incoming applications at a large company ... could harm hundreds of thousands of applicants.[56]

Of course an individual who experiences the effects of biased AI in such a scenario likely has no easy way to know this has occurred even when they suspect it and they cannot prove this without transparency about the LLM design and algorithmic application. With AI generating disputes while also increasingly being incorporated into different phases of dispute management processes a rich discussion has gotten underway about what the parameters of online dispute resolution (ODR) actually are. This is not merely an intellectual exercise since the framing of parameters of ODR has ramifications for training and the formal education of those in the legal and ADR field, for dispute system design, and of particular importance to our examination, in what forms of oversight and governance mechanisms are required for artificial intelligence and other technologies to protect individual members of society at large and trust in its institutions.

The National Center for Technology and Dispute Resolution[57] noted the robust discussion underway about ODR's parameters among seasoned ODR

---

55 By 2023 there were more than 100 million generative AI users according to the U.S. Government Accountability Office, June 13, 2023. https://www.gao.gov/products/gao-23-106782 Last accessed February 18, 2024. PricewaterhouseCoopers predicts "that 45% of total economic gains by 2030 will come from product enhancements, stimulating consumer demand. This is because AI will drive greater product variety, with increased personalisation, attractiveness and affordability over time." "PwC's Global Artificial Intelligence Study: Exploiting the AI Revolution." https://www.pwc.com/gx/en/issues/data-and-analytics/publications/artificial-intelligence-study.html Last accessed February 18, 2024.

56 Hilke Schellmann in Lytton, C. "AI hiring tools may be filtering out the best job applicants." *BBC*, February 16, 2024. https://www.bbc.com/worklife/article/20240214-ai-recruiting-hiring-software-bias-discrimination Last accessed February 17, 2024.

57 The National Center for Technology and Dispute Resolution (NCTDR), where ODR first began, is, (despite its name), an international organization that supports and sustains

practitioners as well as the greatly expanded number of new adherents in the wake of lockdown. In recognition of how significant the articulation of the boundaries of ODR are to ethical practice, NCTDR developed and issued an ODR Framework[58] that provides a continuum based on the amount of reliance on humans and technology and it can serve as a useful tool for examining the complex, changeable, and interwoven roles that technology can play within dispute management systems and processes along with their attendant risks and opportunities. The continuum is presented as a *description* of the discussion in the field – *not a proscription*–about the depth and breadth of what can be considered ODR. It includes a broad framing of ODR such as being 'inclusive of any process or intervention used to handle disputes that employs electronic communications and other information and communication technologies'[59] and as such, that could encompass the entire ODR Framework from Levels 1–5 in [Figure 5.2]. Alternatively, for those viewing ODR within more limited parameters, they can use the Framework to articulate where they see the boundaries of ODR, placing restrictions on technology's usage–its purpose, role, impact, the amount of reliance on it, who can employ it, or when it can be used – for example, and where it may fall along the continuum either by Level or by usage within Levels. No doubt as new technologies emerge and as experimentation continues with incorporating AI in new and varied ways, the boundaries of ODR's parameters will continue to be discussed and therefore, it was presented as a living ODR Framework with future updates to be anticipated.[60]

For our purposes, an examination of the ODR Framework can illustrate the multiple entry points in a system or process where AI can have an impact: on the creation and dissemination of data by and to all the parties; on the roles of disputants, human third parties, and fourth parties; and thus, impacting process and outcome. The ODR Framework in [Figure 5.2] provides examples of 'moments' referred to as Levels within a dispute resolution process in which technology may be included. Levels are articulated for

---

the development of information technology applications, institutional resources, and theoretical and applied knowledge for better understanding and managing conflict. At the time of writing, NCTDR has 54 Fellows from 26 countries on six continents and has served as an international leader and resource in developing the field of online dispute resolution since its founding in 1998.

58 Wing, L. with Draper, C., principal authors. *Framing the Parameters of Online Dispute Resolution*. National Center for Technology and Dispute Resolution, 2022.

59 National Center for Technology and Dispute Resolution. *Ethical Principles for Online Dispute Resolution*, http://odr.info/ethics-and-odr/.

60 At this point, we can envision an upcoming revision to include the fifth party – whether human or artificial intelligence – that function as dispute system designers, software developers, and AI generators, for example.

Used with permission from Chris Draper and Leah Wing

**Level 0: Dispute Handling with No Technology**
Any dispute handling process that is executed without any assistance from technology (e.g.: no electronic document sharing, shared e-calendars). When a Level 0 system includes a mediator, arbitrator, judge, or some other neutral party, it would be considered mediation, arbitration, a court proceeding, etc. When a Level 0 system does not include a neutral party, it would be considered a negotiation. *Note: Two disputing parties are shown for illustrative purposes only, it is also relevant to scenarios with multiple parties negotiating.*

**Level 1: Technology Assisted Dispute Handling**
Any dispute handling process that includes technology assistance (e.g.: case management, real-time video conferencing, or asynchronous tools like document sharing and collaborative writing). Technologies used in a Level 1 system will not take actions without direction from a human participant. These technologies in a Level 1 third party process (such as mediation or arbitration) will typically be provided or controlled by the third party and will not connect to any platform that may be used by any of the participants. For example, any documents shared in a video conferencing platform would not automatically transfer into any of the parties' storage systems in the cloud. In a Level 1 negotiation, these technologies will typically be jointly controlled by the parties. For example, if video conferencing were used in Level 1 mediation, the third party would start the session, invite the parties in, and manage access to the system. In a Level 1 negotiation, no third-party human is responsible for the management of the technology.

**Level 2: Partially Automated Dispute Handling**
In Level 2, independently directed technology platforms may employ process automations or directly communicate with each other to perform specific tasks supporting a dispute handling process (e.g.: process automations could include automated incident submission or automated acknowledgement). For example, in Level 2, the parties could each choose to use different document management systems to communicate with a third party or each other. A Level 2 third party process could include grievance handling systems where a user submitting an issue via a form prompts the technology to create a case, conduct an intake, notify all parties, and assign a mediator; it could also provide an AI-generated analysis for decision making by the disputing parties or a third party. Level 2 negotiation could include systems that use natural language processing to read a party submission, perform a sentiment analysis, and offer the receiving party insights that may influence that party's next action.

**Level 3: Human Managed Technological Dispute Handling**
In Level 3, fully integrated technology systems automate many elements of the ODR process, yet human third-party oversight is required to ensure compliance with the process; (e.g.: technology provides adherence to all procedural and ethical obligations; offers choice or direction to the parties for utilizing the technology). Level 3 would be considered "human in the loop" systems that cannot be completed without actions being taken by the third party or negotiators. Level 3 negotiation systems would restrict the actions that could be taken by a party (e.g.: tools that facilitate the sharing of monetary proposals), yet not restricting party choices during negotiation.

**Level 4: Technology Directed Dispute Handling**
In Level 4, fully integrated technology systems do not require input from a human third party, yet a human third party may influence the ODR process (e.g.: through system design or help desk assisting with a technical or process problem). Level 4 would be considered "human on the loop" systems that may use event or decision trees, expert systems, or other guiding technologies to assist as parties reduce the number of available options during the decision-making process. Decision support technologies incorporated into a Level 4 system are human designed and outcomes or recommendations can be overridden by humans. *Note: Most eCommerce platforms and many filtering ODR technologies are Level 4 ODR.*

**Level 5: Fully Automated Dispute Handling**
Level 5 fully integrated technology systems do not allow a human third party to influence the process. Level 5 would be considered "human out of the loop" systems that may rely on anything from human designed to AI-based algorithms to drive any decision-making process in a manner that prevents influence by any human third party, negotiator, or human administrator. An example could be a workplace insurance policy that requires an AI-driven arbitration. In this case, if an individual is injured at work, the Level 5 ODR system would determine if a payout is awarded and how much. The system could scan the actuarial tables and the individual's claim history, medical records, and social media feeds; evaluate them in terms of consistency, legitimacy, and the compensation value of the claimed injuries; and provide a decision that all parties previously agreed could not be appealed to any human.

FIGURE 5.2 ODR framework
WING, L. WITH DRAPER, C., PRINCIPAL AUTHORS. *FRAMING THE PARAMETERS OF ONLINE DISPUTE RESOLUTION*. NATIONAL CENTER FOR TECHNOLOGY AND DISPUTE RESOLUTION, 2022, 7.

the purpose of highlighting increased reliance on technology and reduced reliance on humans along an ODR Technology Dependence Continuum; beginning in Level 0 with no use of technology (thus, not considered part of ODR) and proceeding to Level 5 which has no possibility of human intervention. In reality of course, dispute handling processes have more fluidity and travel with multi-directionality between Levels sometimes multiple times in the course of a case. Despite this, distinguishing between the Levels can help us identify opportunities, risks, and responsibilities that attend increasing reliance on technology and decreasing reliance on humans.[61] Several examples are provided to illustrate the relationships between humans, AI, and other technologies to highlight the fact that the impact of technology can manifest differently within the Levels relating to: who must or can choose to rely on it, its role (ie: administrative functions, security, diagnosis, option generation, decision-making, etc.), the point in a process when it is employed (ie: prevention, management, resolution, implementation, etc.), and the types and amount of human involvement and control.

Articulating what the parameters are for the actual and potential use of artificial intelligence and other forms of technology in ODR makes clear how impactful they can be on the process and outcome far beyond merely enhancing efficiency, by exponentially expanding the knowledge base humans and AI can employ to prevent, identify, analyze and resolve conflicts. The ODR Framework could be useful in a myriad of ways to enhance ethical dispute processing that incorporates AI and other technologies. This framing of the parameters could be used to examine the impact of a role for AI and, for example, illustrate an in/appropriate time in a process when it could be used to influence options generation. And whether this enhances or raises risks to procedural or substantive fairness could depend on if, by that point in the process, participants were informed about their loss of control over decisions or are given the choice to gain insights from artificial intelligence generated responses. It could also be used to consider how AI can serve in multiple roles to support the implementation and monitoring of a final decision or agreement.

Given the tremendous potential, demonstrated abilities, and ubiquitous presence of AI in other aspects of our lives, we should anticipate that it will become increasingly embedded in dispute handling inside and outside of the field of dispute resolution. The ODR Framework is but one tool to help us contemplate this burgeoning reality, to find additional ways to incorporate technologies to resolve conflicts and further understanding and healing. And given the present and predicted exponential increase in the power of

61 And, some may argue, the reverse.

AI,[62] its replication of biases, and in the on-going inequalities in access to justice, the Framework will hopefully stimulate further thinking about the necessary mechanisms of governance for AI usage in ODR.

> Without addressing bias within AI, we will risk adding creativity and efficiency to our ODR processes on the backs of some of the same people and viewpoints already burdened and excluded from equal access to justice offline.[63]

In other words, we must develop structures of accountability so that rather than compound bias, 'ODR design and delivery must respond to inequalities in society: No code, no justice'.[64] Guardrails are clearly required as well as incentives to accomplish these goals wherever technology is at play – whether creating conflicts or being employed to resolve them. They are therefore needed both locally and on an international scale–in ways that are relevant within and across sectors, legal jurisdictions, and cultures. And there are a growing number of efforts globally to enact AI governance measures in a variety of fields and jurisdictions.[65] Similar calls for attention to

---

62 See PricewaterhouseCoopers. "PwC's Global Artificial Intelligence Study: Exploiting the AI Revolution." https://www.pwc.com/gx/en/issues/data-and-analytics/publications/artificial-intelligence-study.html Last accessed February 18, 2024 and Katsh, E. and Rabinovich-Einy, O. *Digital Justice: Technology and the Internet of Disputes*. Oxford: Oxford U. Press, 2017.

63 Wing in Katsh, E., Draper, C., Ebner, N., Loebl, Z., Rainey, D., Ross, G., Rule, C., Vilalta, L. and Wing, L. "Comments on Artificial Intelligence." *International Journal of Online Dispute Resolution*, (9)2, 2022, 176.

64 Wing, L. *Tech Infused Dispute Resolution: Creativity for Social Good. Poetry in Motion.* International, Comparative, Foreign and Domestic: A Virtual Gathering of Friends, University of Toledo College of Law, January 22, 2021.

65 As noted in earlier chapters, and see International Association for Privacy Professionals (IAPP), 'Global AI Law and Policy Tracker', *Research and Insights*, January 2024. https://iapp.org/media/pdf/resource_center/global_ai_law_policy_tracker.pdf Institute of Electrical and Electronics Engineers, *Ethical Principles & Standards for Artificial Intelligence and Autonomous Systems*. IEEE Standards Association 2016; European Parliament, *Proposal for a Regulation of the European Parliament and of the Council Laying Down Harmonised Rules on Artificial Intelligence (Artificial Intelligence Act) and Amending Certain Union Legislative Acts*. 2021/0106(COD) Draft [Final draft as updated on 21/01]. 21-01-2024 at 17h11; Prime Minister of Vietnam, Decision No. 127/QD-TTg by the Prime Minister on the National Strategy on AI research, development and application until 2023, adopted on January 26, 2021; U.S. Government Accountability Office, June 13, 2023. https://www.gao.gov/products/gao-23-106782 (last accessed February 18, 2024); and *The Blueprint for an AI Bill of Rights: Making Automated Systems Work for the American People*. The White House Office of Science and Technology Policy, October 2022.

this within the dispute resolution field[66] have not gone unheeded. And fortunately, they are beginning to bear fruit in ways that mirror the positive disruptive nature of technology – following its pathways across the silos and boundaries of disciplines and legal jurisdictions.

## 7 ODR Standards and AI: State of Play

With the growth over the past 25 years of the use of technology in dispute resolution there has been a slow development of governance mechanisms for ODR in general and, only recently for ODR and AI in particular.

What follows is a brief overview of the context of the development of ODR Standards and the state of play regarding the relatively recent inclusion of artificial intelligence in them and other ODR governance tools. The National Center for Technology and Dispute Resolution (NCTDR), the international organization that is the birthplace of ODR, issued a first set of international ODR Standards in 2009 (which did not reference AI) to assist in the development of its governance and further the conversation about how technology impacts the ethics of dispute generation and management.

These Standards had immediate international impact through their adoption in 2009 by the Internet Corporation for Assigned Names and Numbers (ICANN) in its handling of Internet domain name disputes. Awareness of the benefits and potential of ODR grew particularly in the commercial sector and some international bodies began to discuss regulation that could promote trust in cross-border e-commerce. For example, the *2009 EC Directive*

66 Cuellar, M., and J. L. Mashaw. 2016. *Regulatory Decision-Making and Economic Analysis.* Working Paper Series, Paper No. 525, John Olin Program in Law and Economics, Stanford Law School; Scherer, M.U. "Regulating Artificial Intelligence Systems: Risks, Challenges, Competencies, and Strategies." *Harvard Journal of Law & Technology.* 2016, 29(2): 353–400. Wing, L. "Artificial Intelligence and Online Dispute Resolution Systems Design: Lack of/Access to Justice Magnified." *International Journal of Online Dispute Resolution,* Vol. 4, No. 2, 2017, 16–20; Wing, L., Martinez, J., Katsh, E. and Rule, C. "Designing Ethical Online Dispute Resolution Systems: The Rise of the Fourth Party." *Negotiation Journal* 37(1), Special Issue: Artificial Intelligence, Technology, and Negotiation, Winter 2021, 49–64; Alessa, H. "The role of Artificial Intelligence in Online Dispute Resolution: A Brief and Critical Overview," *Information & Communications Technology Law,* 31:3, 319–342, 2022; Joint Technology Committee of the Conference of State Court Administrators (COSCA), the National Association for Court Management (NACM) and the National Center for State Courts (NCSC). *Introduction to AI for Courts.* Version 1.0 Adopted 27 March 2020; Ngo Nguyen, T.V. "AI Implementation in ODR: A Game-Changer or a Troublemaker of Data Protection." *Vietnamese Journal of Legal Sciences,* 2023, Vol. 08, No. 01, 01–24; and Abbott, R., Brinson, S.E., and The Cantellus Group. *Putting the Artificial intelligence in Alternative Dispute Resolution: How AI Rules Will Become ADR Rules.* 685Amicus Curiae, Series 2, 2023, Vol 4, No 3, 685–706.

*of the European Parliament and Council on Injunctions for the Protection of Consumers' Interests*[67] and the *2013 Regulation of the European Parliament and Council on Online Dispute Resolution for Consumer Disputes*[68] were issued although neither made explicit mention of standards for ODR or of AI usage within it. International collaboration was undertaken by the United Nations Commission on International Trade Law (UNCITRAL) regarding regulating technologies for online dispute resolution and resulted in an issuance of Technical Notes (with no mention of AI). In 2010 UNCITRAL observed that due to:

> the sharp increase of online cross-border transactions and the parallel need for mechanisms for resolving disputes arising from such transactions, the United Nations Commission on International Trade Law (UNCITRAL) agreed, at its forty-third session,[69] to undertake work in the field of online dispute resolution. UNCITRAL finalized and adopted the Technical Notes on Online Dispute Resolution at its forty-ninth session in 2016. The Technical Notes on Online Dispute Resolution are non-binding, and take the form of a descriptive document, reflecting elements of an online dispute resolution process.[70]

Seeking to further the work on ODR governance, in 2016, NCTDR published Ethical Principles for Online Dispute Resolution,[71] stating that the purpose was:

> to enhance the quality, effectiveness, and scope of dispute resolution processes with technological components ... [to] provide a touchstone for best practices, standards, rules, qualifications, and certification efforts in dispute resolution and related fields that address dispute resolution processes and practices. This document builds on previous work by the National Center for Technology and Dispute Resolution on principles and standards of practice as well as the growing body of

67 See Directive 2009/22/EC of the European Parliament and of the Council of 23 April 2009 on Injunctions for the Protection of Consumers' Interests.

68 See Regulation (EU) No 524/2013 of the European Parliament and of the Council of 21 May 2013 on Online Dispute Resolution for Consumer Disputes and Amending Regulation (EC) No 2006/2004 and Directive 2009/22/EC (Regulation on Consumer ODR).

69 Official records of the General Assembly, Sixty-fifth Session, Supplement No. 17 (A/65/17), para. 257.

70 United Nations. *UNCITRAL Technical Notes on Online Dispute Resolution*. United Nations: United Nations Commission on International Trade Law. April 2017, iii. These Technical Notes do not directly address AI.

71 See https://odr.info/ethics-and-odr/

> literature and the standards of numerous professional, governmental, and commercial bodies concerning ODR and dispute resolution more generally … With the rapidly growing adoption of ODR in a number of sectors it is timely to produce a living document of ethical principles integral to the design, structure, practices, and implementation of online dispute resolution systems. Therefore, while debate will likely continue over time about the definition and scope of ODR and what practices and standards should be formalized, if any, it is hoped that the creation of these Ethical Principles for Online Dispute Resolution can provide a benchmark for these discussions and for systems development, usage, and the integration of ODR into existing institutions.[72]

Having articulated a set of shared values and not standards it was hoped that the Principles could serve as aspirational guidance for very diverse stakeholders, including dispute resolvers with no training on the implications of deploying technology, courts concerned about due process, consumers' rights advocates, and businesses and legislative bodies invested in fostering cross-border trade. And importantly, given the dearth of governance for ODR, it was hoped that the Principles could go some way to fill the gap and stimulate further development of such mechanisms.

In the late 2010s, a growing body of scholarship and rich discussions were taking place as stakeholders explored ODR's value-add, its risks, and ways to address them. In this landscape it became increasingly clear to greater numbers of people that technology impacts process, can impact outcomes and, in fact, arguably that once utilized in dispute resolution, it 'becomes a party to the dispute in that it alters the dynamics of the dispute engagement process'.[73] This led to increasing calls from within and outside the field for necessary guardrails for the use of technology since it was unaccounted for in traditional ethical standards for dispute resolution.[74] As part of these efforts,

72 National Center for Technology and Dispute Resolution. *Ethical Principles for Online Dispute Resolution*. 2016. https://odr.info/ethics-and-odr/

73 Rainey, D. *Making Friends with the Fourth Party: Integrating Technology into Your Dispute Resolution Practice*. The Hague: Eleven Publishing, 2022, 15.

74 See Wing, L., Martinez, J., Katsh, E. and Rule, C. "Designing Ethical Online Dispute Resolution Systems: The Rise of the Fourth Party." *Negotiation Journal* 37(1), Special Issue: Artificial Intelligence, Technology, and Negotiation, Winter 2021, 49–64; Anderson, Dorcas Quek. "Ethical Concerns in Court-Connected Online Dispute Resolution." *International Journal of Online Dispute Resolution*, Vol 5 issue 1–2 (2018), 20–38; Cortés, P. "Regulatory Developments in Mediation and in Technology Supported Mediation Schemes in the UK." *Computer and Telecommunications Law Review*, (2017) 23(8),

NCTDR used the Ethical Principles for ODR as a foundation for issuing an updated set of ODR Standards in 2017 and that same year it founded the International Council for Online Dispute Resolution (ICODR)[75] as a standards-setting and membership organization.

The pandemic lockdown exponentially grew the numbers of courts and ADR practitioners applying tech to their processes, with necessity driving those who may have never have previously considered using video conferencing, for example. With arguably hundreds of thousands of practitioners globally now experimenting with at least some forms of ODR, along with the millions they were serving, new adherents were born along with

---

208–212.; Cortés, P. and Cole, T. "Legislating for an Effective and Legitimate System of Online Consumer Arbitration" in M. Piers and C. Aschauer, *Arbitration in the Digital Age: The Brave New World of Arbitration*. Cambridge: Cambridge University Press, 2018, 207–243; Ebner, N., and J. Zeleznikow. 2016. No Sheriff in Town: Governance for the ODR Field. *Negotiation Journal* 32(4): 297–323; Katsh, E., Draper, C., Ebner, N., Loebl, Z., Rainey, D., Ross, G., Rule, C., Vilalta, E. and Wing, L. "Comments on Artificial Intelligence." *International Journal of Online Dispute Resolution*, (9)2, 2022, 147–176; Katsh, E. and Rabinovich-Einy, O. (2017). *Digital Justice: Technology and the Internet of Disputes*. Oxford: Oxford U. Press; Liyanage, K. C. 2012. "The Regulation of Online Dispute Resolution: Effectiveness of Online Consumer Protection Guidelines." *Deakin Law Review* 17(2): 251–282; Daniel Rainey. "Creating Standards for ODR." "*International Journal of Online Dispute Resolution*, 2017 (4) 2, 21–26; Raymond, A. H., and S. J. Shackelford. 2014. "Technology, Ethics, and Access to Justice: Should an Algorithm be Deciding Your Case?" *Michigan Journal of International Law* 35(3): 485–524; Amy J. Schmitz. "A Blueprint for Online Dispute Resolution System Design." *Journal of Internet Law*, (2018), 21(7), 3–11.; Amy J. Schmitz. "Expanding Access to Remedies through E-Court Initiatives," *Buffalo Law Review*, 67, 2019, 101–173; Amy J. Schmitz and Colin Rule, *The New Handshake: Online Dispute Resolution and the Future of Consumer Protection*. American Bar Association Section on Dispute Resolution (2017); Wing, L. "Artificial Intelligence and Online Dispute Resolution Systems Design: Lack of/Access to Justice Magnified." *International Journal of Online Dispute Resolution*, Vol. 4, No. 2, 2017, 16–20; *Joint Technology Committee of the National Center for State Courts that has developed a set of Court Technology Standards*. https://www.ncsc.org/About-us/Committees/Joint-Technology-Committee/JTC-Court-Technology-Standards.aspx Last visited November 30, 2019; *Civil Legal System Modernization*, at https://www.pewtrusts.org/en/projects/civil-legal-system-modernization Last visited Dec. 18, 2019; Jim Melamed, *Establishing Standards for Online Domestic Relations Mediation*, MEDIATE.COM (July 2019), https://www.mediate.com/articles/OnlineDomRelMediationStandards.cfm Last visited Jul 22, 2019; Joint Technology Committee of the Conference of State Court Administrators (COSCA), the National Association for Court Management (NACM) and the National Center for State Courts (NCSC). *Introduction to AI for Courts*. Version 1.0 Adopted 27 March 2020. And for a detailed overview of additional earlier literature through 2016, see Wing, L. "Ethical Principles for Online Dispute Resolution: A GPS Device for the Field." 3 *International Journal of Online Dispute Resolution*, 12–29, 11–15 (2016).

75 https://icodr.org/

expectations that the benefits gained should not be lost once lockdown ended. More people joined the conversation about how to deliver quality services without compromising cherished rights and values of dispute handling processes. A number of regional governing bodies, courts, and ADR organizations responded by issuing some form of guidance or guardrails regarding ODR[76] and at the time of writing, a few have addressed artificial intelligence.[77]

76 An archive of ODR Standards and Guidance is accessible to the public for free on the NCTDR website: https://odr.info/. What follows are a number of examples. Asia-Pacific Economic Cooperation (APEC). *Study on Best Practices Using ODR*, January 2023; The National Center for Technology and Dispute Resolution and International Council for Online Dispute Resolution. *Online Dispute Resolution Standards*, May 2022; The International Institute for Conflict Prevention and Resolution, Inc. *Annotated Model Procedural Order for Remote Video Arbitration Proceedings*, 2021; APEC Committee on Trade and Investment. *Public-Private Dialogue (PPD) on Promoting Consumer Protection in the Dispute Resolution and Redress Mechanisms of eCommerce Summary Report*, September 2021; Council of Europe. *Guidelines of the Committee of Ministers of the Council of Europe on Online Dispute Resolution Mechanisms in Civil and Administrative Court Proceedings*, 2021; American Arbitration Association-International Centre for Dispute Resolution. *Model Order and Procedures for a Virtual Hearing via Videoconference*, 2021; American Arbitration Association-International Centre for Dispute Resolution. *Virtual Hearing Guide for Arbitrators and Parties Utilizing Zoom*, 2021; The Chartered Institute of Arbitrators (CIArb). *Guidance Note on Remote Dispute Resolution* Proceedings, 2020; International Chamber of Commerce. *Guidance Note on Possible Measures Aimed at Mitigating the Effects of COVID-19*, 2020; International Chamber of Commerce. *Interim Measures: Practical Considerations for Arbitrators*, 2020. Hong Kong International Arbitration Centre. *Guidelines for Virtual Hearings*, 2020; International Council for Commercial Arbitration, New York City Bar, and CPR International Institute for Conflict Prevention and Resolution. *Protocol on Cybersecurity in International Arbitration*, 2020; African Arbitration Academy. *Protocol on Virtual Hearings in Africa*, 2020; Korean Commercial Arbitration Board International. *Seoul Protocol on Video Conferencing in International Arbitration*, 2020; Michigan Supreme Court Office of Dispute Resolution. *Using Zoom to Conduct Online Mediation: Considerations and Resources for Community Dispute Resolution Program Centers*, 2020; American Bar Association, Section of Litigation and Judicial Division. *Virtual Courts in the COVID-19 Era and Beyond*, June 2020; APEC. *Collaborative Framework for Online Dispute Resolution of Cross-Border Business to Business Disputes*, 2019.

77 For some examples, see African Arbitration Academy. *Protocol on Virtual Hearings in Africa*, 2020; Asia-Pacific Economic Cooperation (APEC). *Collaborative Framework for Online Dispute Resolution of Cross-Border Business to Business Disputes*, 2019; Asia-Pacific Economic Cooperation (APEC) Committee on Trade and Investment. *Public-Private Dialogue (PPD) on Promoting Consumer Protection in the Dispute Resolution and Redress Mechanisms of eCommerce Summary Report*, September 2021; Asia-Pacific Economic Cooperation (APEC). *Study on Best Practices Using ODR*, January 2023; and Council of Europe. *Guidelines of the Committee of Ministers of the Council of Europe on*

Below are a few examples presented in chronological order of their issuance, highlighting areas of foci regarding AI:

Asia-Pacific Economic Cooperation (APEC):

> The use of artificial intelligence or other modern technology is encouraged in any of the three stages [negotiation, mediation arbitration].[78]

African Arbitration Academy:

> Where possible, procure the use of Artificial Intelligence for continuous user authentication, facial recognition, silhouette tracking, and multifactorial authentication.[79]

The Global Initiative for Inclusive ICTs:

> Artificial Intelligence (AI) and machine learning could help courts digitize important legal documents that, unlike paper or images, can be read by assistive technologies for persons with disabilities. Similarly, technology, including video and collaboration software as well as artificial and virtual reality, can support remote participation of persons with disabilities in court proceedings, including with live captioning to provide additional support for those with auditory and other disabilities.[80]

Asia-Pacific Economic Cooperation (APEC):

> Artificial intelligence can play a valuable role in advancing and facilitating Online Dispute Resolution (ODR), but the development of Artificial Intelligence (AI) and algorithms must be based on ethical

---

*Online Dispute Resolution Mechanisms in Civil and Administrative Court Proceedings*, 2021. The Global Initiative for Inclusive ICTs (G3ict). *Advancing the Rights to Digital Access for Persons with Disabilities*, June 2020. Stockholm Chamber of Commerce. *SCC Guide to the Use of Artificial Intelligence in Cases Administered Under the SCC Rules*, October 2024.

78 APEC. *Collaborative Framework for Online Dispute Resolution of Cross-Border Business to Business Disputes*, 2019, 1.

79 African Arbitration Academy. *Protocol on Virtual Hearings in Africa*, 2020, 12.

80 The Global Initiative for Inclusive ICTs (G3ict). *Advancing the Rights to Digital Access for Persons with Disabilities*, June 2020, 5.

> principles and be free of bias or other features that would lead to unfairness in its decision-making process. Online Dispute Resolution (ODR) systems should undergo regular and systematic review of the rules and algorithms to ensure that they are unbiased and result in fair outcomes.[81]

Council of Europe:

> *Right to a reasoned decision*[:] Sufficient reasons should be given for decisions reached using ODR or with the assistance of ODR, in particular the decisions reached with the involvement of AI mechanisms.[82]
>
> *Right to judicial review in cases involving purely automated decisions*[:] Where national law allows for purely automated decisions, such decisions should be open to review before a judge.[83]
>
> The guidelines do not apply to internal management systems of electronic case files by the courts. This includes, for example, the algorithm for allocation of cases among the judges.[84]
>
> The guidelines cover such ODR techniques as: … iii. artificial intelligence systems, big data analysis techniques and automation, to the extent that they affect court proceedings.[85]
>
> Guideline 32[:] 67 … Special consideration should be given by member States to the Guidelines on Artificial Intelligence and Data Protection

81 APEC Committee on Trade and Investment. *Public-Private Dialogue (PPD) on Promoting Consumer Protection in the Dispute Resolution and Redress Mechanisms of eCommerce Summary Report*, September 2021, 17.

82 Council of Europe. *Guidelines of the Committee of Ministers of the Council of Europe on Online Dispute Resolution Mechanisms in Civil and Administrative Court Proceedings*, 2021, 9. Italics in the original.

83 Council of Europe. *Guidelines of the Committee of Ministers of the Council of Europe on Online Dispute Resolution Mechanisms in Civil and Administrative Court Proceedings*, 2021, 9. Italics in the original.

84 Council of Europe. *Guidelines of the Committee of Ministers of the Council of Europe on Online Dispute Resolution Mechanisms in Civil and Administrative Court Proceedings*, 2021, 19.

85 Council of Europe. *Guidelines of the Committee of Ministers of the Council of Europe on Online Dispute Resolution Mechanisms in Civil and Administrative Court Proceedings*, 2021, 21.

> adopted in 2019 by the Consultative Committee of the Convention for the Protection of Individuals with regard to Automatic Processing of Personal Data (T-PD) of the Council of Europe.[86]

National Center for Technology and Dispute Resolution (NCTDR) and International Council on Online Dispute Resolution (ICODR):

An updated set of Online Dispute Resolution Standards issued in May 2022 by NCTDR and ICODR articulates nine standards, each of which have relevance to artificial intelligence and three of which explicitly discuss it:

> 2. Accountable[:] ODR systems must be continuously accountable to the institutions, legal frameworks, and communities that they serve. ODR platforms must be auditable and the audit made available to users. This must include human oversight of: i) traceability of the originality of documents and of the path to outcome when artificial intelligence is employed, ii) determination of the relative control given to human and artificial decision-making strategies, iii) outcomes, and iv) the process of ensuring availability of outcomes to the parties.[87]
>
> 5. Equal[:] ... ODR must provide access to process instructions, security, confidentiality, and data control to all parties. ODR must strive to ensure on an on-going basis that no process or technology incorporated into ODR provides any party with a technological or informational advantage due to its use of ODR. Bias must be proactively avoided in all processes, contexts, and regarding party characteristics. ODR system design must include proactive efforts to prevent any artificial intelligence decision-making function from creating, replicating, or compounding bias in process or outcome. Human oversight is required in ODR system design and auditing to identify bias, make

86 Council of Europe. *Guidelines of the Committee of Ministers of the Council of Europe on Online Dispute Resolution Mechanisms in Civil and Administrative Court Proceedings*, 2021, 39.

87 The National Center for Technology and Dispute Resolution and International Council for Online Dispute Resolution. *Online Dispute Resolution Standards*, May 2022, 2. https://odr.info/wp-content/uploads/2022/05/NCTDR_and_ICODR_ODR_Standards_2022.pdf

> findings transparent to ODR providers and users, and eliminate bias in ODR processes and outcomes.[88]
>
> 9. Transparent[:] … The sources and methods used to gather any data that influences any decision made by artificial intelligence must be disclosed to all parties. ODR that uses artificial intelligence must publicly affirm compliance with jurisdictionally relevant legislation, regulations, or in their absence, guidelines on transparency and fairness of artificial intelligence systems. ODR must clearly disclose the role and magnitude of technology's influence on restricting or generating options and in final decisions or outcome.[89]

Asia-Pacific Economic Cooperation (APEC):

> Advanced technologies like Artificial Intelligence (AI) and machine learning, which are an integral component of ODR, remain largely untapped by ADR providers and the justice system.[90]
>
> C. The ODR Platform Should Include Algorithmic Tools to Help Parties Find a Resolution Without the Help of a Neutral Third Party[:] … During the negotiation stage, algorithmic tools enable the parties to communicate and negotiate within the online platform … The computer-led ODR process saves on the cost of hiring lawyers, neutrals, or arbitrators, at least during the initial stage, where most disputes are being resolved. Algorithms deliver instant answers, greatly reducing timelines for dispute resolution.[91]
>
> D. ODR Should Include the Use of Advanced Technology Such as Artificial Intelligence[:] The APEC ODR Collaborative Framework states that modern technologies such as artificial intelligence should be

---

88 The National Center for Technology and Dispute Resolution and International Council for Online Dispute Resolution. *Online Dispute Resolution Standards*, May 2022, 3. https://odr.info/wp-content/uploads/2022/05/NCTDR_and_ICODR_ODR_Standards_2022.pdf

89 The National Center for Technology and Dispute Resolution and International Council for Online Dispute Resolution. *Online Dispute Resolution Standards*, May 2022, 4. https://odr.info/wp-content/uploads/2022/05/NCTDR_and_ICODR_ODR_Standards_2022.pdf

90 Asia-Pacific Economic Cooperation (APEC). *Study on Best Practices Using ODR*, January 2023, 6.

91 Asia-Pacific Economic Cooperation (APEC). *Study on Best Practices Using ODR*, January 2023, 9.

> incorporated into the design of ODR platforms whenever possible.[92] … Artificial Intelligence, or AI, could power the components of ODR, such as handling multiple languages, guiding dispute resolution, evaluating cases, facilitating mediation, or AI-only mediation and adjudication. AI has the potential to simplify, accelerate, and even out the dispute resolution process. By its nature, AI improves as it accrues data. However, today's AI algorithms still struggle to make sense of unstructured data, which explains the limited use of AI in ODR. AI also carries risks, including reliance on inaccurate data leading to incorrect results. Machine learning and AI rely on data and software engineers that could be biased. The line of reasoning is scripted in code and not easily accessible or understandable by the parties to the ODR process. The APEC PPD Recommendations on Promoting Consumer Protection in Dispute Resolution state that "Artificial intelligence can play a valuable role in advancing and facilitating Online Dispute Resolution (ODR), but the development of Artificial Intelligence (AI) and algorithms must be based on ethical principles and be free of bias or other features that would lead to unfairness in its decision-making process."[93,94]

The document then quotes all the May 2022 NCTDR/ICODR ODR Standards that reference artificial intelligence.

Stockholm Chamber of Commerce (The entire document issued in 2024 speaks to AI and arbitration):

> Artificial intelligence ("AI") is a rapidly evolving and transformative field with no universal definition. At the same time, international arbitration has in recent years been the subject of criticism for perceived increases in time and cost. AI offers exciting possibilities to reverse this… The SCC Arbitration Institute ("SCC") … has prepared this Guide to the Use of Artificial Intelligence in Cases Administered Under the SCC Rules[95] ("AI Guide") to provide flexible guidance to

92 The citation within the text makes reference here to the *APEC ODR Collaborative Framework*, Overview, https://www.apec.org/SELI/Overview; APEC ODR Collaborative Framework, para, 1.2.

93 APEC PPD Recommendations on Promoting Consumer Protection in Dispute Resolution, supra note 16 at 17.

94 Asia-Pacific Economic Cooperation (APEC). Study on Best Practices Using ODR, January 2023, 10.

95 Defined in Article 1 of the SCC Arbitration Rules as "the Arbitration Rules of the SCC (the "Arbitration Rules"), the Rules for Expedited Arbitrations of the SCC (the "Rules

participants in an SCC case without imposing specific obligations ... Arbitration practitioners are already deploying AI in numerous ways, with new uses and tools developing and evolving at an impressive pace ... The list of AI's uses in arbitration continues to expand, with significant potential.

Managing AI's potential[:] The use of AI in dispute resolution has significant potential to reduce cost and increase efficiency. Because of the societal importance of binding dispute resolution, the EU Act qualifies as high-risk AI systems used by an Arbitral Tribunal "in researching and interpreting facts and the law and in applying the law to a concrete set of facts."[96] The SCC encourages Arbitral Tribunals using AI systems for this purpose, and as appropriate other participants in arbitration, to bear in mind the following.

Confidentiality: Many users value arbitration's ability to respect accords on confidentiality. The use of some AI tools may have unintended consequences for the confidentiality of an arbitration. Participants, in particular the Arbitral Tribunal, are therefore encouraged to inform themselves as to how any data input is employed and deployed when using AI.

Quality: At the present state of development, the use of some AI systems may contribute to the perpetuation of biases or generate incorrect or false information. AI systems may also produce false or manipulated evidence. Therefore, AI systems should be equipped with technical solutions to mark and detect AI-generated or manipulated content, using reliable and interoperable methods. Arbitral Tribunals should ensure any use of AI does not lead to any reduction in the quality of their decisions. To ensure effective human oversight, Arbitral Tribunals should apply an appropriate level of review and verification to any outputs of AI systems before making use of such outputs in an arbitration.

Integrity: The integrity of arbitration is essential to its continued success. Transparency and accountability are key components of integrity.

---

for Expedited Arbitrations") and other rules and procedures adopted by the Stockholm Chamber of Commerce".

96 EU AI Act, Recital 61, Annex III, 8 (a).

> Arbitral Tribunals are therefore encouraged to disclose any use of AI in researching and interpreting facts and the law or applying the law to facts. Such disclosure may assist in ensuring the parties' rights to be heard, and that the Arbitral Tribunal does not exceed its mandate.
>
> Non-delegation of the decision-making mandate: AI tools may be used to support arbitral decision-making but cannot replace it. Arbitral Tribunals cannot delegate the decision or the reasoning leading to it to anyone or anything.[97]

The overarching themes in these documents include 1) references to the value of ODR; 2) the importance of aligning ODR and AI usage with principles, standards, regulations, and legislation that uphold common values in ADR and rights enshrined in law such as those regarding procedural rights, confidentiality, and data security; and 3) seeking to address the increased risk of data bias when AI is employed. With the exception of the NCTDR-ICODR ODR Standards, the documents are guidelines, observations, or summaries of some best practices on what should be valued or that raise concerns about using AI when handling disputes. Also noteworthy is that they, with the same exception, are designed to address a particular sector (ie: the economy), form of dispute resolution (ie: arbitration, civil and administrative courts, or more than one form of ADR), or particular populations (ie: APEC countries, countries under the European Council, persons with disabilities, arbitrators and arbitrations in African countries, and arbitrators and arbitrations under the jurisdiction of the Stockholm Chamber of Commerce). In these ways, they appear to seek to address specific sectors and/or constituencies and thus follow common approaches in the development of governance mechanisms as discussed in previous chapters. Alternatively, the NCTDR-ICODR Online Dispute Resolution Standards (May 2022) that are outlined in detail further below, is an international standards document that addresses AI, is inclusive of any dispute handling process and of any type of dispute from any sector of society (ie: labor, environmental or other public policy, commercial, educational, family, community), and is designed to be used in any jurisdiction and across jurisdictions.

The standards work of NCTDR and ICODR was designed to follow the disruptive nature of technology as, in reality, it has broken down silos be-

97 Stockholm Chamber of Commerce. *SCC Guide to the Use of Artificial Intelligence in Cases Administered Under the SCC Rules*, October 2024, 1–2.

tween disciplines, professions, legal jurisdictions, and sectors of society – all places where conflict arises. Thus, these two international organizations considered that architectures of governance needed to address this reality as well. In addition, the standards were designed to not only seek to prevent and reduce risks due to the disruptive nature of technology, but to capitalize on the new opportunities to transform conflict handling systems beyond merely replicating or enhancing their efficiency. And they seek to respond to calls[98] for such new opportunities to be oriented towards increasing access to justice for those for whom barriers exist and for whom the application of technology can either reduce or exacerbate them.

Recognizing that with tech innovation there would continue to be an ongoing need to revise governance mechanisms, NCTDR and ICODR framed their NCTDR Ethical Principles, ICODR 2017 ODR Standards, and the NCTDR-ICODR May 2022 ODR Standards as living documents, with the assumption that they would very likely need to be updated with changes in technology. For similar reasons, these international Standards were crafted to be thin enough to be relevant and able to be interpreted across different sectors of society and national, regional and international legal jurisdictions, recognizing that their manifestation would be influenced in their operation by other governance mechanisms whether they be legal, regulatory, ethical norms, or other professional standards.

At the time of writing, The International Organization for Standardization (ISO) 'working group on Transaction Assurance in E-commerce – Guidelines for Online Dispute Resolution (ISO/TC321/WG 3), is using the NCTDR/ICODR ODR Standards [May 2022] to develop Basic Principles for ODR'[99] to be included in ISO's new standard *Transaction Assurance in E-commerce – Guidance for Offering Online Dispute Resolution Services* with a target publication date of 2025. The International Organization for Standardization is 'an independent, non-governmental international organization with a membership of 174 national standards bodies'[100] whose standards impact stakeholders, users and regulators in these countries in the areas of technology, management and manufacturing. The NCTDR-ICODR ODR Standards (May 2022) have also been cited as valuable guidance and support for endorsement and integration into the standards of other bodies internationally. A few examples at the time of writing include work

98 See for example, G. LaForge, R. Muggah, and G. Seiler *Bridging the AI Governance Divide*. Task Force 5, Inclusive Digital Transformation, G20 Brasil 2024.

99 Asia-Pacific Economic Cooperation (APEC). *Study on Best Practices Using ODR*, January 2023, 7.

100 https://www.iso.org/about-us.html

by the Asia-Pacific Economic Cooperation (APEC),[101] The Republic of India government-wide policy think tank (NITI Aayog) and the country's central bank and body responsible for regulation of the Indian banking system (Reserve Bank of India),[102] and Canada's self-regulatory professional dispute resolution organization (the ADR Institute of Canada–ADRIC). It is interesting to consider if this experiment in creating international ODR Standards from within a professional field that include artificial intelligence and are designed to have relevance across jurisdictions and all sectors of society may have something illustrative to share about international standards setting; while arguably, only as a snapshot in time since disruption will no doubt lead to new challenges and future pathways to respond to them.

## 8 Online Dispute Resolution Standards

The NCTDR-ICODR Online Dispute Resolution Standards (May 2022) are presented below followed by an exploration of how artificial intelligence is addressed within them. These Standards[103] were crafted to serve as a baseline of acceptable dispute handling practices and processes that utilize information and communication technologies and to explicitly address the use of artificial intelligence. They are designed to be utilized together, interlocking, and relating to each other as a cohesive whole. The Standards are purposefully thin to provide for the necessary flexibility to be made relevant and appropriate through interpretation by culture, sector, and jurisdiction. What follows are the NCTDR-ICODR Online Dispute Resolution Standards:

> ODR Standards require that online dispute resolution platforms and processes must be:
>
> **Accessible:** ODR must be easy for parties to find within a system and participate in and not limit their right to representation. ODR should be available in communication channels accessible to all the parties, minimize costs to participants, and be easily accessed by people with different types of abilities.

101 See Asia-Pacific Economic Cooperation (APEC). *Study on Best Practices Using ODR*, January 2023.

102 See NITI Aayog. *Designing the Future of Dispute Resolution: The ODR Policy Plan for India*, 29/11/21.

103 As opposed to being guidance, recommendations, or a set of best practices.

**Accountable:** ODR systems must be continuously accountable to the institutions, legal frameworks, and communities that they serve. ODR platforms must be auditable and the audit made available to users. This must include human oversight of: i) traceability of the originality of documents and of the path to outcome when artificial intelligence is employed, ii) determination of the relative control given to human and artificial decision-making strategies, iii) outcomes, and iv) the process of ensuring availability of outcomes to the parties.

**Competent:** ODR providers must have the relevant expertise in dispute resolution, legal, technical execution, language, and culture required to deliver competent, effective services in their target areas. ODR services must be timely and use participant time efficiently.

**Confidential:** ODR providers must make every genuine and reasonable effort to maintain the confidentiality of party communications in line with policies that must be articulated to the parties regarding i) who will see what data, ii) how and to what purposes that data can be used, iii) how data will be stored, iv) if, how, and when data will be destroyed or modified, and v) how disclosures of breaches will be communicated and the steps that will be taken to prevent reoccurrence.

**Equal:** ODR providers must treat all participants with respect and dignity. ODR must seek to enable often silenced or marginalized voices to be heard and strive to ensure that offline privileges and disadvantages are not replicated in the ODR process. ODR must provide access to process instructions, security, confidentiality, and data control to all parties. ODR must strive to ensure on an on-going basis that no process or technology incorporated into ODR provides any party with a technological or informational advantage due to its use of ODR. Bias must be proactively avoided in all processes, contexts, and regarding party characteristics. ODR system design must include proactive efforts to prevent any artificial intelligence decision-making function from creating, replicating, or compounding bias in process or outcome. Human oversight is required in ODR system design and auditing to identify bias, make findings transparent to ODR providers and users, and eliminate bias in ODR processes and outcomes.

**Fair and Impartial:** ODR must treat all parties equitably and with due process, without bias or benefits for or against individuals, groups, or entities. Conflicts of interest of providers, participants, and system administrators must be disclosed in advance of commencement of ODR services. The obligation to disclose such circumstances shall be a continuing obligation throughout the ODR process.

**Legal:** ODR providers must abide by, uphold, and disclose to the parties relevant laws and regulations under which the process falls.

**Secure:** ODR providers must make every genuine and reasonable effort to ensure that ODR platforms are secure and data collected and communications between those engaged in ODR are not shared with any unauthorized parties. Disclosures of breaches must be communicated along with the steps taken to prevent reoccurrence.

**Transparent:** ODR providers must explicitly disclose in advance and in a meaningful and accessible manner: i) the form and enforceability of dispute resolution processes and outcomes and ii) the risks, costs including for whom, and benefits of participation. Data in ODR must be gathered, managed, and presented in ways to ensure it is not misrepresented or out of context. The sources and methods used to gather any data that influences any decision made by artificial intelligence must be disclosed to all parties. ODR that uses artificial intelligence must publicly affirm compliance with jurisdictionally relevant legislation, regulations, or in their absence, guidelines on transparency and fairness of artificial intelligence systems. ODR must clearly disclose the role and magnitude of technology's influence on restricting or generating options and in final decisions or outcomes. Audits of ODR systems and platforms must identify metrics used to assess system performance, making the accuracy and precision of these metrics known and accessible to any ODR system operator and user. Users must be informed in a timely and accessible manner of any data breach and the steps taken to prevent reoccurrence.

*Implementation of ODR Standards*

We recommend practitioners, platform and system designers, and managers of any form of online dispute resolution process commit to these ODR Standards. We encourage dispute resolution membership organizations and other entities–whether public or private–with responsibility and/or authority over ODR-related processes, practices, and practitioners, to incorporate these standards and create appropriate mechanisms for accountability and monitoring including through the examination of impacts of different technological design and use across disputant demographics and case types.[104]

## 9 Analysis of AI within the ODR Standards

The three ODR Standards that make explicit reference to artificial intelligence are Accountable, Equal, and Transparent. The Accountable standard addresses issues of the auditability of ODR that employs AI, the maintenance of human oversight of the audit and the process – including the determination of how much control humans and AI have over decision making. Note the relationship here between Level 5 in the ODR Framework and this standard. Level 5 would entail humans "out of the loop", unable to intervene or have oversight of the process. Such a process would clearly violate the Accountable standard which requires 'human oversight of: i) traceability of the originality of documents and of the path to outcome when artificial intelligence is employed, ii) determination of the relative control given to human and artificial decision-making strategies, iii) outcomes, and iv) the process of ensuring availability of outcomes to the parties.'[105] This will become even more important as we move closer to singularity and need to retain human control over the development and deployment of AI. A future revision of the ODR Standards may speak to the role of AI as a fifth party, able to create new forms of AI that could otherwise circumvent these guardrails designed for human oversight of ODR.

The Equal standard speaks to this to some extent as well. It highlights that human oversight is necessary in ODR system design and auditing to proactively prevent, make transparent, and eliminate any AI bias found in process and outcome. Beyond these important measures to reduce risks of bias that can re/produce disadvantages to some and privileges to others, the standard articulates the requirement for ODR to seek to 'enable often silenced or marginalized voices to be heard.'[106] This charges ODR practitioners, providers, system designers, and other fifth parties to consider ways to harness technologies including artificial intelligence to address access to justice gaps.

---

104 The National Center for Technology and Dispute Resolution and International Council for Online Dispute Resolution. *ODR Standards*. © May 2022. Accessible at: https://odr.info/wp-content/uploads/2022/05/NCTDR_and_ICODR_ODR_Standards_2022.pdf

105 The National Center for Technology and Dispute Resolution and International Council for Online Dispute Resolution. *ODR Standards*. May 2022, p. 2.

106 The National Center for Technology and Dispute Resolution and International Council for Online Dispute Resolution. *ODR Standards*. May 2022, p. 3.

The requirement within the Transparent standard that 'ODR providers must explicitly disclose in advance and in a meaningful and accessible manner: the risks, costs including for whom, and benefits of participation'[107] can be used to proactively ward off the creation of differing ODR processes and outcomes that could deploy AI in ways that – whether purposefully or not – could result in favoring one category of party over others as was discussed earlier. The requirements of audits and their transparency can help to identify unforeseen bias re/production by AI in the system. Requiring 'meaningful and accessible' transparency provides a clear window into what is usually a "black box". In addition, requiring transparency about the level and type of human agency versus artificial intelligence and each of their impacts (ie: regarding the generation of options and outcomes), can increase party agency, informed consent, and trust in the process. Beyond its positive contribution for involved parties, the visible and proactive application of the Transparent standard may help to enhance overall trust in the usage of AI in courts and alternative dispute resolution. This can be valuable given some of the pressing legal, ethical, and practical concerns raised about artificial intelligence discussed earlier that relate directly to the lack of transparency. These include concerns about the ability to know what algorithms are used that influence the process and case outcome[108] and other concerns that AI disproportionately affects some groups more than others, for example, in the use of facial recognition algorithms and job selection[109] and emotion detection software in hiring.[110] These disconcerting realities have resulted in demands for stronger public oversight and

---

107 The National Center for Technology and Dispute Resolution and International Council for Online Dispute Resolution. *ODR Standards*. May 2022, p. 4.

108 See for example, legal decisions impacting a person's right to know what algorithms are utilized that influence the outcome of the legal judgments in their case: Loomis v. Wisconsin, 881 N.W.2d 749, 749–57 (Wis. 2016), cert. denied, 137 S. Ct. 2290 (2017); Adam Liptak, "Sent to Prison by a Software Program's Secret Algorithms." May 1, 2017. https://www.nytimes.com/2017/05/01/us/politics/sent-to-prison-by-a-software-programs-secret-algorithms.html?_r=0. See Buolamwini, J. *Written Testimony*. Hearing on Facial Recognition Technology (Part 1): Its Impact on our Civil Rights and Liberties, United States House Committee on Oversight and Government Reform, May 22, 2019, 7.

109 Ifeoma, A. "Unfair Automated Hiring Systems Are Everywhere." *Wired*. May 15, 2023. https://www.wired.com/story/unfair-automated-hiring-systems-are-everywhere-ftc/; Urbi, J. "Some Transgender Drivers are Being Kicked Off Uber's App." *CNBC*. August 8, 2018, updated August 13, 2018. https://www.cnbc.com/2018/08/08/transgender-uber-driver-suspended-tech-oversight-facial-recognition.html

110 Information Commissioner's Office (ICO). "'Immature Biometric Technologies Could Be Discriminating Against People' Says ICO in Warning to Organisations." October 26, 2022. https://ico.org.uk/about-the-ico/media-centre/news-and-blogs/2022/10/imma

methods of accountability for artificial intelligence usage[111] and the ODR Standards can be seen as a contribution to these efforts. The assertion within the Transparent standard that 'ODR that uses artificial intelligence must publicly affirm compliance with jurisdictionally relevant legislation, regulations, or in their absence, guidelines on transparency and fairness of artificial intelligence systems'[112] holds those designing and providing ODR accountable for knowing and complying with other relevant governance mechanisms. The language here is an example of how the ODR Standards can and need to be interpreted in jurisdictionally appropriate ways and how they can be integrated rather than compete with other tools of public accountability and of self-governance.

While these three Standards explicitly address AI, all nine of the standards can be interpreted to have relevance to artificial intelligence. For example, given that the Fair and Impartial standard requires treatment of 'all parties equitably and with due process, without bias or benefits for or against individuals, groups, or entities',[113] then active efforts to prevent, reduce and address the risks of hallucinations and biased data usage by LLMs is a must. Similarly, when forms of AI are used that could affect the security of data and in jurisdictions with laws on AI, then the Legal and Secure standards are directly relevant to AI.

## 10 So What?

The development and response to these international ODR Standards may offer some reflections about AI standards promulgation in the future. As explored elsewhere in the book, standards and regulations often emerge from within silos and reflect particular divisions based on disciplines or

ture-biometric-technologies-could-be-discriminating-against-people-says-ico-in-warning-to-organisations

111 See *Buolamwini, J. and Costanza-Chock, S.* "Announcing the Sunset of the Safe Face Pledge." *Algorithmic Justice League,* February 8, 2021. https://medium.com/@Joy.Buolamwini/announcing-the-sunset-of-the-safe-face-pledge-36e6ea9e0dc5. Rauenzahn, B., Chung, J., and Kaufman, A. "Facing Bias in Facial Recognition Technology." *The Regulatory Review,* March 20, 2021. https://www.theregreview.org/2021/03/20/saturday-seminar-facing-bias-in-facial-recognition-technology/

112 The National Center for Technology and Dispute Resolution and International Council for Online Dispute Resolution. *ODR Standards.* May 2022, p. 4.

113 The National Center for Technology and Dispute Resolution and International Council for Online Dispute Resolution. *ODR Standards.* May 2022, p. 3.

professions. And regulation reflects jurisdictional divisions – municipal, state, provincial, national, regional, for example. However, AI has disrupted boundaries between professions and fields as well as across all other boundaries – sectors of society, between nations, etc. In the face of these common standards development traditions, the ODR Standards were developed by two international bodies to be cross-sectoral, trans-disciplinary, trans-professional, and trans-jurisdictional and they appear likely to be poised for adoption in some form if not in their entirety by ISO, a leading body for international standards – one which focuses on economies not on dispute resolution. What might, if anything, this story tell us about a standards governance mechanism for AI that doesn't fit into a traditional box of 'domestic or international' or just for one profession or practice or sector of society? While it will not be the only governance mechanism to do so, will the ODR Standards contribute to a story about the disruption of the typical boundaries of governance? Will similar types of responses to how AI has infiltrated across all boundaries be a way of the future as we seek to productively control AI to foster the best and prevent and reduce the worst that it can be used for?

Simultaneous with continued research and innovation in artificial intelligence is the need to significantly enhance mechanisms of governance and accountability for its deployment in dispute resolution and other arenas. These on-going 'efforts will need to be focused on developing the appropriate institutional mechanisms for detecting, monitoring, and correcting for bias in AI decision tools'.[114] As legal institutions and ADR entities employ AI, we must face the reality that the hegemonic approaches to coding and use of AI tools have for decades continued to replicate AI bias despite our knowledge that this is the case, as well as is the fact that even newly created hallucinations often replicate the patterns of who is negatively impacted. This raises important questions for every society about how it will protect all its members including the most vulnerable. If market forces have so far proven insufficient, we may ask why we should anticipate that excluded stakeholders are suddenly going to be present and attended to at the table; and if not, then whose values, needs, and voices will be listened to in the creation of design specifications, systems implementation, and necessary oversight to address inaccurate and dangerous outputs that undermine equal access to justice? So often it is those profiting by building such tools

114 Engstrom, D. F., D. E. Ho, C. M. Sharkey, and M.F. Cuellar. 2020. *Government by Algorithm: Artificial Intelligence in Federal Administrative Agencies.* NYU School of Law Research Paper No. 20–54, 81.

who are the ones 'seeking closure that stabilizes their approach to fairness, while others – usually those subject to the effects of technology – have little voice at all'.[115] This points towards the value of continuing to build the necessary standards, regulations, and legislation, as well as guidance, best practices, and appropriate incentives for the design and implementation of dispute resolution systems which require that technology design and usage reflects the needs and voices not only of a broad range of stakeholders, but specifically those with the most at risk when AI is utilized.[116]

Collaboration can serve us well as we seek to structurally determine an increase in access to procedural and substantive fairness in dispute resolution processes that harness artificial intelligence and other forms of technology. All hands on deck are needed to address not only the historic patterns of inequality in dispute handling but also in the impact of AI. If preventing encoding of bias and if reducing inequality in access to procedural and substantive justice are not goals tied directly to the requirements of each element of a dispute resolution process and system, they are not likely to be outcomes. Therefore, they must become core to dispute system design: the system design goals, problem definition, decision making matrices, and accountability mechanisms must each respond to the reality of unequal risks in terms of AI usage. A focus on equity cannot be an add on ... it must *be code not a coda*. Further research is required to strengthen the ability of AI to account for context and the human social actors who will use it – a significant challenge in the face of demands for abstraction for portability and efficiency. Multidisciplinary research collaboration that includes ODR stakeholders offers promise in tackling historic and emerging issues of bias and inequality that are magnified by the application of AI to dispute resolution.

---

115 Virginia Eubanks. 2018. *Automating Inequality: How High-Tech Tools Profile, Police, and Punish the Poor.* New York: Picador, St. Martin's Press, 65.

116 See Amsler, L. B., J. K. Martinez, and S. E. Smith. 2020. *Dispute System Design: Preventing, Managing, and Resolving Conflict.* Stanford, CA: Stanford University Press. Also see the Online Dispute Resolution Party Engagement (OPEN) project, dedicated to increasing access to court resources for self-represented litigants, particularly those with low-literacy and the project's publications: Feinstein, R., Shack, J., and Henry, J. *Focus Group Participant Perspectives on ODR and the Barriers to Its Use.* Resolution Systems Institute, 2024 and Feinstein, R., Henry, J., and Shack, J. *Communicating Effectively on ODR: A Guide for Courts.* Resolution Systems Institute, 2024. For a useful applicable framework, see Matsuda, M. "Looking to the Bottom: Critical Legal Studies and Reparations." *Harvard Civil Rights-Civil Liberties Law Review*, Vol. 22, 1987, 323–399.

ODR practitioners and users are stakeholders with important roles to play in what protections should be provided for in governance measures. We can continue to advocate for the benefits of self-regulation, formal and non-formal education, training, development of best practices, expansion of funding and incentives for related research, and importantly, increased oversight and methods of accountability about AI and ODR. These efforts can help reduce the creation of greater inequality due to AI[117] as well as assist with more ethical system design and delivery of public and private alternative dispute resolution and judicial services.

The adoption and adaption of international ODR Standards within and across sectors, cultures, and legal jurisdictions can bring them to life and embed them as appropriate in additional governance structures, strengthening the delivery of ethical ODR to all, including the most under-resourced and vulnerable parties in the face of AI. However, in realistic tension with such adoption and embeddedness is the importance of on-going attention

117 See the landmark European Union Artificial Intelligence Act (2023) that is being referred to as the world's first comprehensive legal framework on AI. While providing for specific law enforcement exceptions, the Act states that by "Recognising the potential threat to citizens' rights and democracy posed by certain applications of AI, the co-legislators agreed to prohibit: biometric categorisation systems that use sensitive characteristics (e.g. political, religious, philosophical beliefs, sexual orientation, race); untargeted scraping of facial images from the internet or CCTV footage to create facial recognition databases; emotion recognition in the workplace and educational institutions; social scoring based on social behaviour or personal characteristics; AI systems that manipulate human behaviour to circumvent their free will; AI used to exploit the vulnerabilities of people (due to their age, disability, social or economic situation)." "Artificial Intelligence Act: Deal on Comprehensive Rules for Trustworthy AI." *News*, European Parliament. December 9, 2023. https://www.europarl.europa.eu/news/en/press-room/20231206IPR15699/artificial-intelligence-act-deal-on-comprehensive-rules-for-trustworthy-ai. See also, Hadnes, A., Yaros, O. Prinsley, M.A., De, R., Leipzig, D.S., Kourinian, A., Lilley, S., Waltzman, H.W., and De Moncuit, A. "Certain applications will be banned under the EU AI Act, including AI systems used for emotion recognition in the workplace, for untargeted scraping of facial images from the internet or CCTV footage to create facial recognition databases. Using AI systems to conduct remote biometric identification in public will be allowed when strictly necessary for law enforcement purposes. However, safeguards will need to be put in place, such as limiting the use of these systems to conducting searches for people suspected of the most serious crimes" with potentially significant financial penalties for violating the Act." "EU AI ACT: European Parliament and Council Reach Agreement." *Meyer Brown*. December 12, 2023, 2. https://1npdf11.onenorth.com/pdfrenderer.svc/v1/ABCpdf11/GetRenderedPdfByUrl/eu-ai-act-european-parliament-and-council-reach-agreement.pdf/?url=https://www.mayerbrown.com/en/pdf/insights/publications/2023/12/eu-ai-act-european-parliament-and-council-reach-agreement?countrycode=US

to revising and improving ODR Standards as artificial intelligence and other technologies rapidly change the landscape of ODR. Fortunately, this is a group project.

> As he logged off his laptop for the night, he reflected on the fruitful discussion he had that day with ODR stakeholders from around the world. Some he knew well and others not at all, for they had cast the net widely to engage a diverse and robust group, building on the valuable lessons of effective stakeholder inclusion from standards development, dispute system design, and inclusive research studies driven by the needs of those most under-resourced. The AI tools the group had used in their discussion had provided opportunities for asynchronous brainstorming by human group members as well as AI generated suggestions based on the RAG and the LLM they employed. The fact that they had designed it so that the AI generated ideas were distinguishable from those that were human generated led to discovering that the RAG database still remained incomplete in need of additional sources to reflect more perspectives, experiences, and diverse approaches to cases. They also contemplated the implications of the fact that the LLM they were using was both generating hallucinations and also providing some useful and creative suggestions. Relying on the ODR Standards had been key to setting their goals when they had begun designing the databases their RAG would access and it was serving as a touchstone as they continuously worked to improve it to enhance the output of the LLM they employed. He reflected how deeply satisfying it was to be a part of a group harnessing innovation while intrepidly seeking to tackle what were age-old problems of inequality and lack of equal access to justice. This was a forever project – for, after all, innovation would continue rapidly and before long AI would be functioning as a 5th party – with the capacity to create new 4th parties! More opportunities and more risk would mean more urgency and more importance to be placed on collaborating for a better future.

# Conclusion – Directions Forward

Governing AI is, as we have suggested, a complicated and perhaps Quixotic enterprise. Regulations can give certainty with the force of law to basic requirements that ensure a baseline of development and use that reduces the risk of danger or harm to the public. International standards can fine tune the concerns addressed by law and regulation and serve an important role when laws are missing or outdated, and standards have the advantage of crossing borders and being as close to universal as possible – assuming the universe buys into the standards. International standards, statements of ethics, and standards of practice specifically developed by professional fields that routinely feature interaction between information and communication technology and humans can also cross borders and offer guidance for developers and users.

Ultimately, we argue that the only way to effectively govern artificial intelligence is to foster a governance ecosystem that combines, coordinates, and seeks to harmonize the promulgation of laws and regulations, international standards that cross disciplines, and international standards of practice from related academic and professional fields. Simply put, in order to be successful, any AI governance ecosystem must include regulation and laws from nation states, international standards, and internationally recognized professional standards.

Successful attempts to govern AI must address both process and content. In terms of process, governance efforts must consider the elements that go into building and reinforcing regulations, laws, and standards. In terms of building, all of these elements must be designed for inclusive stakeholder participation, foster either formal or informal relationships that are vigorous and lasting, and must develop methods to update and improve based on what may be absent in any iteration of governance. This will require initial work, and, importantly, the creation of feedback loops like those used routinely in international standards development and management. In terms of content, the governance ecosystem must address the aspirational (the 'good' we wish to promote) and the cautionary (the harms we are trying to prevent). And throughout, a workable governance system must consider the range of individuals and organizations that will be affected by AI (e.g., designers, suppliers, vendors, users, regulators, educators, etc.) and design guidance and information for those entities with attention to those most vulnerable to the dangers that AI can (re)produce.

© KONINKLIJKE BRILL BV, LEIDEN, 2025 | DOI:10.1163/9789004737389_008

The work already done by nation states, regional governance entities, and standards organizations can offer some guidance regarding the key components required to address the good and the cautionary elements of AI that should become part of the governance ecosystem. And the international ODR Standards discussed earlier can offer one example of a governance framework born of a profession that is finding support and incorporation across different sectors and jurisdictions.

While it is axiomatic that all of the interested parties will bring to the discussion of governance their own political and cultural views, we think there are some basic issues that cut across at least most interests. Standardization and regulation efforts should include:

- Governance that is Human Centered – focus on the human impact of the applications versus the technology itself.
- Governance that features Feedback Loops – focus on continual stakeholder feedback that incorporates independent voices at a narrow, use-case level, like Safety Review Boards that will ensure technological progress does not outpace public safety.
- Governance that considers Consolidation of Use Cases – use of safety oversight boards until enough consistency across use cases allows for similarities to emerge and be standardized. For example, safety standards for AI digital assistants in marketing may reveal enough similarities with AI digital assistants for insurance claims evaluation to the point that the standards could be found for AI digital assistants that can cover use cases for both industries.
- Governance that goes from the Real World to Governance – consolidation and a sufficient number of use cases to allow for standards that are robust enough for regulatory inclusion.
- Governance that uses Regulations that are Use Specific – targeting what is useful to specific entities within the AI ecosystem.
- Governance that goes from Standards to Regulations – harnessing the consensus of international standards to serve as a useful basis for their incorporation into regulations and law in relevant ways by sovereign governmental bodies.

The importance of these basic issues suggests that full AI governance will not reside in one document or set of standards, but will instead consist of multiple regulations and standards that offer guidance to developers and offer some sense of safety and accountability for users. While simultaneously, attention to harmonization across standards and regulations can strengthen the governance ecosystem, facilitating greater international cooperation in offering protection from AI's threats and access to its positive potential.

## 1 How to Coordinate

Coordinating among the three realms we have discussed throughout the book, standards of practice from existing technology-based fields (such as online dispute resolution), international standards, and traditional regulation, will require a level of cooperation across borders, both national and professional, that heretofore have been far too rare. So what will make this approach more frequent and workable?

First, it will be necessary to continue the conversations underway among nations to identify the basic protections that all societies want to ensure as AI continues to develop, with attention to the inequities within nations and between the Global North and South that affect the impacts of AI and access to the use of technologies. The list may include the obvious ones: data security, personal privacy, protection of intellectual property, human rights, etc. But the list may also include items that are not immediately apparent and which may be revealed only as new technologies and their implications emerge, and in honest discourse between and among sovereign actors and their constituents.

Second, international organizations must look at the ethics and standards of practice that should guide developers of AI systems, providers of AI services, and consumers of AI services. This, again, is an international enterprise, with as many of the stakeholders as possible at the table to add ideas, objections, and directions, all of which may lead to identifying new opportunities and bring to light concerns that those with formal decision making power might miss. This can proactively foster a more robust set of protections and trust in the international consensus that emerges.

Third, academic and professional fields, like the example of online dispute resolution, must consider and incorporate ethics about the impact of AI on modes of practice, including where they can create or aggravate inequalities such as access to justice or protection. Much of this information will, undoubtedly, cross over and be relevant to associated fields. For example, the standards of practice involving AI for mediators may be very closely related to the standards of practice for executive coaches using AI, or for counselors, or for attorneys.

Each of these three types of efforts can be exponentially enhanced by being attuned to the others; to learn from and build upon them, to enhance an integrated and synergistic ecosystem. While jurisdictional and sector-specific regulations and standards will no doubt continue to be required, the internationalization of AI governance is becoming imperative given the reality of its global disruptive positive and negative forces. Such a stance can assist in fostering increased collaboration, feedback loops to strengthen governance mechanisms already in place, and to identify and address gaps in the perpetual chase to catch up to AI innovations.

If there is forethought and communication between and among all of these players, the answer to our opening question – is it possible to govern AI? – is at least a qualified yes.

## 2 What Developers and Providers Need

With the caveat that those who wish to use AI for destructive or nefarious purposes will not be bound by any governance, however rational and universally accepted, there are basic things that developers and providers of AI services should be able to recognize as broadly or universally acceptable or required as they create AI systems, or offer AI platforms to the public. And while some have been addressed by existing legislative or standards efforts, they will undoubtedly need to be updated, and for those yet to be addressed, they must be as the technology continually changes. Below are some of the key topics that need to be addressed in order to prevent the worst harm and reduce risks:

- Accessibility – who has access and through what means? Is access denied, *de facto* or *de jure*, to some? What are the implications of any unequal access?
- Accountability – who is responsible for the structure of the AI systems, and who is responsible for the harm they may do?
- Accuracy – how is the accuracy of the information generated by the AI measured and reported, to whom, and under what circumstances?
- Auditability – what is the process for looking "behind the curtain" at AI structure and performance, and who is negatively impacted when transparency is absent?
- Bias Prevention and Management – what are the evaluative approaches that ensure that attempts to prevent and reduce bias in data or programming are continually addressed? That those biases that exist can be identified? Competence – what is the baseline measure of competent AI development or use, and how is that competence measured and acknowledged and to whom?
- Confidentiality – how can AI providers and users clearly communicate the parameters of what an AI platform and its use offers in this regard? Does the platform ensure that personal and professional information supplied by the users will not be seen by unauthorized persons?
- Conflicts of Interest – is the nature of conflicts of interest defined, and is there a mechanism for disclosing? To whom and how is it disclosed?

- Consumer Protections – if there are disputes or harm done through use of the platform, are there redress or dispute resolution protocols for addressing the disputes?
- Data Security – how does the platform ensure that information generated during its use will not be distributed or obtained by unauthorized actors?
- Data Use – does the platform clearly identify if and how information generated by interaction with the platform is used, including in increasing the AI's data set or learning base and any decisions or outcomes rendered by the system? Is there a declaration that use of data is not presented out of context and to whom and how is it provided?
- Efficiency – does the AI platform make efficient use of time and do minimal ecological harm?
- Equality – does the AI platform treat all participants with respect and dignity? Does it seek to enable often silenced or marginalized voices to be heard and strive to ensure that offline privileges and disadvantages are not replicated through its usage?
- Human Oversight – are there humans in or on the loop as the AI is used? Are users informed of the parameters of human influence or lack thereof when AI is used?
- IP Protections – is the platform clear about the data set from which the AI learns, and does it ensure that the intellectual property of individuals is protected or compensated?
- Human rights – how does the use of the AI conform to relevant human rights definitions, standards, laws, and treaties?
- Legality – is the AI platform operating in a legal manner in all of the jurisdictional venues in which it is used?
- Transparency – to what degree is the development, management, and use of AI and its data sets visible to potential users?

These do not represent a comprehensive list of basic protections that could be established in law or regulation or standards, and we would recommend that any governance mechanisms consider the level of requirements or guidance appropriate to address the necessary performance goals and standards that those developing, managing, or using AI should have access to or be required to understand and use as a base for behavior.

## 3 What Users Need to Know

An important element in the ultimate utility of AI governance is the ability for the regulations and standards to guide users (whether government agencies, private entities, or individuals) as they undertake to commission the creation of, evaluate and choose AI platforms.

Ultimately, much of what has been outlined above that developers need to know, end users need to know as well; however, there are other topics that may be different and more specific to them. As we begin the new age in which AI will be ubiquitous–incorporated into a dizzying array of almost all services and activities that affect us, we offer below a short, but in no way a comprehensive list of a number of questions that at this time are worth consideration by potential consumers of AI, whether they are using an AI platform for their own use or for providing services to others. Robust governance of AI should ensure that potential users of AI systems can get answers to these (and potentially other) questions.

- What regulations and standards affect my responsibility and liability in offering a service that involves AI?
- What is the data set from which the AI learns?
- What are the confidentiality and data security policies?
- What are the data security risks and to whom? What are the benefits and for whom?
- How can I ensure that the outputs are not violating intellectual property rights or presenting data out of context?
- What on-going testing and by whom is needed to ensure that the AI functions do not reflect bias in the private or public service we offer?
- What is the level of human oversight over the AI functions?
- Is support and training offered to potential users?
- What is the initial or on-going cost and what are the terms of service?
- What are the updates and maintenance policies and costs?
- Will it integrate with other tech platforms?
- Can you customize the look and feel of the platform?
- Is there a track record of reliability and accuracy? Does an independent entity provide an audit or review?
- What legal liability and ethical responsibility do I have regarding the use and impact of AI in the process and outcome?
- What changes are needed to the present protocols, systems, or practices that we use so that when adding an AI tool we can ensure that we are maximizing benefits for all and protecting those most vulnerable to its potential risks?
- What protections of the public are needed by government agencies approving use of or utilizing AI in the delivery of public services?
- Can we add the use of a RAG to strengthen the data set and make it most relevant for our purposes?

– How can I/we participate in the development of AI standards and regulations? In a feedback loop to those developing or overseeing AI standards and regulations?

## 4 Coda

The ubiquitous and profound impact of AI on our societies has arrived. When viewed through the lens of other transformative technologies, we can learn from history how other disruptive technologies were given space to safely innovate, mature through the development and acceptance of internationally recognized standards efforts, and gain societal acceptance through the adoption of regulation within sovereign nation states. From mail service to mining asteroids, many of the products and services developed share the same governance risks and this review of history demonstrates how vital inclusive stakeholder engagement is in each step of these collaborative technology journeys from concept to maturity in order to maximize their benefits and protect society from their worst impacts. At every point along the path the danger of the known and unknown must be balanced against the promise of a better, technology augmented future.

This book explores the fact that while there are many similarities between AI and other technologies, it is also indeed different. And this difference should significantly impact our journey in seeking to govern it. AI will continually raise profound risks that cannot be prevented or accounted for unlike other technologies, since it has an exponentially growing capacity to create actions without human initiative and that can remain beyond human understanding or control. Therefore, the difference is not seen in its underlying math or computational demand but rather in our expectation that users will design AI systems to function as humans without us.

This work confronts the notion that our full acceptance of this difference is trapped by our desire to see AI as separate from us. We want to see a technology layer where engineers smarter than us can collaboratively arrive at an algorithmic "safety" akin to the mechanism which prevents a trigger from being pulled. The safety of a gun is a mechanical lever whose design and operation will remain consistent from the time it is installed until the time its components are recycled. Its use remains dependent upon human actions, yet the technological means of making that weapon safe will always remain the same for each specific weapon. This is not the case in a probabilistic tool like AI. When the human instructs the system to be "safe," the path that system takes to safety will more likely than not be different every time, especially as AI innovation continues to iterate. We cannot currently create the same physical lever that prevents the firing pin from arriving at the bullet or the multiple checks that involve humans before a nuclear button is pushed. We cannot provide this mechanical level of certainty in these tools because these systems are traversing probability models that are simultaneously attempting to learn both what we mean and what we expect, producing outcomes that may be contrary to our interpretation or intentions. Our own multiplicity of and uncertainty of purposes are hard coded into probabilistic instruments that are by their very nature designed to offer us outputs that will never be as certain as a mechanical safety because they reflect the uncertainty of our very nature. We want to believe that AI is a disruption that is not embedded in us, that it can be designed to operate without the uncertainty that defines us, when it is nothing more than a reflection of us.

AI elevates long simmering risks that differentially impact various populations who, for too long, have lurked below the surface for so many in our society. AI must be seen and governed as the societal augmentation that it is, accelerating and amplifying the best and worst of us without sufficient protection. AI can provide one human the digital significance of thousands, regardless of borders, cultures, norms, or even regulations and standards. And it is the application of this technology to the service of human actions which are rapidly transforming societies in unpredictable and likely drastic ways that this work asks the reader to keep in focus.

Given the cross-jurisdiction reality of AI's impact, the project of developing a robust governance ecosystem has become an urgent need that can be furthered by international cooperation at every level. This work must be done with human impact remaining squarely at the center of a technology that has yet to be fully defined, with its limitations and consequences yet to be fully known, and innovation already occurring unbridled in the beating heart of our communities. Unlike in years past when nations tested nuclear bombs in far away deserts to protect the general population, too often blissfully unaware that the dangers would remain and reemerge far after a test bomb was dropped, the full might of AI is being iteratively refined behind closed doors that produce opaque 'black boxes' which are immediately deployed on millions of human test subjects despite many of its harms already being made unavoidably apparent. And much of the danger our minds can dream up for AI has yet to come to pass.

Keeping AI a technology whose opportunities outweigh its risks across all stakeholders impacted within the broad and disparate communities sharing our Earth will require rigorous, thoughtful, clear eyed collaboration. We hope this book goes some way towards contributing to these efforts.

# Postscript

Immediately prior to going to press, we received notification that the International Organization for Standardization (ISO) has adopted the NCTDR-ICODR ODR Standards in full,[1] with attribution provided, incorporating them into ISO Standard 32122.[2] This marks what may be a watershed in international standardization for artificial intelligence and other forms of technology utilized in dispute handling for international commerce.

Given the history of success of ISO standards being embraced by sovereign nations, regional governance bodies, private enterprise, and professional entities, it is hoped that the international ODR Standards as adopted as ISO Principles for ODR will lead to wide-spread global adoption in each of these arenas. This would bode well as another example of how committed engagement by multi-disciplinary international stakeholders (including from the academy, private industry, the public sector, professional organizations, and users) can result in the incorporation of their creative consensus into regulations and legislation by sovereign nations and the private sector. Importantly, in this case, it would mean that global consensus is harnessed to foster both cross-border and more localized jurisdictionally relevant protections against the worst artificial intelligence can offer while hopefully cultivating conditions to harvest its positive potential.

1 Referred to as Basic Principles, the only alteration made was to comply with ISO requirements, thus the word "must" in each NCTDR-ICODR ODR Standard was changed to a verb indicating best guidance such as "should."

2 ISO 32122 *Transaction Assurance in E-commerce – Guidance for Offering Online Dispute Resolution Services* was published on March 10, 2025.

© KONINKLIJKE BRILL BV, LEIDEN, 2025 | DOI:10.1163/9789004737389_009

# Index

www.ingramcontent.com/pod-product-compliance
Lightning Source LLC
Chambersburg PA
CBHW051358240926
51852CB00001B/61
*9789004736290*